Acoustic Profiles

The Oxford Music / Media Series
Daniel Goldmark, Series Editor

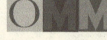

Tuning In: American Narrative Television Music
Ron Rodman

Special Sound: The Creation and Legacy of the BBC Radiophonic Workshop
Louis Niebur

Seeing Through Music: Gender and Modernism in Classic Hollywood Film Scores
Peter Franklin

An Eye for Music: Popular Music and the Audiovisual Surreal
John Richardson

Playing Along: Digital Games, YouTube, and Virtual Performance
Kiri Miller

Sounding the Gallery: Video and the Rise of Art-Music
Holly Rogers

Composing for the Red Screen: Prokofiev and Soviet Film
Kevin Bartig

Saying It With Songs: Popular Music and the Coming of Sound to Hollywood Cinema
Katherine Spring

We'll Meet Again: Musical Design in the Films of Stanley Kubrick
Kate McQuiston

Occult Aesthetics: Synchronization in Sound Film
K.J. Donnelly

Sound Play: Video Games and the Musical Imagination
William Cheng

Sounding American: Hollywood, Opera, and Jazz
Jennifer Fleeger

Mismatched Women: The Siren's Song Through the Machine
Jennifer Fleeger

Robert Altman's Soundtracks: Film, Music and Sound from M*A*S*H to A Prairie Home Companion
Gayle Sherwood Magee

Back to the Fifties: Nostalgia, Hollywood Film, and Popular Music of the Seventies and Eighties
Michael D. Dwyer

The Early Film Music of Dmitry Shostakovich
Joan Titus

Making Music in Selznick's Hollywood
Nathan Platte

Hearing Haneke: The Sound Tracks of a Radical Auteur
Elsie Walker

Unlimited Replays: Video Games and Classical Music
William Gibbons

Hollywood Harmony: Musical Wonder and the Sound of Cinema
Frank Lehman

French Musical Culture and the Coming of Sound Cinema
Hannah Lewis

Theories of the Soundtrack
James Buhler

Through The Looking Glass: John Cage and Avant-Garde Film
Richard H. Brown

Sound Design is the New Score: Theory, Aesthetics, and Erotics of the Integrated Soundtrack
Danijela Kulezic-Wilson

Rock Star/Movie Star: Power and Performance in Cinematic Rock Stardom
Landon Palmer

The Presence of the Past: Temporal Experience and the New Hollywood Soundtrack
Daniel Bishop

Metafilm Music in Jean-Luc Godard's Cinema
Michael Baumgartner

Acoustic Profiles: A Sound Ecology of the Cinema
Randolph Jordan

Acoustic Profiles

A Sound Ecology of the Cinema

RANDOLPH JORDAN

OXFORD
UNIVERSITY PRESS

Oxford University Press is a department of the University of Oxford. It furthers the University's objective of excellence in research, scholarship, and education by publishing worldwide. Oxford is a registered trade mark of Oxford University Press in the UK and certain other countries.

Published in the United States of America by Oxford University Press
198 Madison Avenue, New York, NY 10016, United States of America.

© Oxford University Press 2023

All rights reserved. No part of this publication may be reproduced, stored in a retrieval system, or transmitted, in any form or by any means, without the prior permission in writing of Oxford University Press, or as expressly permitted by law, by license, or under terms agreed with the appropriate reproduction rights organization. Inquiries concerning reproduction outside the scope of the above should be sent to the Rights Department, Oxford University Press, at the address above.

You must not circulate this work in any other form
and you must impose this same condition on any acquirer.

Library of Congress Cataloging-in-Publication Data
Names: Jordan, Randolph, author.
Title: Acoustic profiles : a sound ecology of the cinema / Randolph Jordan.
Description: New York, NY : Oxford University Press, 2023. |
Series: Oxford music/media series | Includes bibliographical references and index. |
Contents: Introduction. Acoustic Profiling—Audible Transparency : Modernist Acoustic Design in Jacques Tati's Playtime—Immersive Reflexivity : Documenting the Inaudible in Peter Mettler's Picture of Light—Reflective Empathy : Soundscape Composition and the Spatialization of Music in Gus Van Sant's Last Days—The Schizophonographic Imagination : Visualizing the Myth of Sonic Fidelity in David Lynch's Twin Peaks—Unsettled Listening : Tracking Vancouver's Contested Acoustic Profiles across Media—Conclusion. A Position Piece.
Identifiers: LCCN 2023011412 (print) | LCCN 2023011413 (ebook) |
ISBN 9780190226145 (paperback) | ISBN 9780190226077 (hardback) |
ISBN 9780190226176 (epub)
Subjects: LCSH: Film soundtracks—History and criticism. |
Motion picture music—History and criticism. | Sound (Philosophy)
Classification: LCC ML2075 .J7 2023 (print) | LCC ML2075 (ebook) |
DDC 781.5/42—dc23/eng/20230523
LC record available at https://lccn.loc.gov/2023011412
LC ebook record available at https://lccn.loc.gov/2023011413

DOI: 10.1093/oso/9780190226077.001.0001

Paperback printed by Marquis Book Printing, Canada
Hardback printed by Bridgeport National Bindery, Inc., United States of America

*Dedicated to my father, Robert Christopher Jordan (1933–2020),
who taught me how to listen.
And to my colleague and friend, Danijela Kulizic-Wilson (1966–2021),
with whom I enjoyed listening.*

Contents

Acknowledgments   ix

Introduction: Acoustic Profiling   1

1. Audible Transparency: Modernist Acoustic Design in Jacques Tati's *Playtime*   29

2. Immersive Reflexivity: Documenting the Inaudible in Peter Mettler's *Picture of Light*   61

3. Reflective Empathy: Soundscape Composition and the Spatialization of Music in Gus Van Sant's *Last Days*   97

4. The Schizophonographic Imagination: Visualizing the Myth of Sonic Fidelity in David Lynch's *Twin Peaks*   127

5. Unsettled Listening: Tracking Vancouver's Contested Acoustic Profiles across Media   171

Conclusion: A Position Piece   211

Notes   227
Index   231

Acknowledgments

The road to this book has been longer than I wanted it to be. It began as a simple plan to revise my PhD thesis (Concordia University, 2010), and ended up becoming a major re-imagining of my interest in acoustic ecology following my postdoctoral research fellowship (Simon Fraser University, 2012–14). Originally contracted by Oxford at the end of my postdoc, the project slowed under the burden of a seemingly endless stream of short-term yet demanding teaching contracts over the past ten years, none of which came with much (if any) provision for research activities. It is largely due to the patience of my editor, Norman Hirschy, that this project has finally seen the light of day. His willingness to wait out those periods during which I was not able to produce any work, while maintaining his encouragement and enthusiasm for the project, is the reason this book is finally being published. Thanks, Norm. You have been wonderful to work with. Here I must also thank series editor Daniel Goldmark and the various anonymous reviewers who have provided valuable commentary on this work throughout the various stages of the project.

My family also needs a hearty thanks up front. If it wasn't for the openness and support of my parents, Maya and Robert Jordan, I would never have found my way into the field of film studies and this book never would have materialized. I have wanted to write books since I was a kid, and they encouraged my writing at every turn. They are also responsible for bringing music and the arts to my life at a very early age, my dad a professional classical guitarist and my mom a potter, and in my passion for film I found a way to bring attention to music and sound into my writing. All along the way my younger brother, Ed, has been a kindred spirit in the endless quest for new experiences in sound and image, and we have shared countless hours in meaningful contemplation of art and life as we forged our often intersecting paths through the world. I have dedicated this book to my dad who was born in Oxford and would have been thrilled to see his son's first monograph emblazoned with the name of his hometown. Sadly, he died two years ago in my own hometown of Vancouver, British Columbia, where he lived most of his life after leaving England in the early 1950s. I offer some thoughts about his influence on my work in this book's conclusion.

And then there's my new family. My partner, Sarah, entered my life just as I was starting my doctoral studies twenty years ago, so she has been there to suffer through the entire process. During that process we've had three children of our own. Keelia was born during the last year of my dissertation and she took her first steps just before I submitted—we found our legs at the same time. Myla was born just as I began my first full-time teaching contract at Concordia University, and Drake was born right in the middle of my subsequent postdoctoral fellowship. The nature of contract teaching is such that my writing has always been a separate activity from my paid employment and is generally done during evenings and weekends, which is time I could have been spending with my family. While I often chose to back-burner the book for the sake of family time, my general anxiety surrounding the ever-incomplete project has been hard to manage and has often spilled over into our home life. It has been largely thanks to Sarah's rare combination of stable employment and lifestyle flexibility that we have been able to make this all work. Here I must also offer thanks to her side of the family, Phyllis, Laura, John, and Chris, for frequently stepping in to help with child care when needed. We all look forward to a better work/family balance now that this project has come to a close.

Since this book is the result of several distinct stages in my academic career, there are a few clusters of people that have had a major influence on what is contained in these pages. This goes all the way back to my first advisor, Mario Falsetto, who died a few years ago. I wrote my MA thesis (Concordia University, 2003) on sound in the films of David Lynch, and some of that material has come full circle here in my chapter on Lynch's *Twin Peaks* (1990–2017). Mario's guidance during my first experience with long-form writing laid the foundation for all the work to follow. Mario also introduced me to the wonderful world of experimental cinema through his grad seminar on the American avant-garde, which helped me understand what I loved so much about filmmakers like David Lynch and Gus Van Sant, for whom Mario and I had a mutual passion, an influence that can felt across this book. During my doctoral studies, Mario gave me the opportunity to workshop my early ideas around Gus Van Sant in his grad seminars on the director, and this work has taken shape in the form of my chapter on Van Sant's *Last Days* (2005) here.

Then there's my PhD thesis committee, consisting of Catherine Russell, Rosemary Mountain, and Jonathan Sterne. Katie was a fabulous thesis advisor, providing timely feedback and useful advice through all stages of that process. Her scholarship has been influential on my thinking about both experimental and documentary film, an influence that is clearest in my chapter on Peter Mettler's *Picture of Light* (1994). And her continuing support for my work after graduation has been very important to my development. It has been a pleasure to spend several years on faculty with Katie in the cinema department at Concordia.

Rosemary Mountain's guidance through the world of electroacoustic music was formative for my early thinking about intersecting acoustic ecology with film studies, and it was thanks to her that I was able to work with R. Murray Schafer as a teaching assistant for an interdisciplinary theater course at Concordia in 2005, an experience that exposed me not only to a broader scope of Schafer's work but to the very man himself, an important step toward articulating my thoughts about his work and influence in these pages. Rosemary and her husband, Harry, also provided a real feeling of family during my doctoral years with frequent occasions to dine with them at their home just two blocks from my own in Montreal's NDG borough.

Jonathan Sterne's influence on this work cannot be overstated. He arrived in Montreal to take a position at McGill University one year after I started my doctoral studies, and his first seminar on sound studies in 2004 (to which I was alerted by my friend and colleague Mike Baker) was a revelation to me. I invited him to come on as an external advisor after the very first class and he did not hesitate to accept. His knowledge of, and contributions to, the field of sound studies are all over this book (maybe a little *too* much), and some of my work for that class has found its way in here, too, particularly around the issue of sonic fidelity. But Jonathan's influence on my career has moved well beyond scholarship; he has become a long-term mentor to me through the trials and tribulations of the academic marketplace in the years following my graduation. Much of the material in this book has been workshopped through his graduate working groups at McGill University, including the book proposal itself, and it was Jonathan who introduced me to Norman Hirschy at the SCMS conference in 2013, which opened the door to discussions about working together on this project. The rest, as they say, is history.

I will take a moment here to also thank my friend Donato Totaro, who teaches in the cinema department at Concordia University and is founder and editor of the online film journal *Offscreen*. I have been a regular contributor to *Offscreen* since the early days of my MA, and Donato has given me several dissertations' worth of space in the journal to wax at great length about my cinematic fixations, particularly around festival coverage here in Montreal. He and his partner Sandra also provided valuable commentary on the last draft of my dissertation, which has gone on to inform the revisions present in this book. Through all of that we have become good friends and he and his family have provided an important base to help make my adopted city of Montreal feel like the home that it is now.

For the postdoctoral fellowship phase of this work, funded by the Fonds de recherche du Québec (FRQ), I am greatly indebted to my supervisor Barry Truax at Simon Fraser University. As an original member of the World Soundscape Project he was a wealth of information and lived experience about the formation of the field that I was researching. He provided me with boundless resources, including his own working group at the Sonic Research Studio, where I was able to present various stages of my research and learn about related work being done by others in the school. It was there that I met a remarkable group of colleagues including Vincent Andrisani, Nathan Clarkson, Milena Droumeva, Dave Murphy, and Jennifer Schine (who where collectively dubbed the "acoustic crew") along with Tim Newman, a fellow historian of BC film completing his PhD at SFU, and a former student of my father. Over my two years in town we had wide-ranging conversations about our work and the state of acoustic ecology today, sometimes while playing bocce on Vincent's carefully groomed lawn. I will remember this time as the most rewarding period in my academic life, carrying the skills I had honed during my doctoral studies into two years of intensive discovery and relative freedom. This was also the period during which my book project became something quite different from my dissertation, and I thank everyone associated with the Sonic Research Studio during my time there for their input into reshaping my thinking about how acoustic ecology might intersect with film studies. Milena and I went on to edit the recent collection *Sound, Media, Ecology* (Palgrave, 2019) that offers new accounts of the history of acoustic ecology and a survey of new work that extends the scopes of the field for the twenty-first century. In turn, materials in this collection are cited frequently throughout my book here.

In 2017–18 I spent a year on faculty in the School of Image Arts at Ryerson University, where I was given space to present my work in a variety of ways, including teaching courses on Vancouver cinema and sound production, a faculty talk on my research, and gallery space for an installation version of my related multimedia project *Bell Tower of False Creek* (which I reference in the conclusion to this book). I have also worked with colleagues there in ways that have shaped this book, including filmmaking collaboration with fellow Concordia PhD and long-time friend Gerda Cammaer, an aspect of my creative practice that has been an important part of my research process and methodology. I have also contributed chapters to several books edited by Gerda and other Ryerson faculty that have helped shape my present arguments around acoustic ecology and cinema. I am also grateful for my friendship with Karla McManus, who arrived at Ryerson for a limited term contract at the same time as I did, and who was also commuting weekly from Montreal for the gig. Karla and I spent a great deal of time in discussion around our mutual interests in ecology and media, the books we were deep in the middle of writing, the job market we were both navigating, and the neck pain induced by long train rides. Karla's encouragement during these challenging times is one of the reasons I got this book done.

Every chapter in this book once lived in the form of conference presentations, and I am grateful in particular to the Film Studies Association of Canada, the Society for Cinema and Media Studies, and the Canadian Communications Association for providing platforms and audiences to get this material rolling with a great deal of valuable feedback along the way, including an award of second place in the 2011 SCMS student writing competition for a draft of my chapter on Jacques Tati's *Playtime* (1967). But there is one conference that stands out from all the rest, becoming a true community well beyond academic networking: Music and the Moving Image (MaMI), hosted by New York University and organized by Ron Sadoff and Gillian Anderson. I have presented at the conference every year since 2011, where I have met the most incredible group of scholars dedicated to the study of film music and sound, gathered in a spirit of exuberant exchange and camaraderie that I have not seen matched anywhere else. There I have made lifelong friends in Eric Dienstfrey, Kevin Donnelly, Rebecca Fülöp, Liz Greene, Danijela Kulezic-Wilson, Anthony Linden Jones, Mike Miley, Katie Quanz, Katherine Spring, and Elsie Walker, among others with whom I have shared many a post-conference meal, film, and/or concert, and who produce work that continues to intersect with my own in a variety of ways. I will single out two from this list for special mention. I first became aware of Katherine Spring's work when she presented on the pedagogical value of soundwalking for film studies, in which she cited my dissertation. We went on to collaborate on related projects, including the organization of a yearly soundwalking event for the MaMI conference, and an entry to the *Journal of Cinema and*

Media Studies Teaching Dossier. And more than anyone else at the conference, Danijela Kulezic-Wilson shared my passion for the experiential qualities of sound design and her work has shown me the value in accounting for these qualities in the context of academic scholarship. Danijela died last year, shortly after the publication of her last book, *Sound Design is the New Score* (2019). I was honored to serve as a reviewer on her manuscript, for which I broke anonymity so as to foster a deeper dialogue with her around this provocative material. I had hoped that she would be able to return the favor on my own book, but I was too slow to make it happen in time. Thankfully we have had many discussions about my work over the years, particularly around the films of Gus Van Sant, about whom she also wrote quite a bit. These conversations have informed my work here. Above all else, though, I cherish our time out on the streets of New York City during the MaMI conference year after year. Danijela was always game to venture into lesser charted territories like John Zorn's jazz club The Stone and the *Dream House* installation by La Monte Young and Marian Zazeela. I last saw Danijela in person on the night of our *Dream House* excursion in 2019. We spent some good time in there, wandering amidst the layering frequencies blasting from the four corners of the room, lying on the floor, inviting the heavy continuous multi-tonal droning to work its vibrational magic on our collective consciousness. I would like to think of her this way now, at rest in the house of dreams. In that spirit, this book is dedicated to Danijela as well.

Like the listener in the *Dream House*, this book resonates at the intersection of multiple sources firing from all directions with simultaneously overlapping tones. As you can imagine, for a project that came together over such a long period, various elements in these pages have had lives in prior publications. The threads across my previous work are too complex to account for here, and the relevant works have been cited appropriately throughout the book. But I would like to acknowledge a few works that were particularly important in transitioning from my dissertation to the present book by way of my postdoctoral research. Key aspects of my general methodology for intersecting acoustic ecology with film studies were laid out in my essay, "The Ecology of Listening while Looking in the Cinema: Reflective Audioviewing in Gus Van Sant's *Elephant*" (2012), which also provided the basis for my opening analysis of *Elephant* (2003) in this book's introduction and my discussion of Gus Van Sant's subsequent film *Last Days* in Chapter 3. My work on phonograph turntables in the films of David Lynch in Chapter 4 reaches back to arguments and analyses found in my MA thesis, but this material has been greatly reworked and expanded in the wake of Lynch's filmography since 2003, which has confirmed my original arguments while allowing room to substantiate my claims across a much broader scope of the director's work. On the occasion of the return of *Twin Peaks* for Season 3 in 2017, I published some initial thoughts about sound in the new series in the francophone journal *24 Images*, translated as, "Interference: Le geographie sonore chez David Lynch" (2017a), which I revised for English publication in *Offscreen* as, "Three Soundtrack Albums and a Record Player: A *Twin Peaks* Music Review (Sort Of)" (2017b). Finally, Chapter 5 is based on my postdoctoral research into the use of sound in the cinemas of Vancouver, British Columbia. This research has yielded a number of publications containing material that has been adapted for this book, beginning with a pair of blog posts on *Sounding Out!* for a series edited by Katherine Spring (2014) and another by yours truly (2015). These posts were revised and expanded for the essay, "Unsettling the Soundtrack: Acoustic Profiling and the Documentation of Community and Place," published in *The Routledge Companion to Screen Music and Sound* (2017c), edited by MaMI organizer Ron Sadoff and conference regulars Miguel Mera and Ben Winters, and this essay formed the basis for the even greater expansion in Chapter 5 here. I am grateful to all the reviewers and editors who have provided feedback on this work over the years as I developed the methodology and analyses that are now formalized into a sustained argument across this book.

Finally, I am particularly grateful to Hildegard Westerkamp for her availability to discuss my interest in her work over the years, and especially for her essay, "The Disruptive Nature of Listening: Today, Yesterday, Tomorrow," (2019), in which she offers thoughtful responses to my critiques of the early work of the World Soundscape Project found in some of my writing about Vancouver cinema. In turn, I have been able to take these responses into account for my revised analyses in this book.

I conclude by acknowledging that this book was written on the unceded lands of the Kanien'kehá:ka Nation of the Tiohtià:ke region, now called Montreal, where I live and work, and in the territories of səlilwətaʔɬ (Tsleil-Waututh), Sḵwx̱wú7mesh Úxwumixw (Squamish), səlilwətaʔɬ (Tsleil-Waututh) and xʷməθkʷəy̓əm (Musqueam) Nations in the region now called Vancouver, the subject of Chapter 5 and about which I follow up in the conclusion to this book.

References

Droumeva, Milena, and Randolph Jordan, eds. 2019. *Sound, Media, Ecology*. New York: Palgrave Macmillan.

Jordan, Randolph. 2003. *Starting From Scratch: Turntables, Auditory Representation, and the Structure of the Known Universe in the Films of David Lynch*. MA Thesis, Film Studies Program, Concordia University.

Jordan, Randolph, 2010. *The Schizophonic Imagination: Audiovisual Ecology in the Cinema*. PhD Dissertation, Humanities Program, Concordia University.

Jordan, Randolph. 2012. "The Ecology of Listening while Looking in the Cinema: Reflective Audioviewing in Gus Van Sant's *Elephant*." *Organised Sound* 17, no. 3 (December): 248–256.

Jordan, Randolph. 2014. "Unsettled Listening: Integrating Film and Place." *Sounding Out!* blog (August 14). https://soundstudiesblog.com/2014/08/14/unsettled-listening-integrating-film-and-place/

Jordan, Randolph. 2015. "Unsettling the World Soundscape Project: The Bell Tower of False Creek, Vancouver." *Sounding Out!* blog (September 3). https://soundstudiesblog.com/2015/09/03/unsettling-the-world-soundscape-project-the-bell-tower-of-false-creek-vancouver/

Jordan, Randolph. 2017a. "Interference: la geographie sonore chez David Lynch." *24 Images* 184 (October/November): 31–35.

Jordan, Randolph. 2017b. "Three Soundtrack Albums and a Record Player: A *Twin Peaks* Music Review (Sort Of)." *Offscreen* 21, nos. 11–12 (November/December).

Jordan, Randolph. 2017c. "Unsettling the Soundtrack: Acoustic Profiling and the Documentation of Community and Place." In *The Routledge Companion to Screen Music and Sound*, edited by Miguel Mera, Ron Sadoff, and Ben Winters, 590–602. New York: Routledge.

Westerkamp, Hildegard. 2019. "The Disruptive Nature of Listening: Today, Yesterday, Tomorrow." In *Sound, Media, Ecology*, edited by Milena Droumeva and Randolph Jordan, 45–64. New York: Palgrave Macmillan.

Introduction
Acoustic Profiling

Early in Gus Van Sant's film *Elephant* (2003), loosely based on the Columbine High School massacre in Colorado, USA, we find student Alex (Alex Frost) mapping out the space of the cafeteria in preparation for the shooting spree that he'll soon embark upon with his friend Eric (Eric Deulen). In the final shot of this sequence, he pauses for a moment and glances around the room in distress as the noisy lunchtime crowd rises to higher levels of amplitude and reverberation. The shot ends as he raises his hands to his head, wincing as though in pain.[1] The next time we find Alex in this space it has been emptied of all life, his own footsteps now reverberating through the vacant space as the chaos of the mid-day bustle has been replaced with the sounds of a forest environment underscored by electronic drones. For a moment he can sit in peace, having violently banished the sounds he apparently found so disturbing the previous day, able now to hear his own place in the world again. Yet the peace is disturbing, a forced emptying of interior space into its surrounding exterior reflected by the bizarre co-existence of electronics, birds, and wind-rustled branches within the boundaries of an institutional enclosure.

The soundtrack we hear at this moment is a combination of the location recording made during the shoot and a pre-existing piece by electroacoustic music composer Frances White entitled "Walk Through Resonant Landscape #2" (1992).[2] White's piece provides the climax to the film's recurring use of *soundscape composition*, a musical genre based on field recordings as the basis for sound art that invites listeners toward a heightened environmental awareness, a goal imported from the field of acoustic ecology out of which the practice developed. Acoustic ecology was born of Canadian composer R. Murray Schafer's program of public education about the sonic environments in which we live, which he began in the 1960s at Simon Fraser University in Vancouver, British Columbia, Canada. Schafer called for an interdisciplinary approach to thinking about the role of sound in our lives, lending a composer's ear to hearing the soundscapes of the world as compositions that can and should be orchestrated according to taste. Instead of joining the chorus of noise abatement campaigns that had been dominating public discourse on urban sound, he proposed *acoustic design* as the goal of acoustic ecology: the creation of better sounding sonic environments through increased attention to the auditory aspects of architecture and urban planning. Some of his colleagues took the idea of acoustic design as the premise for creating soundscape compositions that called attention to the reorchestration of specific sound environments as acts of media intervention, which could then inspire interventions into the design of the built environments.

Van Sant's decision to use Frances White's piece, along with two other soundscape compositions by Schafer's colleague Hildegard Westerkamp, invites an intertextual reading of the film through the field of acoustic ecology and its emphasis on acoustic design, whether in musical composition or the architecture of public space. In *Elephant*, Alex takes a militant approach to the reorchestration of his acoustic environment, the extreme end of the negatively charged noise abatement that Schafer hoped to steer away from. Yet in framing this horror by way of intersecting film sound design with the art of soundscape composition, the filmmakers invite us to reflect upon the narrative situation by way of its formal execution, a reflexive call to open our ears wider to the environments outside the walls of our screening rooms.

No doubt it is a cynical move to suggest that we think of something as harrowing as a high school shooting spree as a kind of militant acoustic ecology. But the loaded nature of such a claim brings the key premise of this book to the fore: that hearing films through the tenets of acoustic ecology can reveal powerful themes of environmental (dis)engagement at work in their narrative, aesthetic, and industrial contexts that would otherwise go unaddressed. The confluence of soundscape composition and film sound design in *Elephant* provides a way of thinking about this film as inviting a level of audience engagement unaccounted for by the common critical description of the film as inevitably distancing, the film that prompted Kent Jones to crown Van Sant as "the prince of calculated disaffection" (2003, 28). If we listen to the film as a call to reflect upon the mutually affecting relationship between people and their soundscapes, we find an alternative way into the sociopolitical issues at its heart. At the same time, we can cast a necessarily critical ear toward the work of acoustic ecology, a field that has sustained a great deal of critique over the years, largely directed toward the didacticism of Schafer's prescriptions and biases (both implicit and explicit).

Acoustic ecology was created to get people thinking about the relationships between our sonic environments and the social contexts that sustain them. The field hasn't (yet) managed to prompt the mass awareness of environmental sound or shift in approaches to urban planning that Schafer had hoped for. Yet acoustic ecology's mandate for listening has been taken up in a broad variety of fields interested in the relationship between sound and culture, loosely associated through the World Forum for Acoustic Ecology founded in 1993 (see Droumeva and Jordan 2019). Indeed, you would be hard pressed to find a work of contemporary sound studies that doesn't make some reference, however small, to the concepts developed by Schafer and his colleagues. Yet there exists no model for the systematic exploration of acoustic ecology's potential contribution to other fields. I argue that broadening the scope of acoustic ecology for media studies will help open soundscape research to new models of analysis, while also opening the ears of media studies scholars to issues of sound ecology embedded in our objects of research. In this book I begin the work of making acoustic ecology and media studies work for each other through the intersection of film sound and the media practices of soundscape researchers. While I focus on "cinema" as more traditionally defined around design for theatrical exhibition and operating in mode of the European art film, the later chapters expand into the worlds of television, contemporary streaming content, and expanded cinema forms that blur the lines between fiction/nonfiction and modes of exhibition/reception, to demonstrate how thinking about sound in film can serve as the basis for considering a broader array of audiovisual works in a variety of contexts. I conclude with an example of how the methodology I propose here can transition from a tool for analyzing audiovisual media to a tool for conducting research, producing creative works, and affecting a change in ideology around settler positionality.

Thinking about film sound through acoustic ecology, and vice-versa, addresses a major issue in contemporary sound studies: the consistent emphasis on recording and transmission as inexorably transformative acts of mediation. The new wave of film sound theory that kicked off in the 1980s is premised upon this line of thinking, scholars like Rick Altman and James Lastra calling to abandon the language of "reproduction" when discussing recorded sound and moving instead to the idea of "representation" to acknowledge the mediation at work in the construction of all film soundtracks (Lastra

2000, 153). This has been an important thrust in documentary film studies as it moves away from naïve notions of film's ability to offer unmediated access to real world events, perhaps finding its most provocative expression in Jonathan Sterne's equation of recording with embalming, the "resonant tomb" in which the interior of a sound event is utterly transformed while its exterior might continue to serve a social function for listeners (2003, 290). These are essential conceptual moves for the climate of twenty-first century media literacy, understanding how the construction of listening practices by individual filmmakers or major technology companies has revolved around selling ideas about transparency that mask the machinery animating the product. However, I have long felt that these arguments overstate the idea of mediation; in compensating for the dangers inherent in uncritical acceptance of the media we lose an appreciation for the power of technologies to facilitate real and deep engagement with the world.

Consider the role of Frances White's "Walk Through Resonant Landscape #2" in *Elephant* more closely. Van Sant and sound designer Leslie Shatz map White's work onto the film as a way of turning the space of the high school inside out, calling attention not only to the narrative situation that finds the student body scrambling about trying to find exits to the outside world, but also triggering reflection upon how the film is connecting with the world outside of its own making. Most obviously we are meant to meditate upon events like the Columbine shootings, the reality outside the film that its audiences cannot escape. But we can also meditate upon what it means to create an intertextual relationship with White's material at such a loaded moment in the film, prompting us to think about similarities between White and the filmmakers in their aesthetic strategies and thematic concerns. In so doing we can become attuned to the role of media practice in raising important ecological issues equally applicable to the film as to the world to which it refers and in which the audience takes it in.

"Walk Through Resonant Landscape #2" enacts the process of engaging with the world by way of sound technologies. It is based on recordings that White made when she first moved from Brooklyn, New York, to Princeton, New Jersey, and was hearing the wooded environment around her new house for the first time. Out of these recordings she created an installation piece that allowed users to control the movement and the layering of recorded elements by way of a computer interface, constructing virtual "walks" through this space that rendered the materials differently each time. The piece now exists only as a recording of one such "walk," opening a window into one person's reorchestration of a sonic environment experienced by another (Pritchett 2007, 2–3). As such, "Walk Through Resonant Landscape #2" is an extension of the practice of *soundwalking* born of acoustic ecology. Soundwalking is a form of spatial practice that calls for individuals to shift their auditory attention while moving through and listening carefully to their sound environments, becoming aware of their component parts and how they are being combined, and emphasizing the role of active attention in constructing these soundscapes within the mind (see Westerkamp 1974). Initially conceived as a listening practice without aid of sound technologies, White's piece offers one example of how sound technologies can aid the process of enhancing environmental awareness through the art of the soundwalk.

Van Sant and Shatz extend White's electroacoustic soundwalk by mapping her sounds onto a new space of their own construction to aid in their own powerful exploration of the audiovisual practice of space. Much of the film is comprised of long tracking shots following characters as they move through the space of the high school as we hear a wide variety of auditory material that prompts reflection upon these environments in various ways. In conjunction with the film's structural loops, continually revisiting the same narrative events from different perspectives and with changing soundscapes, *Elephant* can be understood as a walk through the resonant landscape of its own making, and an invitation for the audience to become aware of the process of this continual reorchestration of the space in order to reflect upon the events taking place within it. Alex has enacted his own reorchestration of the high school soundscape, and it is this reorchestration that White's piece emphasizes. As the soundscape shifts on the soundtrack, the audience is made privy to the film's overt construction of audiovisual space. This is a reflexive move, but one that is designed to bring the audience in rather than push them away, a key strategy for soundscape composition as well.

Film sound design shares with soundscape composition the power of enacting new forms of spatial practice that call attention to our own practices in the spaces we occupy every day, and considering these art forms relationally is ideal for exploring acoustic ecology in the context of media studies. It is the argument of this book that a literal connection between acoustic ecology and film sound design, such as we find here in *Elephant*, can inform our understanding of *all* sound films. In turn, understanding how films work to shape our experience of space, inside and out of the screening room, can help us understand the value of making acoustic ecology work in a media studies context.

A Sound Ecology of the Cinema

This book proposes a sound ecology of the cinema by way of establishing an interdisciplinary methodology for hearing film sound through the tenets of acoustic ecology. In so doing I reveal the commonalities between sound design practices for the cinema and the media practices that drive soundscape research. My method is to draw on the discourse of acoustic ecology to engage in close readings of specific films and audiovisual works across a range of international narrative fiction, documentary, and experimental forms. Through my analyses I address ecological issues at play within the aesthetic and thematic content of these works while rethinking acoustic ecology as a set of media practices, which Jonathan Sterne has likened to early manifestations of what we now call the "digital humanities" (2019). To that end, I demonstrate how the creative use of media technologies in different fields can be understood relationally through the ecological issues that connect them, revivifying acoustic ecology for media studies while broadening the latter's ecological scope. With my film analyses I provide a tool kit for my readers to hear films with new ears, to think critically about this new listening practice, and to extend that engagement beyond the walls of the screening room by opening works of audiovisual media up to the consideration of soundscape research.

I focus on the framework for acoustic ecology established by the practices of the World Soundscape Project (WSP), which began in 1970 at Simon Fraser University (SFU) in Vancouver as a case study of that city (which continues to this day). The basic frames of reference that coalesced in their methodology continue to inform soundscape research across the globe today while also inspiring heated debate. There are four key dimensions to the WSP's practice: field recording in specific sonic environments to document and "preserve" aspects of these environments for posterity and analysis; establishing secondary accounts of the soundscapes of the present and past through appeals to painting, literature, interviews, and other sources; prescribing acoustic design practices for the built environments of the future; and the creative practice of soundscape composition that explores all three previous areas through the use of field recordings as the basis for musical composition with the intention of fostering environmental awareness. All of these areas involve the use of media as tools for engaging the soundscapes of specific geographic locales, hence my assertion that acoustic ecology functions as a set of media practices.

The key question driving my inquiry is how the use of media technologies can facilitate a closer connection with the world rather than putting us at a mediated distance from it. I first encountered the work of the World Soundscape Project through their 1996 CD release entitled *The Vancouver Soundscape/Soundscape Vancouver 1996*, which contained a selection of recordings made in the 1970s and 1990s, along with audio documentaries about the changing soundscape and some soundscape compositions designed to promote reflection upon the sonic distinctiveness of the city (World Soundscape Project 1996). I had recently moved cross-country from Vancouver to Montreal for graduate school and there was something compelling about hearing my city through these recordings, filtered through the WSP's media practices and my new geographical separation from home. The profundity of my engagement prompted questions beyond the glint of nostalgia with which my personal association with the city was charged. In particular, I asked how it is that the naturalistic approach of these recordings meshed ideologically with their composed counterparts on the disc to heighten my experience of engagement, changing the way I interacted with the city upon subsequent visits while prompting me to take a new approach to my academic investigations of film sound. My graduate work was founded upon a love for art cinema, while my postdoctoral research dove into the location-specific cinemas of my hometown. This trajectory is mapped in this book so as to demonstrate the value of embedding traditional appreciations of film as art into investigations of how films are embedded in the sociopolitical dimensions of the spaces in which they are made, and how the tools of acoustic ecology can inform that bridge.

So much contemporary sound studies theory focuses on the idea of mediation as distanciating, but it was clear to me that the World Soundscape Project was driven by a profound belief that such recordings and compositions could engender a deep connection to the world. There is a level of naïveté present in the work of the WSP, which has resulted in a lack of self-reflection upon their practices—particularly in the early days. Yet it would be to the great benefit of sound studies to think through just how their enthusiasm for the power of recording to provide access to the world in front of the microphones might be brought to other areas of inquiry within the world of sonic representation. I begin by demonstrating this value for the field of film studies by way of examining how acoustic ecology allows us to engage more deeply with films, recognizing how they invite us to rethink our experience of the spaces we occupy every day. In turn, I show

how the tools provided by film sound studies can fuel critical reassessment of the work of acoustic ecology.

Film sound theory offers a rich discursive framework through which to account for the use of media technologies in the work of acoustic ecology, an essential move for taking a media studies approach to understanding the field's desire to foster environmental awareness through attention to the role of sound in culture. My approach is based on a double critical movement. On the one hand, a sound ecology of the cinema entails the application of acoustic ecology's prescribed listening practices to film sound studies. On the other hand, my approach implies a new way of thinking about acoustic ecology born *of* film studies, a way to consider acoustic ecology's practice through film studies' long history of dealing with problems of fidelity and realism through recording technologies. Learning to hear the practical and aesthetic commonalities between the work of film sound design and acoustic ecology's media practices enriches soundscape research by opening up a vast collection of recorded film materials for inclusion in the document pool under consideration by acoustic ecology. At the same time, this intersection of fields also offers a necessary critical discourse for handling the challenges inherent in navigating acoustic ecology's media practices.

In the chapters that follow, I address each of the four dimensions of acoustic ecology—documentation, analysis, prescription, and composition—through a set of films that demonstrate, enact, and challenge these dimensions. I argue that these films invite audiences to reflect upon their approaches to the audiovisual construction of space so that we may carry this reflection out to the world beyond the frame of the screen and its surrounding walls. In so doing I demonstrate how the intersection of acoustic ecology and film sound studies can make films work as both extensions of acoustic ecology and means for critically rethinking the field.

Keeping the Faith

At the core of my investigation lies the notion of fidelity, a long-standing emblem of the relationship between recordings and the world they record, enshrined equally in the languages of sound reproduction and visual documentary media. What it means for a film or sound recording to be faithful to that which it represents has long been debated amidst the shifting tides of sound studies and documentary studies alike, and these debates have informed the practices of acoustic ecology as well. It is productive to consider how these areas overlap as a key aspect of my methodology. Across this book I intersect the language developed for soundscape research in acoustic ecology with key concepts from film sound theory, and this intersection centers on the discourse of fidelity that has been fundamental to sound studies at large, long governing debates about realism and representation in film sound and equally applicable to acoustic ecology's interest in the functioning of the sonic environments in which we live.

Schafer developed his general program for acoustic ecology within the heyday of hi-fi stereo culture, and he used the language of this culture in the listening pedagogy he developed as a way of attuning his students to the sounds of their daily environments. As Jonathan Sterne reminds us, the term soundscape itself, popularized by Schafer (though it was in use prior to Schafer's first publications), must be understood as the product of this culture: "Soundscape was shaped by a relationship to recording, reproduction and Western art music concert tradition.... Soundscape implies a way of listening to compositions—a rapt, total attention—and a sense of the world that is much like a compositional work" (Sterne 2013, 191). Once we are listening to our sonic environments as an audiophile might listen to her stereo, Schafer evocatively uses descriptors like *hi-fi* and *lo-fi* to refer to different kinds of balance between various categories of sound in any given environment. In his words, "the quiet ambiance of the hi-fi soundscape allows the listener to hear farther into the distance just as the countryside exercises long-range viewing," the opposite of the lo-fi soundscape that Schafer associates with urban settings in which "perspective is lost" when "individual acoustic signals are obscured in an overdense population of sounds" (1977, 43). Here Schafer deliberately draws on the inherent bias in the language of hi-fi stereo culture with its emphasis on a high ratio of "signal" to "noise" that allows listener's awareness of the media itself to disappear from our attention, a *vanishing mediation* made possible by differentiating between those characteristics that studio engineers want listeners to focus on and which they would like us to ignore (Sterne 2003, 285). Schafer has been all too happy to play off that bias in his own writings about what kinds of sounds might constitute valuable signals in our everyday environments, and what kinds of sounds should be banished as unwanted noise.

While Schafer was an early advocate for the use of sound recording technologies to document bits of the sonic environment to aid analysis and track changes (while attempting to "perverse" aspects that disappear), he also displayed a vocal distaste for the presence of sounds emanating from loudspeakers in our daily environments. He famously coined the term *schizophonia* to describe an imagined state of anxiety and alienation provoked by the experience of sound that is transmitted electroacoustically (1977, 90–91). Many have taken Schafer's term to be the guiding concept of acoustic ecology in general. As Timothy Morton puts it, through the concept of schizophonia, acoustic ecology "criticizes disembodiment as a feature of modern alienation. Like forms of Romanticism, acoustic ecology yearns for an organic world of face-to-face contact in which the sound of things corresponds to the way they appear to the senses and to a certain concept of the natural" (2007, 43). This concept of the natural is tied directly to Schafer's idea of "human scale" as the defining concept for the ideal soundscape (Schafer 1977, 207), or what Jonathan Sterne has called "the spatiality of the unamplified voice" (2003, 342).

Schafer's notion of human scale is incompatible with the technological realities that govern our daily activities of communication in the world today, and as such Schafer's anti-technological bent has been the subject of much critique. Indeed, it is perhaps the most common criticism of Schafer's writings that he uses language borrowed from hi-fi stereo culture to make arguments against the effects of sound technology in modern sonic environments, all the while advocating the use of this technology in the study of our environments through the World Soundscape Project. Andra McCartney extends these critiques to question the ethics of conducting soundscape research guided by the discourses of fidelity that have so problematically constructed ways of thinking about the relationship between sound technology and sonic objects in the world (2010). The model listener implied by Schafer's writing has also been critiqued for its lack of diversity in addressing a variety of listening positions, whether in terms of general listening practice (attentive vs. distracted) or along intersectional lines (race, class, gender, etc.), with some scholars suggesting ways of incorporating a broader array of listening positions into the way we theorize our relationships with the sonic environment (see Bijsterveld 2008, 23; Birdsall 2012, 21–23), a move Barry Truax began when he laid out a continuum of listening positions in *Acoustic Communication* (first published in 1984 and revised for the second edition in 2001). Some have called Schafer out on the explicit racism on display in some of his writings, most powerfully in the opening to Dylan Robinson's book *Hungry Listening*, in which he quotes Schafer belittling Inuit throat singing, an all-too-common example of how colonial encounters with indigenous music have typically unfolded (2020, 1). And Hildegard Westerkamp has recently gone on record about her experiences as the only female member of the WSP and the gender biases she faced from Schafer and other members of the team (see Westerkamp 2019). All of this is to say that the theoretical biases in play in Schafer's writings are part and parcel of the real-world context of social inequities that need to be accounted for in any discussion of acoustic ecology's influence and relevance on the broader field of sound studies. The problematic construction of fidelity takes center stage in these conversations, and will serve as the basis for how I address these issues in the chapters that follow.

Given that the discourse of fidelity lies at the heart of the development of acoustic ecology, it is essential to keep this discourse in mind when addressing the media practices at work in the field, with all their problems taken alongside their benefits. Fidelity, for Schafer, is characteristic of a sonic environment in which sounds do not compete with each other for our attention, and in which human communication is unhindered—in essence: a fantasy, along the same lines as the fantasy of transparency that holds the possibility that sound technology could provide direct and unmediated access to the sound event that was recorded. The fact that Schafer can use the language of fidelity to describe environments free of the kinds of technology for which this language was invented is not a paradox or contradiction: it is Schafer developing a theoretical construct for an idea of fidelity that is in line with the fantasy of transparency espoused by hi-fi stereo culture, carrying the biases of his own privileged positionality along with it. Schafer and the proponents of hi-fi technologies want us to learn to listen in the ways that suit their positionality the best. Recognizing the constructed nature of these ideas about fidelity, and the role of media technologies in shaping these constructions, makes acoustic ecology especially well-suited for application to the analyses of media arts. Across this book, I endeavor to illustrate how starting with the problems embedded in the theoretical constructs of Schafer and the WSP, like fidelity, provides the basis for a deeper understanding of how acoustic ecology can inform our knowledge of film sound, and how engaging with film sound in this way can, in turn, offer pathways into rethinking acoustic ecology for the twenty-first century.

The Medial Move

Each of the films I discuss in this book enact what I will call a *medial move*: a reflexive strategy designed to call particular attention to the ways in which technologies of sound create portals of access to the world through conventional notions of mediation. Through a medial move, that which is frequently considered distanciating shifts to an alternative notion of mediation that emphasizes inclusion; audiences are brought in rather than pushed away. Such medial moves frequently hang on foregrounding problems with the construct of fidelity as the basis for exploring the cinema's sonic potential, and these problems are my focus in this book.

Jonathan Sterne takes issue with conflating the term *media* with *mediation*, asserting that "Mediation is not necessarily intercession, filtering, or representation. Another sense of mediation describes a form of nonlinear, relational causality, a movement from one set of relations to another" (Sterne 2012, 9). He uses the term *mediality* to address the reality "that communication technologies are a fundamental part of what it means to speak, to hear, or to do anything with sound. Mediality simply points to a collectively embodied process of cross-reference," without assuming that one form of experiencing the world is automatically less mediated than another (10). Sterne's use of the term mediality thus allows for thinking about the use of recording media as ways of engaging with the world rather than exemplifying our removal from it.

For the purposes of this book we will need to understand the value of mediality for discussions of works of sound and film art. Here I turn to Timothy Morton's use of the term *medial* as part of a taxonomy of strategies in play in art works that engage in *ecomimesis*, or "nature writing": developing an idea of nature embedded in the formal strategies through which the idea is expressed. What he calls *medial writing* stands as an interdisciplinary alternative to the literary notion of *phatic writing* designed to call attention to how the act of writing itself invokes the mediation involved in the writing process (2007, 37). In film studies we generally defer to *reflexivity* as the relevant term, most often referred to as a distancing device. Yet Morton argues that medial strategies in nature writing are used not to distanciate the reader, but rather to generate the illusion that the reader is there with the writer to create a sense of immersion (38). Morton's goal in defining medial aesthetic strategies is to illuminate the ways in which ideas about "nature" are constructed in ecowriting so that we may, in turn, recognize these ideas as problematic constructs that stand in the way of addressing nature as it is rather than how we imagine it to be. Understanding the medial quality of art works that represent the world allows us to understand the processes of representation. While Morton wants to call attention to these processes in order to undo our imaginary and learn instead to engage with the world as it is, I argue that it is precisely this mediality that allows for engaging the world by way of our imaginative uses of technologies. The key is to understand how mediality functions to put us in touch with the world, not simply to represent it according to prescribed ideologies.

The most instructive aspect of acoustic ecology lies in the development and proliferation of soundscape composition as an artistic embodiment of the World Soundscape Project's initial impulses toward documentation, analysis, and prescription. Soundscape composition exemplifies the form of mediality that I will be applying across this book. WSP member Barry Truax has identified a continuum of practices within the sphere of soundscape composition. On one end of the spectrum lies what he refers to as "phonography" (2008, 106), privileging the kind of untouched single-take location recordings that make up the bulk of the raw material in the WSP's archive, R. Murray Schafer's preferred approach to both the documentation and presentation of the sounds of Vancouver when he founded the WSP in 1970. On the other end of the spectrum lies the "abstracted soundscape" often including heavily processed recordings in which any material captured on location may no longer even be recognizable as such (106). Soundscape composers like Truax and Westerkamp have moved away from the limitations of the single-take approach to documentation and embraced the power of technology as tool for composition to explore the many ways that alternative recording practices and studio techniques can foster heightened engagement with place. These differing ideologies are partially responsible for the rift that opened up between Schafer and his colleagues on the World Soundscape Project, perfectly illustrated by the differences across the two iterations of the *Vancouver Soundscape* releases. The first in 1973 consists mostly of raw single-take field recordings annotated by audio commentary and notes in the accompanying booklet, while the 1996 release expands the repertoire to include heavily composed sound pieces that offer creative explorations of the changing nature of Vancouver's soundscape across a twenty-year period (Droumeva and Jordan 2019, xiii).

Through the development of soundscape composition as both a mode of research within acoustic ecology and an artistic offshoot of the movement, the WSP shifted from implicit to explicit acknowledgment of the role that sound technology can play in fostering engagement with geographic locations. Soundscape composition thus becomes a useful touchstone for addressing how we can read engagement with place through the recording and transmission of sound across a variety of media. Soundscape composition actively engages acoustic ecology's emphasis on understanding particular geographic locales while foregrounding its own medial processes as part of this understanding. In short, soundscape composition's goal is medial: to promote listener engagement with real-world space through foregrounding the ways in which our experience of this space can be shaped by sound technology.

Katharine Norman uses the term *reflective listening* to refer to a mode of listening based on heightened environmental awareness through the use of sound technologies that guides artists in the creation of soundscape compositions, a mode of listening that these compositions are designed to engender in the audience as well (1996, 5). Central to this mode of listening is the foregrounding of mediality through the balance between the naturalism of the recorded environments that make up the compositional building blocks and their treatment through technologies of electroacoustic recording and transmission, a balance that Barry Truax describes as the "dialectic . . . between the real and the imaginary, as well as between the referential and the abstract" (2001, 237). For Hildegard Westerkamp, the key to linking soundscape composition with acoustic ecology is recognizing this dialectic not only in terms of the aesthetic treatment of field recordings as heard in the finished piece, but in the relationship between the composer and the environments she engages with while making the piece (see Westerkamp 2002). This is a dialectic between the act of recording and the manipulation of these recordings in the studio, both of which involve the use of sound technology to change listening practices. For Norman, reflective listening is applicable both to the composer's listening practice while making the piece and her desire to inspire such reflection in the audience hearing the finished piece.

Later in this book I bring Norman's concept of reflective listening into the audiovisual context of the cinema, deliberately drawing a connection between the work of soundscape composition as an extension of acoustic ecology and the work of film sound designers interested in provoking audience engagement through their contribution to the representation of audiovisual space. Listening to film sound in a reflective way is based on the awareness of various levels of mediality between sound and the built environment, environment and recording, recording and composition, composition and listener, and listener and environment. When we think of acoustic ecology in general as a media practice, it is by folding the ideologies that drive soundscape composition back onto the other dimensions of the field's use of media technologies for soundscape research, particularly as they relate to the four dimensions I have outlined: field recording as documentation, analysis of primary and secondary documents, prescriptions for shaping the soundscapes of the future, and the role of the arts in engaging all of these dimensions to enhance listener consciousness. I argue for the value in considering these practices in relation to the work of film sound design to understand the ecological implications of cinematic spatial practices, while drawing on the rich discourse of film sound theory to bring acoustic ecology into the sphere of media studies.

Acoustic Profiling

To enable my examination of the mediality on display in the films under discussion here I propose a methodology called *acoustic profiling*, a way of intersecting useful terms and concepts from acoustic ecology and the discourse of film sound theory in order to attend to the sonic strategies used in films to articulate space in ways that challenge established notions of sonic fidelity. I begin with film historian James Lastra's use of the term *perceptual fidelity* as a category for auditory representation in the cinema that emphasizes the relationship between a listener's position in the world and the role of technology in constructing this position. In arguing for thinking about all film sound as representation rather than reproduction, Lastra demonstrates that sound recording for film has brought together two traditions of representation: those of the phonographic industry and those of the telephonic industry. The telephonic model emphasizes the intelligibility of speech over all other elements of the soundtrack, often at the expense of realism. The phonographic model, on the other hand, emphasizes perceptual fidelity, referring to the idea that the sound in a film remains faithful to what might be heard if the listener were occupying the space represented on screen (2000, 138–139). Built into these modes of representation are ideologies about what sounds are important and what sounds are not: "The 'fidelity' approach assumes that all aspects of the sound event are inherently significant . . . The 'telephonic' approach ... assumes that sound possesses an intrinsic hierarchy that renders some aspects essential and others not" (Lastra 2000, 139).

The idea of perceptual fidelity is caught between two different conceptual frameworks: on the one hand, it refers to the way an environment would sound to an objective listener; on the other hand, the emphasis on *perceptual* recognizes that no such objective listener actually exists, and that every listener will hear a given soundscape in their own way—what Rick Altman refers to as the *Rashomon* phenomenon in reference to the Akira Kurosawa film (1950) and its play on the idea of subjective realities (1992, 24). So the concept of perceptual fidelity bridges the goals of objective and subjective representation of space, and is as much about human engagement with the sound environment as it is about "faithful" representation of the world.

The term *perceptual fidelity* is useful for present purposes in the way that it calls attention to the relationship between perception and fidelity, a tension that was built into the very definition of soundscape once formalized as a concept for acoustic ecology (Truax 1978, 126–127). This tension can be productively linked to Schafer's problematic formulation of ideal soundscapes operating at a human scale in which all the sounds of the natural world are bent around the basic premise of unamplified human communication, just as filmmakers will adjust music and sound effects around dialogue. It is almost as though Schafer developed his idea of the hi-fi soundscape after listening to one too many movies that privilege telephonic intelligibility over perceptual fidelity. The hi-fi soundscape he wants to live in would be designed around the intelligibility model, but for the purposes of documenting these soundscapes it's the phonographic model all the way. Tellingly, if we address the subjective element in Lastra's configuration of the phonographic model's aim at realistic representation, we find a way out of the Schaferian conundrum.

As Sabine Breitsameter points out, no critic has been able to sort out the many paradoxes present in Schafer's work, and that this gives Schafer's writing a "shimmering" quality that is instructive in its tensions. Schafer's "listening pedagogy ... wants all sound experiences ... to be considered worthy of attention" (Breitsameter 2013, 27), contrary to the judgmental hierarchy set up by the notions of *hi-fi* and *lo-fi* sound. She contends that, for Schafer, it is the very act of filtering according to value judgment espoused by hi-fi stereo culture that leads to impoverished listening practices in society (24–25). Yet Schafer's insistence upon the terms *hi-fi* and *lo-fi*, and the inarguably negative take on sound technologies inherent to his concept of schizophonia, obscure the ecological goal behind his call to hear the world with fresh ears. In short, Schafer's personal biases dominate his writing about the soundscape, and it has been nearly impossible for critics to hear past these to the original spirit of new environmental listening practices that are ultimately open to myriad listening positions within the soundscape. Lastra's move is, in part, to expose the very idea of perceptual fidelity as a representational choice by filmmakers, the first step toward accessing the ecological implications of this choice and how it can speak to acoustic ecology. In this representational choice lies a prescription for listening through technology without bias, and I use this as the basis for intersecting film sound theory with acoustic ecology.

We can refer to the relationship between listener position and choices in representation as "staging" sound following Karin Bijsterveld and her cocontributors to the *Soundscapes of the Urban Past* (2013). Here they bring some of the analytical tools developed by the WSP into a comparative media approach to the historiography of specific urban locales, while addressing key critical issues in the WSP's practice and how these can be worked through the broader field of media studies. They adopt some of the WSP's broad categories of *keynote sounds*, *soundmarks*, and the adapted concept of *sonic icons* to categorize the kinds of sounds presented across various media that stage urban environments (15). Within these categories she then applies her own auditory topoi to determine the role that these sounds play: the intrusive sound, the sensational sound, the comforting sound, and the sinister sound (15). In appealing to representations of urban spaces across a variety of media, the key challenge is to understand that sound in radio, film, television, and so on is always staged for specific purposes, and that these purposes are often specific to the medium for which the sound is produced.[3] With this in mind, questions of "faithful" representation are always at the fore in learning to hear the mediality in play so that the processes of fabrication can be understood as part of a cultural and historical form of engagement. By bringing attention to medium specificity, and situating this within the cultural and historical contexts of production, productive comparisons can then be made across media to flesh out the roles that such media play in establishing the dynamics of particular places at any given historical moment.

I build off Bijsterveld's work by intersecting another handful of terms that allow us to consider listener positionality as a function of fidelity. For example, Michel Chion uses the term *auditory extension* to refer to how far into the distance a film's soundtrack allows us to hear, the auditory equivalent of depth of field (1994, 87). Rick Altman's concept of *spatial signature* similarly refers to the distance between a sound source and point of audition by emphasizing the fact that sound will bear the markers of the space in which it is heard (1992, 24). Both of these simple concepts address how filmmakers can construct hi-fi or lo-fi soundscapes within the world of the diegesis by controlling our sense of space through evocations of the distance between source and listener. Chion's concept of *on-the-air sound* is also pertinent as it addresses sounds that are transmitted electroacoustically within the diegesis, such as music coming from a character's car radio or a voice from a public address system. Chion argues that such sounds "are not subject to 'natural' mechanical laws of sound propagation" and "enjoy the freedom of crossing boundaries of cinematic space" (1994, 76). Sounds that are on-the-air can take on different levels of spatial signature depending upon whether the filmmaker intends them to be grounded within the world of the diegesis, the realm of non-diegetic sound, or ambiguous spaces in between. The on-the-air category of sound is charged with the implications of schizophonia but without necessarily buying into Schafer's ableist bias against the technologies that make it possible. On-the-air sound can be a celebration of schizophonic potential; its use depends upon fluctuating levels of extension and qualities of spatial signature, and as such it acts as a nexus point around which the idea of schizophonia in the cinema can be tied to descriptive tools for film sound analysis.

Each of the aforementioned concepts can be read through the ideological underpinnings of acoustic ecology's project to reveal ecological issues at work in the audiovisual treatment of a film's narrative. In particular, these tools for film sound analysis become significant when read through Barry Truax's extended delineations of Schafer's *acoustic horizon*, *acoustic community*, and *acoustic profile*, each of which define particular acoustic ecologies through the limits that sound events reach and the particularities of their interaction within a given space (see Truax 2001). Particularly interesting, here, is how schizophonia is bound up with Schafer's notion of the hi-fi soundscape, equating fidelity not only with a strong signal-to-noise ratio but also with the ability of sounds to travel a long way in an environment without being masked by density (1977, 43). Here fidelity is embedded within geography as mapped by auditory extension. As such, this geographical fidelity can also map community, allowing us to account for the way that sound within a given acoustic profile can articulate the communities that hear it.

In this book, I use the term acoustic profiling to formalize the process of framing the issue of fidelity around the recognition of how filmmakers articulate the acoustic profiles of their narrative spaces, and how this articulation serves as a medial move to engage audiences with our everyday spatial understanding on deeper levels. This approach provides the possibility of reframing issues of fidelity, typically treated as the relationship between what is in a film and what lies beyond, around mediality as an immersive process that dissolves the boundary line between the two. Attention to how films delineate spaces through sound's capacity to move through them, and be limited by them, puts the audience in a fluctuating position with respect to the films themselves and how they are embedded in our lives. So in *Elephant*, when Frances White's "Walk Through Resonant Landscape #2" opens the high school cafeteria out into spaces beyond and unknown, we have a dramatic shift in the acoustic profile of that location from its previous representation as a noisy but contained environment. For Alex, the contained nature of the space provided the conditions for the noise that contributed to his sense of confinement, a lack of fidelity between his experience in the school and his experience outside. In turning the space inside out, he extended the profile of the space outward into the impossible. We could say that the representation of this space in this moment lacks fidelity in the traditional sense, as the sounds we hear do not reflect what we expect from the space we see on screen. However, when binding the idea of fidelity to the functioning of the acoustic profile as both a cinematic tool and a loaded concept within acoustic ecology, we open to the possibility that Alex's experience in this moment is now more authentic, a successful shift from the lo-fi to the hi-fi environment, expressed by heightened sonic extension, and laden with the troubling implications of the means by which this extension has been achieved.

The Films

In the chapters that follow, I employ the method of acoustic profiling, exploiting the aforementioned terminological intersections, to reveal how a variety of films illustrate principal concepts in acoustic ecology while getting us to think about the role of spatial representation along medial lines. Each chapter addresses a single film or set of films with critical attention to a particular line of division that can be productively analyzed through the idea of the acoustic profile: to what extent do the spaces on either side of the line extend into each other? How can this extension be tracked with attention to sound? What narrative and political purposes do the variable extensions across these lines serve? In some examples, these lines are diegetically physical: the architectural quality of the simultaneously transparent and reflective windows of Jacques Tati's *Playtime* (1967) that demarcate the spaces of modernity and their hindrance to community engagement; or the doorways of Gus Van Sant's *Last Days* (2005) that modulate empathy between friends gathered in a single house. In other examples, these lines are tied to media technologies and their capacity to foster audience engagement with the worlds they represent: Peter Mettler's overtly reflexive attention to the line between cinematic sound and image in *Picture of Light* (1994), exploited through asynchronous aesthetics; or the role of visualized sound technologies like the phonograph in the world of David Lynch's *Twin Peaks* (1990–2017), prompting questions about the possible fidelities that such technologies can afford. In still other examples, it is the very line between real-world locations and their audiovisual treatment on film, as in the tour through the cinemas of British Columbia in the book's final chapter. Of each example, the driving question is this: how does the simultaneous appearance and invisibility of these boundary lines that determine any acoustic profile—their apparitions and vanishings—create the medial moves that can support arguments for the value of including cinema as an important element of media practice in the world of acoustic ecology?

In Chapter 1 I introduce Schaferian acoustic ecology through an analysis of Jacques Tati's film *Playtime*. The film is a meditation on the spaces of modernist architecture as exemplified by the use of glass as building material in the International Style. Emphasizing the fact that glass enclosures are visually transparent while blocking the passage of sound, Schafer has dubbed such spaces as examples of "the glazed soundscape" wherein the view out the window is dissociated from its soundscape, an example of what Schafer laments about the current state of acoustic design (1993, 71–73). Emily Thompson equates this characteristic of the modernist soundscape with schizophonia, establishing architecture as a sound media much like the electroacoustic technologies that Schafer denounces (2002, 321). Yet just as hearing sound emanating from speakers need not be a disjunctive experience, nor should the experience of architectural glass necessarily be. *Playtime* challenges any overt critique of modernist architecture by setting up a rigorously Schaferian glazed environment in the first hour, only to subvert it in the second: by film's end Tati presents a total reversal of the glazed imperative, glass becoming highly reflective while sound is allowed to pass through unhindered. This shift is only detectable through careful attention to the film's handling of auditory extension, with equal attention to sound and image, and as such it provides a clear example of how acoustic profiling provides access to a dimension of the film that would be otherwise inaccessible. The dramatic reversal in the representation of architectural space is the film's mediality on display, emphasizing the fabricated nature of the ideologies that govern not only the construction of physical space but also our habits of experiencing it. To reveal this mediality I refer to the film's shift as an example of *audible transparency*, the glass on display in the film acting as both literalization of, and challenge to, the metaphor of transparency in hi-fi stereo culture (the myth of media's capacity to vanish from its representations) that also forms the basis for Schaferian acoustic ecology. My reading offers a way of rethinking Schafer's thought along perceptual lines by linking the shifting representation of glass in *Playtime* to the creative repurposing of the built environment that formed the basis for the *psychogeographic* practice of space espoused by the Situationists who were contemporaries of Schafer and Tati in the 1960s. As such, acoustic design is as much a function of our perception as it is about the physical environment itself.

With the idea of media transparency as a perceptual construct now firmly in mind, Chapter 2 addresses Peter Mettler's film *Picture of Light* as an exploration of what is at stake in the debates about the documentary recording practices essential to soundscape research. Mettler and his crew travel to Churchill, Manitoba, and attempt to capture the aurora borealis on film. They take an overtly reflexive strategy that foregrounds the filmmaking process while continually questioning if our experience of the lights on film could be anything like being there in person. While the filmmakers do capture some fine images of the lights, Mettler simultaneously asks what it might mean to *hear* these lights, staging the soundscape of Churchill through a combination of location recording and electroacoustic music that he pairs with images in ways that continually challenge the limits of documentary representation while meditating upon the role of media in shaping our engagement with the world they seek to document. The dividing line in *Picture of Light* is that between image and sound, and to what extent the realm of the seen can extend into the realm of the heard, and vice versa. My analysis of the film's acoustic profile works issues of documentary representation through the discourse of fidelity, with a particular emphasis on theories of *performativity* in documentary practice in which reflexivity is shown to have become a norm in the age of media skepticism (see Nichols 1994; Bruzzi 2006). However, I argue that Mettler "performs" his documentary as a way of moving past skepticism about the media's power to provide access to the world. Instead, Mettler calls attention to how we perform *with* our media as the very basis of our engagement with the world. I call this strategy *immersive reflexivity*: the foregrounding of mediality as a tool for engagement rather than distanciation, a mode that draws on the long history of experimental film and its attempts at generating more holistic experiences through self-conscious means, particularly with respect to sound/image relationships. By framing *Picture of Light* through the discourses of documentary and experimental film, I demonstrate how Mettler's film teaches us to address the practice of field recording in soundscape research as highly staged material that can, nevertheless, provide faithful means of engaging with the world that presents itself to the microphones.

The first two chapters explore how two of the core tenets of acoustic ecology, acoustic design and media documentation, play out in films that question the very nature of these tenets through their reflexive approaches to sound/image relationships. In Chapter 3 I make an explicit connection between film sound and another core practice in acoustic ecology, soundscape composition, through an analysis of Gus Van Sant's film *Last Days*. Like his previous film *Elephant*, discussed at the start of this introduction, the sound design for *Last Days* incorporates the soundscape compositions of Hildegard Westerkamp, original member of the World Soundscape Project. I examine how her piece "Türen der Wahrnehmung (Doors of Perception)" (1989) is mapped onto the space of the house occupied by Blake (Michael Pitt), a character loosely based on Kurt Cobain, who spends the days leading up to his suicide wandering around his estate in a drug-addled mental condition, surrounded by people who position themselves as his friends but who do not communicate with him effectively. Westerkamp's piece is premised on the use of door sounds to explore relationships between separate acoustic spaces that can be superimposed by way of the architectural construct of the doorway. The film is preoccupied with how Blake stands at an emotional remove from the people around him, and maps this remove onto the spaces they inhabit through a formal exploration of how the rooms of the house either join together or remain separate by way of the doorways through which the characters must continually pass. In heightening our attention to the architectural space of the house, the film also heightens our attention to the role of music in that space as several pieces—either pre-existing records or live performances—play out spatially. I argue that to properly understand how soundscape composition works as a sound design element we need a new model for theorizing how the compilation film soundtrack makes use of pre-existing pieces of music, extending the work of Anahid Kassabian (2001) on audience identification to undertheorized considerations of the spatial qualities of music. With the goals of acoustic ecology at heart, soundscape composition attunes us to the spatial dimensions of music, and bringing theorizations of the genre to questions of the compilation film soundtrack offers a new pathway into thinking about film music along ecological lines. I demonstrate how the presence of Westerkamp's piece in the film opens up ways of thinking about the function of space across all the sound design elements, as well as the image track, to reveal the heart of the film: *reflective empathy*, the term I use to describe the problems of opening up empathetic space between characters in the film, and between films and their audiences, similar to the problems of vanishing mediation in the discourse of fidelity. The acoustic profile under examination here is demarcated by the boundary line between human individuals, the extent to which any one person can truly experience the world as another, a requirement for empathy. The problem of reflective barriers to empathy is articulated formally by the role of doorways within the diegesis that mirror the boundaries between people, and echoed by the limits to which pre-existing music can enter into an empathetic relationship with films that build them into their soundtracks.

In Chapter 4 I focus on one particular sound technology, the phonograph, as a highly visual marker of the myth of vanishing mediation at the crux of the fidelity thesis, ideal for cinematic evocations of the schizophonic condition. With David Lynch and Mark Frost's *Twin Peaks* saga as a case study, I use the term *schizophonographics* to refer to cinema's capacity to represent the split between sound and source through graphic representation of the materiality of phonographic processes. *Twin Peaks* ties its schizophonographic representations of phonography to questions of neurodivergence in its narrative focal point: the figure of Laura Palmer, the high school senior found murdered in the opening minutes of the pilot episode, and whose troubled life unfolds through the police investigation that follows. *Twin Peaks*, through the original series (the first two seasons, 1990–91), the subsequent theatrical film *Fire Walk with Me* (1992), and the series' return for Season 3 (2017), extends Lynch's long-standing interest in the onscreen presence of sound technologies—especially record players—whose materiality serves as the basis for slippage between worlds, be they psychological states or spatiotemporal territories. For Lynch, dating back to his first feature, *Eraserhead* (1977), it is the material substance of the phonographic process that opens up portals to other times, places, and experiences. These portals are metaphors for the ideal of vanishing mediation, paradoxes that drive his narratives forward, perfectly illustrating the problem of the fidelity thesis at the heart of hi-fi stereo culture. As with the audibly transparent windows in *Playtime*, the immersively reflexive presence of on-screen filmmaking technologies in *Picture of Light*, and the reflectively empathetic relationship between soundscape composition and film sound design in *Last Days*, Lynch's interest in phonography inverts the fidelity thesis by fetishizing the materiality of the medium as the basis for its capacity to vanish. With reference to scholarship on early twentieth century anxieties surrounding sound and image recording technologies, and late twentieth century anxieties around the shift to digital processes, I demonstrate where *Twin Peaks* sits in the context of Lynch's history of schizophonographics to bind alternate modes of perception to medium-specific materiality.

The crux of my investigation into *Twin Peaks* is the fact that in Season 3, for the first time in Lynch's oeuvre, we are presented with a phonograph that emits sounds with no visible media: there is no record on the player—the media has vanished. What are we to make of this shift? This vanishing media is part of how Season 3 extends the pre-digital world of earlier *Twin Peaks* into the digital present, posing questions about the nature of media materiality along the way. The acoustic profile under consideration, then, is the one demarcated by the question of how these phonographic sounds are being transmitted, and from whom, where, and when. In demonstrating how the schizophonographic process works across these shifting manifestations in *Twin Peaks*, I offer an adjustment to the theoretical value of the fidelity thesis, particularly around Michel Chion's figure of the *acousmêtre*: the voice without a body whose evocation of the technological split between sound and image becomes the basis for supernatural powers. The way that Lynch's phonography shifts from materially specific to ethereally vague presents a model for the sound/body split that can help us better understand the issues in play with Schafer's reference to the schizophonic condition. In the figure of Laura Palmer, a character whose psychological instability drives much of the formal experimentation with sound and image in the series, we find a practical use for Schafer's negative evocation of schizophrenia in articulating the presence of sound technologies in our daily lives. The key to understanding the shift in schizophonographic representation is to understand how Laura Palmer, as the center of the *Twin Peaks* universe, has shifted along with it. Her trajectory across the entire *Twin Peaks* cycle maps the acoustic profile of the absent media, charting new ways of thinking about sonic fidelity along the way.

Finally, in Chapter 5 I consider how film sound can become an essential part of soundscape research conducted by acoustic ecology, and how folding the discourse of film sound theory back onto acoustic ecology can correct for a variety of gaps in the field's foundational texts. I use the city of Vancouver, British Columbia, birthplace of acoustic ecology and longest running case study of the World Soundscape Project, as an example of how the sonic environment of a specific geographical locale can be researched through film and audiovisual media. Here I ask: how can the work of the WSP teach us to hear things in films produced in and around Vancouver that have gone unaccounted for in the existing literature? In turn, how can listening to these films through the research of the WSP help us hear things that the WSP themselves failed to acknowledge? Here, the dividing line under consideration is that between the city itself and its appearances in films and media: to what extent can a study of one side of this line inform the other? After an analysis of how the sounds of Vancouver have been staged in the publications of the WSP, I apply my conclusions to an investigation of sound aesthetics and practices in Vancouver-based based film and media production. I use the sound of trains as represented in Vancouver film as the foundation for addressing how sound is tied to geographical specificity in local media, demonstrating why film sound design should be an important area of consideration for soundscape research. In the WSP's original *Vancouver Soundscape* documents of 1973, the sound of trains figured heavily in discussions of the city's geographically specific soundscape and its changes over the decades. This is not surprising, given that Vancouver was incorporated in 1886 as part of an agreement with Canadian Pacific Railway (CPR) that the city would serve as their western terminus, thus earning the name Terminal City. With the birth of cinema around the same time, and the immediate fascination that early filmmakers had for trains, the CPR instantly recognized the medium's potential as promotional tool, ensuring that train travel was a staple of films shot in the region since the beginning. Through a selection of film examples that feature the sounds of trains, ranging from the "silent" era through to the present, I construct a history of Vancouver's soundscape on film that reveals unheard dimensions of local film practices and their intersection with the development of the city.

The sound of the train is the locus for examining the city's acoustic profile: given that the sounds of trains have become a defining characteristic of the city, we can say that the entire city becomes the range across which these sounds can be heard. However, a problem arises when imagining a homogenous set of responses to these sounds within such a highly diverse population as is found in Vancouver. The work of acoustic profiling in this chapter leads to what I am calling *unsettled listening*, following Nicholas Blomley's work on Vancouver in his book *Unsettling the City* (2004), whereby listener positionality is taken into account when trying to understand the relationship between sound and culture within a given acoustic profile. While the work of the WSP was fairly limited in its imagination of what the sound of trains means to Vancouverites, my study of a variety of films and media across a wide range of historical periods, genres, and formats reveals a complex set of overlapping responses to this omnipresent sound. And here I illustrate why the work of film sound studies, informed by acoustic ecology, needs to reflect back onto acoustic ecology itself, bringing new perspectives to bear on their methods for studying the soundscapes in which we live. The issue of fidelity, finally, comes to rest on how well the complexity of overlapping communities can be represented in documentation, analysis, prescription, and composition in and around the spaces they occupy.

I conclude the book with a reflection upon how the methodology I have established for intersecting acoustic ecology with the film and media has influenced my approach to thinking about the spaces I occupy outside the screening room walls. Having examined the four key dimensions of acoustic ecology as established by the World Soundscape Project, and demonstrated the value of intersecting these with the study of film sound, I explain how the revelations about the myth of vanishing mediation that I take away from all the films examined in this book have given me a tool kit for living more consciously of the complexities of the spaces that live in, which, in turn, have informed my approach to creative practice. As a concrete illustration, I explain how some of my own biographical details have informed two artistic projects that I have worked on that both explicitly frame an approach to audiovisual design through the method of acoustic profiling used as an analytical tool throughout this book, now a tool for critically examining my own listener positionality as a settler on indigenous lands. In the end, my wish for this book is not only to inform new ways of thinking about film sound for use in research, analysis, and teaching, but also to inform new ways of thinking about where we stand in relation to the world that we live in. In this time of dire need for full accountability in the relationship between settler and indigenous positionalities, we need ways of listening that provide a foundation for action in the world. Creative practice with full disclosure about settler positionality is one form of productive action that can work to prevent continuing imposition of fixed positions upon the multiply diverse spaces of the world. I conclude by showing how this has begun to work for me, in the hopes that it might also work for you, too.

References

Altman, Rick. 1992. "The Material Heterogeneity of Recorded Sound." In *Sound Theory, Sound Practice*, edited by Rick Altman, 15–31. New York: Routledge.

Bijsterveld, Karin. 2008. *Mechanical Sound: Technology, Culture, and Public Problems of Noise in the Twentieth Century*. Cambridge: MIT Press.

Bijsterveld, Karin, ed. 2013. *Soundscapes of the Urban Past: Staged Sound as Mediated Cultural Heritage*. Bielefeld: Transcript Verlag.

Birdsall, Carolyn. 2012. *Nazi Soundscapes: Sound, Technology and Urban Space in Germany, 1933–1945*. Amsterdam: Amsterdam University Press.

Blomley, Nicholas. 2004. *Unsettling the City: Urban Land and the Politics of Property*. New York: Routledge.

Breitsameter, Sabine. 2013. "Ways of Listening; Figures of Thought." In *Ways of Listening; Figures of Thought: A Festschrift for R. Murray Schafer on the Occasion of his 80th Birthday*, edited by Sabine Breitsameter and Eric Leonardson, 17–36. Darmstadt: Hochschule Darmstadt.

Bruzzi, Stella. 2006. *New Documentary*. 2nd edition. New York: Routledge.

Chion, Michel. 1994. *Audio-Vision: Sound on Screen*. Translated by Claudia Gorbman. New York: Columbia University Press.

Chion, Michel. 2009. *Film, A Sound Art*. Translated by Claudia Gorbman. New York: Columbia University Press.

Dienstfrey, Eric. 2023. *Making Stereo Fit: The History of a Disquieting Film Technology*. Berkeley: University of California Press.

Donnelly, Kevin. 2008. *The Spectre of Sound: Music in Film and Television*. London: British Film Institute.

Droumeva, Milena and Randolph Jordan. 2019. "Historical Timeline for the Development of Acoustic Ecology at Simon Fraser University Through to the Foundation of the World Foum for Acoustic Ecology." In *Sound, Media, Ecology*, edited by Milena Droumeva and Randolph Jordan, vii–xiv. New York: Palgrave Macmillan.

Gorbman, Claudia. 1987. *Unheard Melodies: Narrative Film Music*. Bloomington: Indiana University Press.

Jones, Kent. 2003. "Corridors of Powerlessness." *Film Comment* 39, no. 5: 28.

Jordan, Randolph. 2007. "Case Study: Film Sound, Acoustic Ecology, and Performance in Electroacoustic Music." In *Music, Sound and Multimedia: From the Live to the Virtual*, edited by Jamie Sexton, 121–141. Edinburgh: University of Edinburgh Press.

Kassabian, Anahid. 2001. *Hearing Film: Tracking Identifications in Contemporary Hollywood Film Music*. New York: Routledge.

Lastra, James. 2000. *Sound Technology and the American Cinema*. New York: Columbia University Press.

McCartney, Andra. 2002. "Sharing Experiences Towards the Possibility of an Electroacoustic Ecology." *Soundscape: The Journal of Acoustic Ecology* 3, no. 1: 22.

McCartney, Andra. 2010. "Ethical Questions about Working with Soundscapes." Text from keynote presentation at the World Forum for Acoustic Ecology in Koli, Finland (June 19). http://soundwalkinginteractions.wordpress.com/2010/06/24/ethical-questions-about-working-with-soundscapes/

Morton, Timothy. 2007. *Ecology Without Nature: Rethinking Environmental Aesthetics*. Cambridge: Harvard University Press.

Nichols, Bill. 1994. *Blurred Boundaries: Questions of Meaning in Contemporary Culture*. Bloomington: Indiana University Press.

Norman, Katharine. 1996. "Real-World Music as Composed Listening." *Contemporary Music Review* 15, nos. 1–2: 1–27.

Pritchett, James. 2007. "Frances White: Centre Bridge." Liner notes to *Centre Bridge* by Frances White. New York: Mode Records 184, compact disc.

Robinson, Dylan. 2020. *Hungry Listening: Resonant Theory for Indigenous Sound Studies*. Minneapolis: University of Minnesota Press.

Schafer, R. Murray. 1977. *The Tuning of the World*. Toronto: McClelland and Stewart.

Schafer, R. Murray. 1993. *Voices of Tyranny, Temples of Silence*. Indian River: Arcana Editions.

Sterne, Jonathan. 2003. *The Audible Past: Cultural Origins of Sound Reproduction*. Durham, NC: Duke University Press.

Sterne, Jonathan. 2012. *MP3: The Meaning of a Format*. Durham, NC: Duke University Press.

Sterne, Jonathan. 2013. "Soundscape, Landscape, Escape." In *Soundscapes of the Urban Past: Staged Sound as Mediated Cultural Heritage*, edited by Karin Bijsterveld, 181–192. Bielefeld: Transcript Verlag.

Sterne, Jonathan. 2019. "Multimodal Scholarship in World Soundscape Project Composition: Toward a Different Media-Theoretical Legacy (Or: The W.S.P. as OG DH)." In *Sound, Media, Ecology*, edited by Milena Droumeva and Randolph Jordan, 85–109. New York: Palgrave Macmillan.

Thompson, Emily. 2002. *The Soundscape of Modernity: Architectural Acoustics and the Culture of Listening in North America, 1900–1933*. Cambridge: MIT Press.

Truax, Barry, ed. 1978. *Handbook for Acoustic Ecology*. Vancouver: A.R.C. Publications/The World Soundscape Project.

Truax, Barry. 2001. *Acoustic Communication*. 2nd edition. Westport, CT: Alex Publishing.

Truax, Barry. 2008. "Soundscape Composition as Global Music: Electroacoustic Music as Soundscape." *Organised Sound* 13, no. 2: 103–109.

Verma, Neil. 2012. *Theater of the Mind: Imagination, Aesthetics, and American Radio Drama*. Chicago: University of Chicago Press.

Westerkamp, Hildegard. 1974. "Soundwalking." *Sound Heritage* 3, no. 4: 18–27.

Westerkamp, Hildegard. 2002. "Linking Soundscape Composition and Acoustic Ecology." *Organised Sound* 7, no. 1 (April): 51–56.

Westerkamp, Hildegard. 2019. "The Disruptive Nature of Listening: Today, Yesterday, Tomorrow." In *Sound, Media, Ecology*, edited by Milena Droumeva and Randolph Jordan, 45–64. New York: Palgrave MacMillan.

World Soundscape Project. 1973. *The Vancouver Soundscape*. Sound recording and book. Burnaby: Sonic Research Studio, Dept. of Communications, Simon Fraser University.

World Soundscape Project. 1996. *The Vancouver Soundscape 1973/Soundscape Vancouver 1996*. Sound Recording. Vancouver: Cambridge Street Records (CSR-2CD 9701).

1

Audible Transparency

Modernist Acoustic Design in Jacques Tati's *Playtime*

The 1967 premiere of Jacques Tati's film *Playtime* coincided with the publication of Guy Debord's *Society of the Spectacle* (1967), the most famous of the works to be produced by a member of the Situationist movement that had been functioning in France since the mid-1950s. Perhaps unlikely bedfellows, there is no question that Tati's cinematic explorations of a modernizing France were grappling with many of the same issues that drove the Situationists in their critiques of the alienating qualities of consumer culture. Meanwhile, on the westernmost frontier of Europe's expansion, Canadian composer R. Murray Schafer had just published *Ear Cleaning* (1967) while on faculty as a music educator at Simon Fraser University (SFU) in Vancouver, British Columbia. This is the publication that laid the foundation for what would become the field of acoustic ecology, a call to develop new listening practices that would "clean" our ears in order to be better attuned to the sonic environments in which we live. Ear cleaning is the first step toward Schafer's goal of acoustic design, most fully articulated ten years later in *The Tuning of the World* (1977),[1] which proposes a refashioning of the built environment according to the new listening practices that he espoused. Like Tati and the Situationists, Schafer was responding to a particularly vibrant moment for global urbanism, said to be homogenizing the cities of the Western world through a shared language of urban architecture epitomized by the International Style. While it is fairly common to find discussions of Tati's films contextualized by way of the Situationists, discussions of Schafer's work in relation to either Tati or the Situationists is essentially nonexistent. Bringing Schafer into this discussion allows for addressing important questions of sound in Tati's film that, in turn, opens the door for a way of unpacking Schaferian acoustic ecology and situating it in the context of film sound studies.

In this chapter I offer a reading of *Playtime* at the intersection of Schaferian acoustic ecology and Situationist thought. I argue that the film is a reflexive meditation on the role of cinema in fostering heightened awareness of how we engage the spaces we inhabit by way of the technologies that determine their shape. There is a double benefit to the intersection of Schafer and the Situationists in developing this reading. Firstly, Schafer's concepts allow us to hear Tati's work with fresh ears to acknowledge a highly reflexive approach to the relationship between sound and image in the representation of modernist architectural space that has not yet been critically examined. Tati is foregrounding the medial quality of his aesthetics as a way of inciting reflection upon the real-world architectural spaces through which we move every day. Secondly, this reading of *Playtime* invites us to take a step back from Schafer's emphasis on redesigning our acoustic environments and focus on the role of creative listening practice as his key contribution to acoustic ecology. The humorless didacticism, to say nothing of the settler's impulse, found within Schafer's prescriptions for a "better" sounding environment have soured many on engaging too deeply with his concepts, one of the many reasons why Schaferian acoustic ecology has not yielded large-scale acoustic design in any urban planning project to date. A similar fate befell the Situationists, whose (often humorous and contradictory) prescriptions for ideal urban forms were never realized either. Yet the tools that Schafer and the Situationists provided for new ways of experiencing the built environment are invaluable for the critical reassessment of our worlds whether inside the walls of a screening room or out. *Playtime* presents a perfect storm in which key issues in both Schaferian acoustic ecology and Situationist thought play out. Tati's project ultimately celebrates the process of changing our awareness of urban space by inviting us to become aware of how we engage with such space by way of the technologies of architecture and the media on which they are founded. As such, *Playtime* makes an ideal starting point for introducing the relationships between acoustic ecology and film sound studies that sit at the foundation of this book.

Playtime is dedicated to imagining a Paris of the near future when the glass and steel of the burgeoning International Style, increasingly associated with postwar Americanism, starts to take over Europe as well. The film charts a wide range of the possible interactions that such spaces could engender with its denizens. The key to my analysis is recognizing a major transformation in the aesthetic treatment of glass as a building material—a transformation only accessible by way of equal attention to sound and image. The film's first hour emphasizes glass as a material imbued with an apparent paradox: on the one hand, glass allows for a persistent illusion of community through its visual transparency; on the other hand, glass separates individuals through its effectiveness as a physical barrier against sound (as well as a variety of other elements). These material characteristics of glass are governed by what Michel Chion has termed auditory (and visual) extension: how far we can hear or see into the distance of a film's diegesis (1994, 86–89). By the film's conclusion, however, the formal treatment of architectural space that allows long-range views combined with isolated sonic environments gives way to a situation in which glass—now more reflective than transparent—no longer acts as an acoustic barrier. Visual extension decreases while auditory extension increases. The physical properties of the architecture have not changed, but their formal treatment within the film has. This decisive reversal of sound/image relationships is the crux upon which the substance of *Playtime* hangs, and it is a medial move: it calls attention to the cinematic construction of architectural space as a means of inviting reflection upon the ways in which we all construct our spaces by way of our perceptual processes.

Listening to how sound functions in relation to the visual treatment of architectural space in *Playtime* allows us to trace the film's audiovisual shift through three fairly distinct acts in what has been described as an open form film that resists such linear readings (see Burch 1973, 47). The first act follows characters through various glass enclosures that are presented as agents of separation between individuals and impediments to physical interaction; the second act is a sequence in the Royal Garden restaurant and night club where the people of the city gather in a communal spirit as the architecture begins to lose its divisive qualities; and the third act finds the partygoers on the streets of Paris in the early morning where the same city, once divided, is transformed into a space of heightened human interaction. As such, the progression of the film presents a shifting perspective on the function of modernist architecture exemplified by glass barriers, and ends with a play on the concept of transparency that casts the idea in range of the discourse of fidelity that governs the film's approach to modernist architecture. Three factors will be key to my discussion of this progression: spatial isolation and containment as major goals of modernist architecture; debates in acoustic ecology and Situationist thought about the effect of this containment on the people exposed to it; and the solutions to the problems identified within these debates suggested by the film's shifting approach to the audiovisual representation of architectural space.

Debates continue about whether the film is ultimately a celebration or critique of modern urban spaces and the social practices they situate. As David

Bellos notes, the film "provokes political and historical interpretations, but avoids giving simple confirmation to any one of them" (1999, 274). I argue, however, that the film does confirm one reading when we pay attention to the role of sound in Tati's construction of architectural space: that the film is overtly reflexive about the fabricated nature of this space, and this reflexivity calls attention to the role of ideology in guiding our attitudes toward such spaces. The central issue here is the very idea of transparency, a concept that forms the core of the discourse of fidelity in sound studies. Held up as an indicator of how closely a recording is said to be faithful to whatever presented itself to the microphones, transparency is, in fact, born of a way of listening that aims to ignore mediality. A pane of glass might be transparent in its ability to let us see through to the other side, but this transparency is dependent upon material qualities that also reflect light and impede other sensory information, not the least of which is sound. The notion of transparency is also at the core of critiques of Schafer's use of the language of the hi-fi stereo culture he ultimately decries, using terms like *hi-fi soundscape* to describe idealized rural environments free of the sound technologies that gave rise to the term *hi-fi* in the first place. Tati's reversal of the audiovisual transparency of glass calls attention to the artificiality of transparency as a constructed practice of both listening and looking, and it does so by emphasizing the role of sound technology—whether in the cinematic apparatus or the way architecture shapes sonic space—offering a way of understanding the value of Schafer's evocation of the language of fidelity discourse in articulating his listening practices. I refer to Tati's audiovisual strategies here as *audible transparency*: a false invisibility that makes itself known through sound, a mediation that attempts to vanish but cannot. Rendering the visual transparency of the architecture audible through the soundtrack is the medial move in *Playtime*, and understanding how this works allows for rethinking Schafer's contribution to acoustic ecology as an emphasis on perception as the basis for creatively expressing different ways of engaging with the soundscape by way of media technologies—whether architectural or electroacoustical in nature.

Reversing Tativille

Playtime is a thorough examination of International Style modernism. Not yet the norm in mid-1960s Paris, Tati had limited options for shooting such a project on location—none of which would have allowed the kind of control he needed. So at great personal expense he had a full-scale set built inspired by the works of Le Corbusier and Mies van der Rohe (see Bellos 1999, 241–250). Dubbed "Tativille," this set is the main focus of the film, and his large cast of characters—including the perennial Mr. Hulot, played in all of Tati's films by the director himself—are choreographed to reveal myriad nuances of these architectural spaces. Because Tati's filmmaking is structured around gags, both sight and sound, the most important moments are designed as points of comedy. Tati's comedy is highly sophisticated in that it often depends upon elaborate choreography of character movement within dense mise-en-scène, and so the jokes are inextricable from the architectural space that takes central position in the film. Accordingly, my analysis will focus on those gags that are designed to illustrate the particularities—and peculiarities—of the International Style. It is upon these gags, each exploring the relationship between transparency and reflectivity (both visual and auditory), that the film's mediality rests. I begin my analysis by comparing the opening of the film to the closing in order to chart a dramatic shift in the audibility of the film's architectural transparency.

The film opens with a shot of a glass and steel skyscraper framed against the sky, emphasizing the airiness of the International Style designed to free architecture from the cumbersome weight of stylistic excess and assume a form that aligns with its function, embracing the aesthetic beauty that such an alignment entails. The glass is both reflective and transparent. Some glass panels reflect the clouds to create a continuum between sky and building, while others allow for a view inside the edifice, the space of the sky opening into the offices within. The ability of glass to be both reflective and transparent is the conundrum that rests at the heart of Tati's film: glass can bring spaces together and keep them separate—often at the same time. In purely visual terms, this duality is a function of the angle from which we view a glass pane, and the lighting differential between the spaces on either side. When considering the other senses, however, glass is much less variable in its mediation of space: a closed window allows for a view out into the world while keeping sound and weather out along with their sensorial tactility. Yet what if the glass window's variable transparency were to encompass the other senses as well? This variability is the subject of two key gags that bookend the film in a reversal of how sound and image function through the medium of glass.

From the outset the film establishes a very clear approach to the way that glass enclosures prevent the flow of sound between interior and exterior spaces. One of the first gags comes as Mr. Hulot approaches the Strand building with walls of glass, positioned next to a street with a fair bit of noisy traffic. Before Hulot arrives at the door, we are given a preview of the delineation Tati will continuously draw between inside and outside in the first half of the film. The scene involves a concierge (Léon Doyen) positioned within the lobby area inside the building, and a construction worker on the street just outside. We are presented with an interior medium shot behind the concierge looking out onto the street, but framed in such a way that we do not see the edges of the windowpane. The effect is as though there is no division between the concierge's position inside the building and the street beyond, though the traffic noise diminishes dramatically when the film cuts from the exterior shot to the interior. Tati then builds a sight gag around the effect created by the framing: the construction worker approaches the concierge from the street, asking for a light for his cigarette, not realizing that there is a pane of glass separating him from his fire. The concierge gestures toward the door, and the construction worker indicates that he now sees the edges of the frame. As the two men move toward the door, the camera dollies leftward to follow, revealing the edges of the windowpane. The worker opens the door as the concierge holds out a match, and a rush of environmental noise from the street becomes apparent on the soundtrack once again. We then cut to a shot from outside the building as Mr. Hulot approaches, and the level of the environmental noise remains the same. Here it becomes clear that glass acts as a powerful barrier to sound while remaining nearly invisible to the eye. At this point the film also makes it clear that doors will be positioned as powerful mediators to the flow of sound between interior and exterior spaces.

The rigorous approach to the auditory distinction between interior and exterior space is consistent throughout the first hour of *Playtime* (as I will demonstrate in more detail below). By the end of the film, however, we find a very different treatment of glass and its role in mediating the divide between interior and exterior space. In the film's final moments there is a shot that works in parallel to that involving the concierge and the construction worker. After a series of exterior views onto the city streets transformed into a carnival environment, complete with street noise and suitable music, we then cut to an interior shot of a window cleaner working on a pane of glass at street level. However, the shot begins as a view out onto the street traffic with no indication that we are looking through a window (save for a bit of reflection toward the bottom left). The exterior sound from the previous shots remains constant as we cut to this one, suggesting that we are still being presented with an exterior point of view. The camera then tracks backward revealing the frame of the window and the fact that we are actually positioned in an interior space. The figure of the window cleaner appears and opens the window, begins wiping it down with a rag, and closes it again in the process. As the window opens and closes there is no change in the dynamics or content of the music or environmental sound. To punctuate this point, Tati cuts from interior to exterior as a car drives by with a loud motor sound that bridges the shots with no auditory distinction between these spaces once so divided. Once positioned outside, the camera frames the window so that we can see the reflection of a tour bus and its passengers, who then appear to rise up and down as the window tilts open and closed. The effect renders the bus riders as though on an amusement park ride, and Tati seals the gag by synchronizing a squeaking sound along with each of the window's movements that sounds at once like a wet rag streaking on the glass and the amused exclamations of ride passengers. Here the reflectivity of the glass is made explicit in the gag where it was hidden in the previous example, and this reflectivity is cued to the soundtrack so that we might listen and become aware of the new realities of the film's representation of architectural space.

Like the cigarette lighting gag, the window cleaner sequence uses a visual strategy whereby a shot of activity out on the street is revealed—through a moving camera—to have been filmed through a window. This time, however, the sound does not provide us with a clue that we are inside as it did in the example of the concierge and the construction worker: the bustle on the street is clearly audible during the interior shots, and the presence of music diminishes the possibility of delineating this interior space as being sonically confined. This situation continues as we then cut to shots of a tourist bus, alternating between interior and exterior perspectives. Here we find Barbara (Barbara Dennek), a tourist with a group of Americans who has been crossing paths with Hulot throughout the film, who is seen here unwrapping a gift finally given to her by Hulot. It is a charming statuette of long-stemmed flowers that resembles the assemblage of streetlamps visible just outside the bus window. This visual parallel is emphasized by framing Barbara and the statuette through the window of the bus, then cutting to a wider shot with Barbara, the statuette and the lamps, and then moving the camera left to frame the lamps by themselves. This is a final visual pun on bridging the gap between inside and outside, and as this occurs on the image track we hear the voices of the people along with the street noise and music on generally equal terms—regardless of where the camera is positioned. With this, Tati sends the bus off into the dusk and the film fades to black.

The second of these set pieces inverts the first: glass is first visually transparent and sonically opaque; then glass becomes visually reflective and sonically transparent. This move is medial in that it puts the materiality of the medium of glass on display within the diegesis while, at the same time, calling attention to how the film constructs the audiovisual space. This is a good example of a variance in acoustic profile: the shift from visual transparency to reflection is tied to a similar shift in auditory extension. Neither of these gags work without equal attention to sound and image, both on the part of the filmmakers and the audience. Acoustic profiling allows us to understand how the film can shift its handling of the relationship between sound and image at will, inviting the audience to think of their own perception in the same way. Specifically, this mediality invites us to reflect upon how Tati's handling of architectural space is tied to ideas about transparency in other media technologies, and how it can allow us to understand Schaferian acoustic ecology while moving through it to a better way of accounting for how we live with media technologies as tools for potential engagement.

Glazing the Soundscape

I can think of no better point of entry into the conceptual issues raised by Tati's audiovisual reversal than R. Murray Schafer's notion of the *glazed soundscape*, centered upon an apparent paradox at work in the functioning of glass as architectural material. "Plate glass shattered the sensorium," Schafer says, "replacing it with contradictory visual and aural impressions . . . framing external events in an unnatural phantom-like 'silence'" that ultimately "craves reorchestration" to make these spaces "more sensorally complete" (1993, 71–73). The use of piped-in sound creates a contradiction between inside and outside: "The world seen through the window is like the world of a movie set with the radio as soundtrack" (73), a fitting analogy when addressing how Tati reorchestrates his glazed spaces across the two window gags described above. Schafer's positioning of the window at the center of audiovisual disjunction is heavily loaded with his more general biases against media technologies, and so it is instructive to read his biases through critical discourses on modernist architectural space. At the heart of the matter lies the concept of transparency and how it is constructed according to particular expectations for looking and listening through media technologies, attempting either to make these media disappear or to bring medial qualities to the fore.

It is essential that we situate architecture in general, and windows in particular, as media technologies that can be discussed in the same terms as technologies of sound and image recording and transmission. In *The Virtual Window* (2006) Ann Friedberg traces the evolution of the window from architectural aperture to screen technology, emphasizing the shift from the window as a tool for ventilation to the window as a device for framing a view. A general argument that runs throughout her book is that this framing of views is not in service of making the viewer feel a part of the world pictured within the borders of the frame, but rather keeps the viewer at a distance from it. The frame becomes an agent of modernist isolation, and the window is a way of emphasizing the boundary between the spaces that it separates. The transparency of glass, then, is tempered by its frame, augmented when we account for the medium's reflectivity that can result in a complex layering of spatial representations that Friedberg ultimately traces through to the computer screen as assortment of virtual windows.

Issues of framing, isolation, and virtuality are key to the soundscapes of modernist architecture as well. In *The Soundscape of Modernity* (2002), Emily Thompson charts modernist ideals that sought to banish reverberation from interior spaces and create quiet and direct soundscapes that could be managed independently of the environment that surrounded them. As Thompson notes, "Walls of expansive glass and hard, thin plaster partitions resulted in uncomfortably reverberant spaces that easily transmitted sound" (209). Le Corbusier, among the first to design such a space, was also among the first to try and regulate its sonic effects (209). Eventually, the visually appealing design of modernist glass enclosures was rendered sonically acceptable through acoustical treatments that were developed in the United States. These treatments were refined to the point where reverberation could be effectively banished, leaving a quiet and direct sound to match the clean and airy designs of such spaces. Thus these spaces managed to contain sound and isolate it from the context of its surroundings, ultimately making the perfect vehicles for filling in with electroacoustically transmitted sound (228).

Tati's formal treatment of audiovisual space lives at the intersection of these visual and auditory characteristics of modernist enclosures, exploiting the potential range of possibility in their confluence. Importantly, R. Murray Schafer's critique of modernist architecture also lives at the intersection of its image and soundscapes. In particular, it is the possibility of disjunctive experience between vision and hearing that Schafer finds most offensive, a quality dependent upon a window's apparent visual transparency combined with its auditory opacity. For this visual transparency to work, however, the frame has to be deemphasized—what Ann Friedberg identifies as the project of "dematerialization" that modernist architects sought in expanding the size of glass panes used for construction (2006, 117). These effects are at their peak, Friedberg says, "in the paradigmatic modernist 'glass box'" in which windows give way to transparent walls (117). Here the frame expands, diverting attention away from itself to create a greater sense of transparency, while keeping the containment of the other senses intact. In this sonic containment, the transparency of the glass box is audible.

The cigarette lighting gag reflects Schafer's attitude toward glass very well. The window as framed view is a function of modernist isolation and containment, yet this gag is premised upon a citizen's lack of awareness of the window's frame; the mise-en-scène is framed in such a way that makes the audience complicit in this illusory community between separate spaces. However, the film does not present an auditory equivalent of the visual gag. Once we have cut to the interior shot, the isolationist properties of the building's modernist soundscape take immediate effect, even before we realize that we are now positioned inside. The nature of the interior sound is contained and cut off from the world visible outside. This situation is reversed in the window-cleaning gag at the end of the film in which there is no longer any auditory differentiation between interior and exterior.

Concerns over the isolationist qualities of modernist architecture are echoed in Situationist critique of modern society in general. As Guy Debord reiterates in various different permutations throughout *The Society of the Spectacle*, "Everything that was directly lived has moved away into a representation" (1983, para. 1). This situation creates an experiential paradox: "The spectacle, like modern society, is at once unified and divided" (para. 54) ensuring "a constant reinforcement of the conditions of isolation of 'lonely crowds'" (para. 28). While Debord's prose is often intentionally cryptic, the theme of modern society's thrust toward virtual realms of experience creates illusions of unification between the people in this society when, in reality, the very fact of experience through representation keeps people divided from one another. The planes of virtuality enabled by windows that frame views while reflecting other views are architectural embodiments of the illusion of community that Debord critiques. The same is true for the decontextualization of the modern interior soundscape and its replacement by virtual materials. These aspects of modernist architecture contribute to the Situationist critique of an emphasis on functionalism that results in the fabrication of "uninhabitable ambiances" despite its positive aesthetics (*Internationale Situationniste* 3 [December 1959], para. 5). For Schafer, these "uninhabitable ambiences" come in the form of isolationist and virtualist soundscapes. As he says about the International Style that emerged from the Bauhaus: "Bellevue—mais mauvais son" (1977, 222). In other words: the transparency has a sound, and it isn't good.

Reflecting upon Transparency

It is instructive to situate Schafer's concerns over architectural isolation within the apparent contradiction at work in his distaste for technologies of sound recording and transmission while evoking the language of hi-fi stereo culture to articulate this distaste. Schafer displays his biases most prominently through his concept of schizophonia, first used in *The New Soundscape* (1968) and later developed in *The Tuning of the World* to attribute negative connotations to "the split between an original sound and its electroacoustical transmission or reproduction" (1977, 90). Emily Thompson productively equates this concept with the goal of sonic isolation in modernist architecture: "Fifty years after it was first accomplished," she says, "R. Murray Schafer dubbed this splitting 'schizophonia' to emphasize its pathological nature" (2002, 321). Here Thompson shows how schizophonia can be understood as an architectural possibility as well as an electroacoustical one: the separation of a contained soundscape from the context of the environment just beyond its walls. Thompson's move to situate architecture on the same plane as media technology is the key to understanding how Tati's film puts mediality on display, and how we can follow his aesthetic treatments as a guide to thinking through the oft-critiqued contradictions in Schafer's anti-technological biases.

In Schafer's thought, the fundamental fear underlying the experience of schizophonia is "the complete portability of acoustic space" in which "any sonic environment can now become any other sonic environment" (1977, 91). This is a nearly impossible situation that I have dubbed "space replacement" (2007, 132). Schizophonic space replacement assumes a level of perfection in sound reproduction whereby an electroacoustically transmitted sound could be mistaken for the naturally occurring soundscape of a given environment. To complicate matters, space replacement also has a temporal aspect, since prerecorded sounds piped into other environments are also originating from an earlier time. These factors bind Schafer's evocation of schizophrenic experience to more general critiques of postmodernity, as when Fredric Jameson invokes schizophrenic symptoms to describe what he sees as the fragmentation, isolation, and surface reassemblage of experience characteristic of postmodernist architecture, amounting to a loss of historical context (1991, 21). As Barry Truax has noted, the fear of schizophonia is essentially a fear of virtual reality (2000, 104). The virtuality in question is premised upon the goal of the "vanishing mediator" described by Jonathan Sterne as an impossible situation wherein "the medium produces a perfect symmetry between copy and original and, thereby, erases itself" (2003, 285). Within this construction, any technologies of recording/transmission should vanish from perception when listening to the final product. As Sterne argues, however, the idea of an "original" sound object or event is bound up with the notion of its copy (282), a symptom of the "modernity thesis" governing ideas about sound technology: "First, it posits the moment of unmediated sonic reality prior to sound's technological mediation. Then, it posits the ideal form of mediation as a vanishing mediator" (285). But since technologies of reproduction cannot vanish, Sterne argues that any claims to transparency at the heart of the discourse of fidelity have been programs for development never fully realized by the designers of sound technologies, but happily used as tools for marketing ways of listening to their targeted consumers. These ways of listening are premised upon what Sterne calls an "audile technique" training listeners to "differentiate between sounds 'of' and sounds 'by' the network, casting the former as 'exterior' and the latter as 'interior' to the process of reproduction" (283). With this audile technique, listeners can identify exterior sounds and ignore them, thus using a perceptual trick to render the medium of reproduction transparent.

In film sound theory, the idea of vanishing mediation has been addressed at length by James Lastra. Expanding on the work of Rick Altman and others who have challenged the idea that recording technology can effectively "reproduce" any given sound event, Lastra concludes that we should always think of sound recordings as "representation" rather than "reproduction" (2000, 153). In other words, all recorded sound is acknowledged as a product of mediation. This allows Lastra to move past expectations for a film soundtrack to reproduce some "original" sound events "faithfully," and focus instead on philosophies of representation that guide the choices that filmmakers make when designing their soundtracks. In this way the expectations for fidelity between original and copy can be changed according to an understanding that all copies are little more than representations to begin with. This is a reality compounded by the fact that even the events being copied cannot be pinned down to stable and original wholes either, and are dependent upon listener positionality (Altman 1992, 28). So the distinction between original and copy is rendered artificial, an issue I will address in greater detail in the chapters that follow. For the moment, what is most important is that we recognize the mediation at work in all auditory contexts, cinematic and otherwise. This is the work of Tati in his exploration of transparency here, and it can be used to rethink Schafer's call for fidelity in the soundscape.

Schafer's concept of schizophonia implies the problems within the discourse of fidelity, a fact supported by Schafer's own use of the related concept of the hi-fi soundscape in which one can hear far into the distance because of the absence of the ubiquitous masking sounds that characterize the lo-fi environment (1977, 43). Here Schafer borrows one of the key definitions of fidelity from hi-fi stereo culture: that a good recording is one with a low signal to noise ratio, one of the main factors in striving for the vanishing mediator. Schafer is equating two varieties of noise: system noise, a marker of the recording apparatus, acting as a presence that inhibits our ability to hear through the technology to the recorded event; and urban noise, which similarly prevents us from hearing far into the distance.

Though Schafer doesn't make an explicit connection between schizophonia and the lo-fi soundscape, the two are closely related: the presence of electroacoustically transmitted sound creates an artificial sense of distance while in reality contributing to the density of sound that ultimately hinders long-range listening within the environment. And, of course, the vanishing mediation required to make schizophonic space replacement a reality is an imaginary construct invented by the hi-fi stereo industry itself. Schafer's concept of a hi-fi soundscape, then, is one premised upon a way of listening that requires attention to certain features of that soundscape while ignoring anything that calls attention to how aspects of this environment mediate the sound.

What is missing in Schafer's account of schizophonia is that it can be a productive incitement toward developing an awareness of technological mediation, thereby enhancing our engagement with modern sound environments rather than degrading it. As Barry Truax suggests, "The challenge of the schizophonic situation for the listener is to make sense out of the juxtaposition of two different contexts" (2001, 134), a situation made possible through electroacoustical transmission. Many artists have gravitated toward exploiting schizophonic media in search of what Andra McCartney calls an "electroacoustic ecology," a way of engaging with our environments that acknowledges the electroacoustic portion of the modern soundscape as just another element to be understood and engaged with (2002, 22). As Sterne points out, such "virtuality" is already a feature of what he calls "speaker culture," and a rather banal one at that: "the overlay of physical and mediatic space in digital media *has already happened* in the sonic domain.... [I]t is a basis for the coherence of a modern hearing subject, not its dissolution or supersession" (2015, 120). If we're all taking the confluence of spatiality in stride, then it is acoustic ecology's job to account for this, not argue against it.

Now, a window can only function in a schizophonic way if we don't recognize the medial quality of glass. The contradictory visual impression only comes from the illusion of transparency, hence the key problem with Schafer's figuration. If glass were to be recognized for what it is—a barrier—then the quietude it frames would not seem contradictory. Mediation doesn't vanish in a glaze. One purpose of glaze, whether on a pot or a donut, is to make the glazed object shine, thus calling attention to the surface of the object rather than attempting to make that surface disappear. Therefore, Schafer's notion of the glazed soundscape needs to be rethought along the lines of mediality.

There is also the problem of the ableist stigmatization of mental disability implied by evoking the condition of schizophrenia to support the negative connotations of the schizophonic experience. This aspect of Schafer's figuration can also be instructive when considering the role of neurotypicality in establishing the norms and conventions of audiovisual representation, and the need to break from the neurotypical when exploring alternative perspectives on the experience of sound in space. I will elaborate on this angle of the schizophonic experience in Chapter 4, when I consider the narrative role of neurodivergent experience through the character of Laura Palmer in David Lynch's *Twin Peaks*. For the moment, let us rest on the fact that the neurodivergence implied by the prefix "schizo" might also help explain the transformations of spatial perception in *Playtime* as suggested by the window gags that bookend the film.

With the heavy baggage of the discourse of fidelity in mind when reading Schafer's call for hi-fi soundscapes, we can think more clearly about what is at stake in Tati's reversal of audiovisual glazing across the two window gags described above. The cigarette lighting gag is in line with Schafer's original formulation of the disjuncture at the heart of the glazed soundscape. Yet Tati inverts this in the window cleaner gag, suggesting a way of thinking about glazing from the opposite perspective: attention to the mediality of the window by way of its reflective nature frees us of the burden that comes with labeling its hindrance to sonic flow a bad thing. At the end of the film, Tati makes his surfaces shine to incite audience reflection, and he ties this to a newly liberated soundscape through which the divisive characteristics of these architectural spaces can be rethought.

Tati exchanges one disjuncture for another, never bringing visual and auditory transparency into perfect alignment. Thus the conclusion to *Playtime* is not particularly utopic; rather, it is revelatory in highlighting the contradictions at work in differing perceptions of modernist architectural space, medial in how it asks us to contemplate these contradictions. In the end, we can situate Schafer's contradictions the same way. As I mentioned in the introduction, Sabine Breitsameter ascribes a "shimmering" quality to Schafer's contradictions that is instructive in its tensions. This goes back to Schafer's original intentions for the use of the term soundscape that emphasizes the listener's role in the construction of space (see definition in *The Handbook for Acoustic Ecology* 1978, 126). This emphasis on positionality has been critiqued for its clear settler orientation, another problem that I will take up in Chapter 5 through my call for unsettled listening practices. But in the Schaferian context, Breitsameter insists that, "The soundscape offers a convincing model by which space is brought into existence via an act of perception performatively experienced by the listener/soundmaker" (2013, 35), and this, I argue, is what Tati is after. He makes his spaces shine so that we can perceive their materiality, and thinking this mediality through Schafer allows us to hear the "shimmer" in Schafer's contradictions as instructive in and of itself. The very notion that attitudes toward listening can hold simultaneously contradicting positions, shifting quickly between them, is the premise of Tati's reversal, and the substance of how *Playtime* charts this shift over the progression of its treatment of audiovisual space. So I continue now by investigating the film's processes of highlighting mediality with an emphasis on how Tati constructs gags around the perception of the characters who attempt the navigation of his modernist architectural spaces. This perceptual quality to Tati's audiovisual treatments is the key to the film's punch line in the reversed glazing, and after demonstrating these treatments I will situate their importance within the culture of Situationist thinking in mid-twentieth century France.

Enclosures

The dramatic transformation at *Playtime*'s end depends upon the formal rigor with which Tati sets up the audiovisual functioning of architectural space in the opening half. I now provide a thorough examination of three key scenes in the film's first hour that illustrate a variety of approaches to the representation of the modernist architectural isolation discussed so far. I begin with the scene that follows the above-described gag between the construction worker and the concierge. As the construction worker exits the frame, the concierge ushers Mr. Hulot inside. Hulot has come to meet with an important businessman, Mr. Giffard (Georges Montant), and the concierge has Hulot take a seat while he calls for the man to come down. The events that follow are presented in a single static long take. Hulot is seated screen left next to the concierge who stands in front of a floor-to-ceiling intercom apparatus, all of which occupies the left half of the frame. In the right half of the frame we see a long hallway recedes in deep focus. After a frustrating time fussing with the newfangled intercom system, the elderly concierge assures Hulot that Giffard is on his way down. Footsteps of hard-soled shoes on a hard floor emerge on the soundtrack, and then Giffard appears at the end of the long hallway. The intercom apparatus blocks Hulot's view of the hallway, so he depends upon his ears to judge the man's proximity. Here the film plays with the artificiality of the soundscape of this building by keeping Giffard's footsteps at relatively equal volume even as he draws closer and closer to Hulot. The volume fluctuates only twice, going briefly up and then back down again each time. Iain Borden suggests that the strange consistency of the footsteps, with minor and seemingly random fluctuations, is an example of how Tati explores the illogicality of modern architectural space (2002, 224). Borden is correct in identifying that the logic of the space is skewed in its tendency toward a presentness that denies the natural markers of distance and proximity, particularly through Tati's consistent ratio of direct to reflected sound on the footsteps which would ordinarily increase as the sound source moves closer to the listener. However, Borden misses an important part of the gag: the volume fluctuations, thought to be random, actually correspond with Hulot's subjective auditory perspective. Twice Hulot believes Giffard to be almost at the end of the hallway, each time rising to greet him only to be shooed back to his seat by the concierge. Each time Hulot rises, the volume of the footsteps rises with him, suggesting that these sounds represent Hulot's subjective experience of the sound. As Hulot sits back down, the volume of the footsteps returns to its previous level. Not until Giffard finally arrives in front of Hulot do his footsteps rise in an objective presentation of the man's proximity to the camera.

With the hallway gag Tati is doing two things. First, he is illustrating one of the effects of the dry direct sound of the modern interior: without reverberation, the sense of distance becomes distorted. That Giffard's footsteps sound as loud at the far end of the hallway as at the near end suggests a space in which it is hard to contextualize sound. Second, Tati illustrates Hulot's confusion when presented with this space. Without being able to see the hallway, and with no consistent gradual increase in the volume or decrease in reflection on the sound of the footsteps, Hulot must rely on his instincts as to how close Giffard might be. Twice Hulot believes Giffard should be almost in view, and twice he is wrong. These auditory fluctuations demonstrate the confusion of human perception within the artificiality of the modern soundscape. This is the first of three crucial gags that play on auditory perception that, I argue, are key to understanding the perceptual dimension of modernist space as it transforms over the course of the film. The other two perceptual gags occur during the second and third acts and will be discussed later.

Giffard then instructs Hulot to wait further, and the concierge leads him to a waiting area consisting of a street-level glass enclosure, a quintessential glass box. Here the transparent walls separate interior space from the street visible just outside. Their level of transparency ensures that we can see right through the enclosure, while remaining aware of its presence. As in the example with the construction worker asking for a light, this glass enclosure develops tension between the framing of views and our awareness of the frame. The broadening of the frame of the window, so that it becomes a wall, creates a heightened illusion of unmediated transition between interior and exterior space. Yet once again, sound within this enclosure is cut off from the street, an example of the disjunction at the heart of Schafer's glazed soundscape.

As Hulot waits within the glass box, he strolls about the enclosure poking the furniture, slipping on the buffed floor, and greeting another man who enters, sits down, dramatically signs some papers while waiting for his own appointment, and then exits. As the scene progresses, the film again regularly cuts between interior and exterior shots. As we have heard previously, we find a marked distinction between the ambient sound of the exterior space and the lack of access to this sound on the inside. Again, there is very little distinction between the spaces on the level of the visual. What we also find is that sounds within this enclosure are enhanced: the space is dominated by the sound of electrical humming coming from the overhead lights. Within this highly artificial soundscape Tati delivers moments of punctuation as the cushions on the chairs squeak, hiss, and pop in an exaggerated manner, just as the second man's physical gestures while signing his papers also stand out amidst the relative quiet. We hear nothing of these sounds while watching Hulot from the exterior shots, and the dominating din of the city is reduced to a low rumble for the interior shots. With the modernist soundscape rendering everything clear, direct, and isolated from its surrounding context, these sounds become prone to unusual exaggeration. It is as though the contained nature of these sounds, and their lack of freedom of flow, creates a hyperreality with a disconcerting nature that Tati uses for comic effect. They may be hi-fi in their clarity and lack of obfuscation, as Iain Borden suggests (2002, 222), but for Schafer the artificiality of this clarity would trump the theoretical benefits of a high ratio of signal to noise. Were it not for a measure of reflectivity and the need for support structures, the glass box would be an invisible barrier between the waiting area and the street. This illustrates the modernist tendency to push the framing of views to the point of total visual immersion, where any virtuality offered by awareness of the frame as mediation between inside and outside disappears, leaving only the illusion of community between spaces that are actually kept separate.

A while later, as Hulot continues to chase down his appointment with Giffard, the film plays with the disconcerting effect that glass's reflectivity can create within a situation where the glass itself is meant to be invisible. Hulot approaches an exit to the office building with glass walls and door through which he can see a similar space directly across the street. The shot is framed from the interior of the first building looking in deep space through to the second. Hulot catches a glimpse of Giffard seemingly across the street, when he is actually standing directly behind Hulot; the glass wall of the adjacent building is catching Giffard's reflection. The upshot of this routine is that when glass is viewed as transparent, its reflectivity poses disorienting problems of perspective.

This gag depends upon the simultaneous transparency and reflectivity of glass, a distinction that Friedberg discusses in terms of reflective mirror surfaces that create a virtual plane of representation, and transparent plate glass window surfaces creating "an unmediated (yet still framed) view of the world" (2006, 109). Friedberg cites Frederick Kiesler's observation that along with the use of glass walls came a kind of superimposition where, for the first time, glass "expresses surface and space at the same time," where the interior and exterior are visible simultaneously (119). Multiple glass surfaces visible together create not only a framed view from a single perspective, but also a cubist view where multiple spatial planes are seen at once (119). Here Friedberg differentiates between two functions of transparency: "the window as a literal architectural aperture and as a phenomenal space of viewing" (122). The particularly modern qualities of the use of glass are thus two-fold. First, the framed view of the window as architectural aperture separates the viewer and the subject. Second, looking through multiple framed views at the same time creates the possibility for perspectival ruptures where space is broken up into differing planes. In the above gag, Hulot suffers from the disorienting effect of looking through a window without knowing which elements of the visual plane are virtual and which are real. It is his lack of awareness of the medial quality of glass that creates the confusion.

Each of these three examples illustrates the basic premise of the film's first hour: that modernist use of glass windows, doors, and walls creates spaces that are contained and isolated from their surrounding context, while at the same time appearing open and transparent. Tati's various comedic strategies explore a range of different possibilities for the conflict between containment and community, always with an emphasis on how this disjuncture is a function of a character's lack of awareness around the mediality of glass. With all its variety, the film's first hour is absolutely rigorous in the basic auditory distinction it draws between interior and exterior space while exploring the visual variability of glass. The effect of these spaces on Mr. Hulot is clear: however humorous his various confusions are to watch, he is consistently unable to take his meeting with Mr. Giffard. The spaces that Hulot has to navigate in his quest for Mr. Giffard are deceptively divisive, and this quality belies their visual beauty. Designed to be isolationist according to new modern ideals, these spaces prove ineffectual for Mr. Hulot, who seems to have arrived in the new Paris from the old-world suburbs of Tati's previous film *Mon Oncle* (1958).

Transformations

Given the strict treatment Tati gives the enclosed spaces during *Playtime*'s first hour, how is it that the film arrives at such a dramatic reversal in its closing few minutes? The answer: through a good old-fashioned party. The film's centerpiece is the restaurant sequence at the Royal Garden that lasts over forty-five minutes. Here people gather in a communal spirit that moves in a slow progression from civilized eating to frenzied dancing. Along with the progression in activity comes a gradual breakdown in the divisions between people and a return to communal behavior that has been seemingly banished by the architectural tendencies of the modernist environment in which these people spend their days. The space of the restaurant is treated as a kind of intermediary between the two poles that we find at the beginning and the end of the film.

As with the kinds of glass enclosures found early in the film, the restaurant features a glass door that, with the help of a doorman (Tony Andal), controls the flow of both sound and human traffic between the street and the reception area. The interior space of the restaurant is dominated by a large open dining hall lined with glass windows and a door that opens out onto a terrace used by the waiting staff as a place to pause amidst their duties, providing the opportunity for Tati to develop various gags over the course of the sequence. Interestingly, the glass that separates the terrace from the dining floor does not impede the flow of sound to any significant degree. As the action in the restaurant takes place, we regularly cut between shots from within the main dining hall and the terrace with no change in the sound of the restaurant environment populated by people talking, dishes clinking, and a jazz band playing. The glass door to the terrace opens and closes, again with no appreciable change to the soundtrack. At one point, a trumpet player arrives on stage and begins a lively jazz number. Shot from the terrace through the glass, the force of the trumpet player's opening note blasts open a window, yet again there is no corresponding adjustment made on the soundtrack. Given that the restaurant's front door remains an effective sonic barrier while the glass doors and enclosures within the restaurant do not, the space of the restaurant is established as being governed by the communal nature of its intended function regardless of the architectural imperatives set forth in the beginning of the film.

As the party progresses, any lingering divisions between people, and between interior and exterior space, start to break down through the physical collapse of the restaurant. This begins, appropriately, with the front door shattering as Mr. Hulot wrestles with the doorman over his right to enter. This is a key event, as it is the unrestricted flow of people and sound between the inside and outside following the door's destruction that aids in the communal environment unfolding within the restaurant. The doorman tries to maintain control by miming his duties with the use of the door handle, thus playing on the invisibility of glass to comic effect. Here Tati develops the second of three important audiovisual gags based on the role of perception in the relationship between sound, image, and space: in an exterior shot of customers arriving at the restaurant's entrance, the sound of the band playing within is raised on the soundtrack while the doorman mimes the opening of the door; the music is then lowered again as the doorman mimes the door closing once the people have passed through. The gag works because the film has developed glass as a transparent material that divides space invisibly, and it indicates the importance of perception as a function of how Tati's characters operate within architectural space. This is a key moment in identifying the role of perception in the experience of architectural space: if people can be made to believe that a barrier exists where there is none, then the reverse might also be possible. This idea lies at the heart of how the film reverses the properties of glass as building material, and it is within the communal environment of the restaurant that perceptual shifts by the city's inhabitants begin to take effect.

Ultimately the doorman's attempts to control the flow of traffic after the collapse of the door are to no avail, and other aspects of the restaurant's physical construction start to come undone. As Hulot attempts to reach for an ornament caught in some baffling near the stage, he inadvertently pulls the baffling down with it, then causing part of the ceiling to cave in as well. The band stops for a moment, then carries on until a couple more of these incidents convince them to pack it in. As the band leaves, a boisterous American customer takes it upon himself to ask if there is a piano player amidst the diners who might be willing to keep the music going. Barbara volunteers, climbing up onto the stage where she begins to play, transforming herself from member of the audience to performer. This gesture of crossing the divide between the spaces of performance and spectatorship removes boundaries separating people from one another, and is symbolic of the physical destruction of the restaurant's front door. Finally, it is through this absent door that, in the early hours of the morning, the partying crowd will stumble out onto the streets, bringing with them the feeling of community fostered by the events of the evening.

With this feeling of communal sensibility still fresh in their beings they find the streets of Paris bathed in morning sunlight and transformed into a festive atmosphere. Here Tati builds a series of gags here that position characters and their vehicles as carnival rides. In this atmosphere there is always music in the air and something as mundane as traffic gridlock on a roundabout takes on the aesthetics of a carousel. This carnival atmosphere provides the environment in which the final shots of the window cleaner and the tourist bus play out, demonstrating that the permeability of glass found inside the restaurant has now become an architectural fact in the world outside, a world that was once governed by more divisive principles.

In these final moments we find the third important gag that revolves around perceived divisions between spaces represented in the film. At one point the carnival-style music now permeating the environment stops dead, along with the circular motion of the traffic emulating a carousel. Then a man comes along to plug a parking meter, and both the music and traffic start up again. This gag illustrates the artificiality of the distinctions commonly made between diegetic and non-diegetic music in film sound theory. Breaking down this distinction is yet another way in which Tati explores the idea that a communion of spaces is made possible by the flow of sound. This time, however, the gag plays upon the perception of the audience who, by exposure to convention, is likely to initially perceive this music as being non-diegetic. If so, we can then chuckle as we learn that the music might really be emanating from a citywide jukebox controlled by the parking meters.

The invisible divide between the inside and the outside of the diegesis is crossed, as was the divide between the stage and the audience in the restaurant, and the two sides of the glass pane in the window cleaner sequence. The boundary line across the inside and the outside of the diegesis is the cinema's version of the tyranny of glass, an invisible barrier through which no sound should pass—but often does. In the parking meter gag music joins these spaces together, just as music joined people together in dance at the restaurant, music that also joined the spaces of performance and spectator together. So the film's final section is clearly geared toward a very different audiovisual representation of space than we find in the first hour. Yet the question remains: what should we make of the film's conclusion? Is it necessarily intended as a positive spin in answer to the critique of modernist architecture earlier in the film?

Is Modernism the Enemy?

In an essay provocatively titled "Modernism as Enemy," Edwin Heathcote cites the films of Jacques Tati among several examples of films from the 1950s that cast modernist architecture in a negative light, and in so doing he adopts the prevailing opinion on Tati's interest in the cinematic representation of urban spaces (2000, 20–25). Iain Borden agrees that Tati's previous film *Mon Oncle* presents a decidedly favorable view of old-world urban settings, "a fast-disappearing France replete with market, mischievous boys, chattering residents, cafés and horse-drawn carts," as opposed to the new modern suburb and its enclosed private spaces (2002, 217). Yet Borden disagrees that *Playtime* offers a similar view transposed into the heart of the modern city. Borden cites an oft-quoted interview in which Tati asserts that he does not find modern architecture itself to be a problem, but rather the consumerist society for which it is built (218). Indeed, Tati's love of certain strains of modernist architecture prompted him to make such spaces the central aspect of the film, devoting much time and energy to the creation of the grand Tativille set. For David Bellos, the film "is not fundamentally or essentially a satire of high-rise architecture: it is more a celebration of the beauty of large edifices, and an expression of wonderment at humankind's ability to create" (1999, 250). Borden argues that Tati's love for modernist aesthetics shines through the film, and that his comic routines involving the spatial disruptions within this architecture are "overtly positive attempts to reassert the poetic aspects of modern life that are latent within Modernist urbanism" (2002, 218). As such Borden equates Tati's poetics with the Situationist goal of "reasserting the irrational, passionate, performed and contested elements of city life" (218).

Borden's appreciation of the celebratory aspect of Tati's work is essential, but he misses the critique upon which the celebration is based by neglecting to differentiate between the film's beginning and end in his exegesis of Tati's playfulness with urban space. As Brian R. Jacobson puts it, "to negate or smooth over the critique [of modern architecture in the film] as Borden does here is, in a sense, to miss the joke by skipping straight to the punch line" (2005, 32). In so doing, he also misses a key point in tying Tati's work to that of the Situationists, based profoundly on critique as the foundation for the transformation of urban space.

In "Jacques Tati's *Playtime* as New Babylon" (2001), Laurent Marie charts the narrative progression through the film and asserts that the conclusion be read as an illustration of Constant's *New Babylon*, an elaborate series of creative renderings of the ideal Situationist city governed by the principles of Unitary Urbanism. Here people roam nomadically free through spaces that are made habitable by social reorganization (262–263). For Marie, this New Babylonian situation is achieved by way of the transformative environment of the Royal Garden, for it is here that the people's "behavior is no longer controlled by their environment, where they are no longer separated from it, but take hold of the place," embracing "their ability to act on the world, to transform it, to re-create it" (262).

Central to Unitary Urbanism is the idea of free flow between the spaces of society. As Guy Debord writes in 1959, "Unitary Urbanism acknowledges no boundaries; it aims to form an integrated human milieu in which separations such as work/leisure or public/private will finally be dissolved" (2006d, 69, para. 5). Unitary Urbanism does have a goal of physical transformation of architecture "to accord with the whole development of society" (para. 4). However, the Situationists acknowledge that this physical transformation to dissolve all forms of boundaries can come only as the result of changing behavior, "to extend the terrain of play to all desirable constructions" (para. 5). And before behavior is changed, people must change the way they *think* about behaving within the spaces they inhabit. This relationship between behavior and its psychology is what the Situationists have dubbed *psychogeography*: "the study of the precise laws and specific effects of the geographical environment, consciously organized or not, on the emotions and behavior of individuals" (Debord 2006a, 8). So there is a tripartite approach to the reorganization of modern social life: psychogeography pays attention to the effects of the environment on the way people behave within it, and forms the basis for raising awareness about how they think and feel when making use of the environment in which they live; once this relationship is understood, people can begin to behave differently within existing spaces, repurposing its existing forms; finally, new spaces can be constructed based on the new forms of use developed out of the previous two stages. So it is not hard to imagine how readings of *Playtime* that emphasize the film's positive representation of the modern city can be tied to Situationist thought about how to reclaim the city for the people.

Before the ideal Situationist city can be created, citizens must learn to perceive their city with freshly attuned senses. Two key methods for this attunement are the ideas of *dérive* (or "drift") and *détournement*. Guy Debord describes "drifting" through the city as, in part, engaging in "playful and constructive behavior" that allows oneself to be "drawn by the attractions of the terrain and the encounters they find there" (2006b, 62), observing new potential for existing structures that could then be subject to *détournement*, the repurposing of these structures along new principles of use (2006c, 67). For David Bellos, the first half of *Playtime* is an enactment of the Situationist notion of *dérive* while the restaurant sequence acts as *détournement* (1999, 270). Here, however, we need to distinguish between Jacques Tati's role as filmmaker constructing the audiovisual spaces of the film and his role as Mr. Hulot being made subject to these spaces. It is useful to think of filmmaker Tati's creative play with these spaces through the above-described set pieces as a kind of *derive*, allowing the audience to appreciate the playfulness of these spaces anew, as Borden highlights in his analyses. But it is quite another to consider the position of Mr. Hulot, trying desperately to carry out a simple task and being frustrated by the prescribed usage of these spaces by the society that built them. Mr. Hulot is not drifting through these spaces; he does not make creative play out of his navigation of Tativille in the first half of the film. As such Tati the filmmaker is illustrating the constrictive nature of established urban form in modernizing Paris, and in doing so he is offering a critique of this form.

It is also essential to recognize that *détournement* is not redesign or reconstruction; it is repurposing. There is no doubt that the diners at the Royal Garden restaurant repurpose that space over the course of the evening. But the streets of Paris onto which they emerge is not yet the ideal Situationist city. The rest of Paris has not followed the restaurant's collapse. Instead, *détournement* continues in the repurposing of established forms of architecture. Laurent Marie jumps the gun in labeling this New Babylon, although this repurposing is a major step along the way. As Simon Sadler puts it: "Psychogeography was merely a preparation, a reconnaissance for the day when the city would be seized for real" (1999, 81). In the end, *Playtime* is about the psychological aspect of reimagining the city, not about revolutionary redesign.

The key point that most critics miss is that the architecture hasn't changed at the end of the film. Rather, its use has become carnivalized. Is this carnivalization good in and of itself? We could imagine an alternative reading that argues for the negative qualities of this new carnivalized space, continuing to trap its citizens in a set of rules for use, containing them while providing illusions of amusement. I argue, however, that we don't need to settle the issue of whether or not the film is ultimately positive or negative. What we need to do is recognize the audiovisual shift as a reflexive move inviting us to rethink our relationship to the spaces we navigate every day. Tati makes this shift through the *détournement* of the window, once functioning as a visually transparent barrier to sonic flow, now sonically transparent with new emphasis on visual reflectivity. Tati situates the audience as though a drifter in Paris who has been given a map of London to navigate the city, experiencing its forms according to a different set of instructions (an experiment performed by the Situationists). This is where thinking of Tati's shift through Schafer's thought can allow us to hear what Tati is doing in ways that have not been acknowledged, and then use this as a way of rethinking the role that Schafer's flawed but evocative language can play in making acoustic ecology work for media studies.

Schaferian Acoustic Design as Psychogeography

R. Murray Schafer's call for acoustic design shares much in common with the Situationist idea of Unitary Urbanism as an interdisciplinary approach to the reorganization of space. Schafer calls for architects and urban planners to collaborate with musicians, composers, and other people involved with the art of sound, so that the spaces in which we live might be more sonically habitable (1977, 205). The beginnings of acoustic design come with increased awareness of the sonic environment fostered by the practice of *soundwalking*: attentive listening to one's environment with the goal of understanding the soundscape as a "composition" consisting of component parts. Rearranging these component parts in the mind through the act of attentive listening is the first step toward thinking through the ways in which aspects of the soundscape might be reorganized to render the world more sonically habitable (see Westerkamp 1974). As a listening practice geared toward understanding the effects of the soundscape on those that live within it, soundwalking is the acoustic ecologist's version of psychogeography.

The crucial point of connection between Schafer's project of acoustic design and the goals of Unitary Urbanism lies in the psychogeographical basis of each. Neither acoustic design nor Unitary Urbanism resulted in large scale rethinking of urban planning; Constant's New Babylon remained a set of creative propositions, much like Schafer's own musings about ideal sonic environments. Yet within Unitary Urbanism there lies hope for the fate of existing space through changing the way it is used *without* necessarily changing its design, and we can find this potential in Schafer's call for acoustic design as well, ultimately starting with "ear cleaning" exercises that he first published the year *Playtime* was finished (Schafer 1967). As outlined in the third newsletter put out by *Internationale Situationniste*, Unitary Urbanism "is not ideally separated from the current terrain of cities. UU is developed out of the experience of this terrain and based on existing constructions" (1959, para. 8). So for the Situationists, "it is just as important that we exploit the existing decors" in attempts to reappropriate modernist urban space "as it is that we construct completely unknown ones" (para. 8). As the practice of soundwalking illustrates, there may be hope for the idea of acoustic design along the lines of reclaiming urban unity. I suggest that the conclusion of *Playtime* is all about changing thought and use, not about changing the architecture itself. This is akin to the practice of the soundwalk as the first step toward acoustic design: through shifting attention, the soundwalker enacts a change in space through changed use that does not require a change in brick and mortar. Each program begins with an approach to shifting perspective on existing spaces that has, over the decades, proliferated—particularly through the arts.

It is important to understand that the only way to fully account for the change in the treatment of sound in space at the end of the film is to acknowledge the role of the change in attitude experienced by the partygoers who find themselves on the street in the morning. The material properties of glass have not changed here: what has changed is the perspective of the people experiencing spaces dominated by glass. *Playtime* presents an architectural impossibility using the cinema's powers of illusion, but this impossibility is best understood as a metaphor for the psychogeographical shift that allows for previously divisive spaces to become sites of communal activity despite their architectural intent. As such, the film offers a way to draw a relationship between acoustic ecology's emphasis on acoustic design and Situationist articulations of psychogeography: where we are interested in how architecture affects human psychology, we might also be interested in how psychology affects architectural space. To shift one's awareness of space is as powerful as shifting the space itself, and I believe this is the message of *Playtime*. It is here that the three gags on perception described above are most important. First, the fluctuating volume of Giffard's footsteps in the long corridor reflects Hulot's confusion about his proximity as a function of the unnatural qualities of the modern space. Second, the volume of the music fluctuating as the doorman at the Royal Garden mimes the opening and closing of the shattered door reflects the expectations people have of modern architecture even after it has been physically destroyed. Finally, the sound of the music in the air transcending the divide between the inside and outside of the diegesis is a reflexive move that suggests the permeable boundary between different levels of the soundtrack as a reflection on audience expectations.

These gags get increasingly reflexive. As an audience, we are in on the first two gags, able to see what the characters experiencing the fluctuations in volume do not. The third gag, however, is on us. When the parking meter doubles as the coin-box for a musical carnival ride, the film reveals that the division between sound and image is as much about the artifice of cinema as it is about the nature of modernist architecture. Just as the window cleaner sequence demonstrates that the flow of sound between compartmentalized spaces is a function of cinematic representation, so too does the parking meter gag reveal the artifice of the divide between the inside and outside of the diegesis. While the spatial qualities of the carnival music haven't changed, our understanding of its position within the diegesis has. The closing gags demonstrate the power of shifting perceptual awareness to create a different understanding of space, and this is the lesson revealed by careful attention to the film's formal approach to spatial representation, to hear the transparency depicted on screen.

Mediality is on display in each of these perceptual gags: they call attention to Tati's construction of audiovisual space in order that we might reflect upon our own perceptual processes in making sense of this space and, by extension, the other architectural spaces in which we live out our lives. There's a reason to keep the rhetoric of hi-fi stereo culture in mind when addressing Schafer's writing: latent in this rhetoric is the fact that we learn to hear according to a set of ideals. Change the ideals, and we hear differently. So we can come to a new understanding of acoustic ecology—one that eschews Schaferian biases that Tati could have maintained throughout the film, and instead invites new ways of positively understanding urban space, in line with Situationist remapping of existing urban forms through practices of psychogeography.

The Moral of the Story

The proposed utopia that concludes *Playtime* has its problems. The presence of music in the air, a fixture of the diegesis, is one of Tati's trademark symbols of space that is able to support human community. Like the old-world Paris in *Mon Oncle* in which there is always music in the air, the final moments of *Playtime* suggest that this modern urban center has been rendered a space where the free flow of music is emblematic of its reclamation by the people. Interestingly, this idea is inherent to R. Murray Schafer's project of acoustic design, the basis of which is to think of the world's soundscapes as a musical composition (1977, 5) thus ensuring that there is always music in the air. The piped-in music of Tati's Paris serves as a marker of the dissolution of borders between spaces once kept separate. Yet this music in the air speaks to one of Emily Thompson's key points about the soundscape of modernity: that the new dry spaces of contained enclosures are completed by the addition of piped-in ambience, the epitome of Schafer's concept of schizophonia. Sound now moves freely across barriers and music is ever in the air, suggesting an atmosphere of freedom and community. As such, in a way, the entire city has now become homogenized, essentially creating a single space washed in a single soundscape. Is this really the solution to the problems of isolationist containment? The idea of free-flow between all spaces is not necessarily an ideal to be sought at all costs. Indeed, this idealization of homogeneity is one of the key critiques of Schafer's approach to analysis and prescription as well, as I will demonstrate in more detail in Chapter 5.

In the end, I argue that Tati's transformation of the formal treatment of architectural space is best understood as a cinematic metaphor for a different way of thinking about this space, leading in turn to a different way of using it. The real reclamation of the space illustrated by the film's final section is neither in the destruction of modernist architecture nor the magical transformation of its material properties. Rather, reclamation lies in a psychogeographical shift where the distance between individuals inherent in modern society is recognized as a necessary function of any community. This psychogeographical shift is given its punctuation point in the final sequence in which Mr. Hulot gives Barbara the flower statuette. This sequence closes the film by offering us the key to establishing a mindset of community: the gesture of giving, an act in opposition to the capitalist ideology that gave rise to the modernist urban spaces that Tati explores throughout the film.

Mr. Hulot spies the gift in a crowded shop, but finds himself caught at the checkout as he sees Barbara getting back onto her tour bus across the street. Just as the architecture of Paris has not physically changed the morning after the Royal Garden, so too is it still mired in the processes of consumer society—the main target of Tati's criticisms. Yet here Hulot finds a solution: he enlists the help of a stranger on the other side of the check-out who runs with the gift box over to Barbara and gives it to her on behalf of Hulot. This is the key marker of the film's engagement with Unitary Urbanism: the structures of consumer space can be reclaimed through altered use. With the creation of this relay, Hulot takes a consumerist principle—shopping—and turns it into an act of profitless giving. To do this, he establishes a link of community between his position within the shop and Barbara's position on the bus by way of a stranger's help. Without destroying the infrastructure that has Hulot trapped, he charts a path of community within this infrastructure. In short, Hulot renders previously constrictive aspects of modernist architectural form truly transparent.

Barbara accepts the gift happily, and as she rides the bus into the dusk, she opens the box and holds the flower in her hand with delight. In looking at her gift, she finds a parallel between its shape and that of the streetlamps just outside her window. As already noted, this moment takes place in an environment where glass barriers no longer impede the flow of sound, bringing this new architectural fact into alignment with the gesture of giving. Herein lies the film's most overt alignment with Unitary Urbanism. The Situationists argue that while the modern city is a "lamentable spectacle, a supplement to the museums for tourists driven around in glass-in buses, UU envisages the urban environment as the terrain of participatory games" (*Internationale Situationniste* 3, para. 7). Hulot's gift to Barbara is made possible by the relay between two elements of consumerist society, the shop and the bus. This relay becomes a participatory game that is reflected by the lack of auditory barrier posed by the glass that once would have kept the tourists on the bus separate from the environment that they came to see. The gift suggests the simple power of drawing associations between things that are usually thought to be separate, of breaking down the barrier between people in the symbol of passing an item from one person to another. Tati takes this gesture and uses it to create the film's final play on the dissolution of the divisive barriers to community that modern architecture posed in the first half of the film. In so doing, *Playtime* offers the potential to read its formal shifts in the audiovisual representation of modernist architecture as a function of a new communal mindset on the part of those that live within its divisive spaces. This gesture, in turn, emblemizes the film's mediality in the form of audible transparency, as the final sonic barriers between interior spaces vanish, conspicuously, once and for all.

References

Altman, Rick. 1992. "The Material Heterogeneity of Recorded Sound." In *Sound Theory, Sound Practice*, edited by Rick Altman, 15–31. New York: Routledge.

Bellos, David. 1999. *Jacques Tati: His Life and Art*. London: The Harvill Press.

Borden, Iain. 2002. "*Playtime*: 'Tativille' and Paris." In *The Hieroglyphics of Space: Reading and Experiencing the Modern Metropolis*, edited by Neil Leach, 217–235. New York: Routledge.

Breitsameter, Sabine. 2013. "Ways of Listening; Figures of Thought." In *Ways of Listening; Figures of Thought: A Festschrift for R. Murray Schafer on the Occasion of his 80th Birthday*, edited by Sabine Breitsameter and Eric Leonardson, 17–36. Darmstadt: Hochschule Darmstadt.

Burch, Noël. 1973. *Theory of Film Practice*. Translated by Helen R. Lane. New York: Praeger Publishers.

Chion, Michel. 1994. *Audio-Vision: Sound on Screen*. Translated by Claudia Gorbman. New York: Columbia University Press.

Debord, Guy. 2006a. "Introduction to a Critique of Urban Geography." In *Situationist International Anthology*, revised and expanded edition, edited and translated by Ken Knabb, 8–12. Berkeley: Bureau of Public Secrets.

Debord, Guy. 2006b. "Theory of the Dérive." In *Situationist International Anthology*, revised and expanded edition, edited and translated by Ken Knabb, 62–66. Berkeley: Bureau of Public Secrets.

Debord, Guy. 2006c. "Détournement as Negation and Prelude." In *Situationist International Anthology*, revised and expanded edition, edited and translated by Ken Knabb, 67–68. Berkeley: Bureau of Public Secrets.

Debord, Guy. 2006d. "Situationist Theses on Traffic." In *Situationist International Anthology*, revised and expanded edition, edited and translated by Ken Knabb, 69–70. Berkeley: Bureau of Public Secrets.

Debord, Guy. 1967/1983. *Society of the Spectacle*. Detroit: Black and Red.

Friedberg, Anne. 2006. *The Virtual Window: From Alberti to Microsoft*. Cambridge, MA: MIT Press.

Heathcote, Edwin. 2000. "Modernism as Enemy: Film and the Portrayal of Modern Architecture." *Architectural Design* 70, no. 1 (January): 20–25.

Internationale Situationniste. 1959. "Unitary Urbanism at the End of the 1950s." Translated by Paul Hammond. *Internationale Situationiste*, no. 3 (December). Archived online, http://www.cddc.vt.edu/sionline/si/unitary.html

Jacobson, Brian R. 2005. *Constructions of Cinematic Space: Spatial Practice at the Intersection of Film and Theory*. MA thesis. MIT.

Jameson, Frederic. 1991. *Postmodernism, or, The Cultural Logic of Late Capitalism*. Durham, NC: Duke University Press.

Jordan, Randolph. 2007. "Case Study: Film Sound, Acoustic Ecology, and Performance in Electroacoustic Music." In *Music, Sound and Multimedia: From the Live to the Virtual*, edited by Jamie Sexton, 121–141. Edinburgh: University of Edinburgh Press.

Lastra, James. 2000. *Sound Technology and the American Cinema*. New York: Columbia University Press.

Marie, Laurent. 2001. "Jacques Tati's *Playtime* as New Babylon." In *Cinema and the City: Film and Urban Societies in a Global Context*, edited by Mark Shiel and Tony Fitzmaurice, 257–269. Oxford: Blackwell Publishers.

McCartney, Andra. 2002. "Sharing Experiences Towards the Possibility of an Electroacoustic Ecology." *Soundscape: The Journal of Acoustic Ecology* 3, no. 1: 22.

Sadler, Simon. 1999. *The Situationist City*. Cambridge, MA: MIT Press.

Schafer, R. Murray. 1967. *Ear Cleaning*. Reprinted in *The Thinking Ear: Complete Writings on Music Education*, 46–92. Toronto: Arcana Editions, 1986.

Schafer, R. Murray. 1968. *The New Soundscape*. Reprinted in *The Thinking Ear: Complete Writings on Music Education*, 93–169. Toronto: Arcana Editions, 1986.

Schafer, R. Murray. 1977. *The Tuning of the World*. Toronto: McClelland and Stewart.

Schafer, R. Murray. 1993. *Voices of Tyranny, Temples of Silence*. Indian River: Arcana Editions.

Sterne, Jonathan. 2003. *The Audible Past: Cultural Origins of Sound Reproduction*. Durham, NC: Duke University Press.

Sterne, Jonathan. 2015. "Space within Space: Artificial Reverb and the Detachable Echo." *Grey Room* 60 (Summer): 110–131.

Thompson, Emily. 2002. *The Soundscape of Modernity: Architectural Acoustics and the Culture of Listening in North America, 1900–1933*. Cambridge, MA: MIT Press.

Truax, Barry, ed. 1978. *Handbook for Acoustic Ecology*. Vancouver: A.R.C. Publications/World Soundscape Project.

Truax, Barry. 2001. *Acoustic Communication*. 2nd edition. Westport, CT: Alex Publishing.

Truax, Barry. 2008. "Soundscape Composition as Global Music: Electroacoustic Music as Soundscape." *Organised Sound* 13, no. 2: 103–109.

Westerkamp, Hildegard. 1974. "Soundwalking." *Sound Heritage* 3, no. 4: 18–27.

2

Immersive Reflexivity

Documenting the Inaudible in Peter Mettler's *Picture of Light*

In *Picture of Light* (1994), filmmaker Peter Mettler (serving here as director, cinematographer, editor, and sound designer) travels with his crew to Churchill, Manitoba, in an attempt to capture the aurora borealis on film. On the surface, the subject matter of the film consists of the problems inherent in translating the aurora borealis into cinematic visual representation. But Mettler frames this quest with broader questions about the role of recording technologies in mediating our experience of the world, and about the relationship between civilization, the wilderness, and the modern human subject. The film explores these questions through a highly reflexive strategy that emphasizes not only the filmmaker's presence in the process of constructing the film, but also the fundamental division between the cinema's two main channels of transmission: sound and image. This is the line of demarcation that forms this chapter's investigation of acoustic profile: the extent to which image can be heard in the soundtrack and vice versa.

Picture of Light is as much about what we hear as it is about what we see, and the film's ecological theme of human engagement with nature by way of modern technology is positioned within this reflexive approach to audiovisuality. Yet these techniques are not used simply to foreground the distance between subject, film, and audience, as is common for the reflexive documentary film. Rather, the film suggests the possibility of providing the audience with an authentic experience of the aurora borealis based on points of intersection between the external manifestation of the lights and our internal experience of them as mediated by the technology of film.

In this chapter I will demonstrate how *Picture of Light* can be read as an attempt to move past critiques of documentary veracity toward a transcendence of the boundary between subject, film, and audience. I employ the term *immersive reflexivity* to refer to the use of medial strategies to bring the audience closer to the film's subject matter rather than cultivating distanced contemplation. My analysis will situate *Picture of Light* within the discourse of reflexive documentary practice, tying the film's mode of address to the concept of the *performative* documentary theorized (slightly differently) by Bill Nichols and Stella Bruzzi. Though Mettler's film shares much in common with these approaches to the documentary film, I argue that the film's reflexivity is not premised upon an irrefutable skepticism about the connection between film and the pro-filmic world that often informs performativity in documentary film. Instead, *Picture of Light* demonstrates how calling attention to cinematic mediation of reality is a way of finding something within this mediation that can instill an experience equivalent to seeing the aurora borealis in person.

Mettler's approach provides an ideal example of how to address a major issue in play with the work of the World Soundscape Project (WSP) and acoustic ecology at large: the use of sound recording technology to provide accurate documentation of the environments that they set out to analyze, appreciate, and critique. Much criticism has been levied against the early WSP and related work because of their apparently naïve assumption that their recordings could tell accurate stories about the world. Such thinking has long been jettisoned from documentary film sound theory, yet I don't think that the baby should be thrown out with the bath water. I will demonstrate how the idea of immersive reflexivity provides a way to reclaim the value of recording as a means toward accessing and experiencing the world in front of the cameras and microphones, particularly with respect to engaging particular geographic locales. The problems with the early WSP's interest in recording technology as a tool for accessing and preserving the world's sonic environments was not in their belief in the possibility of such access and preservation, but in their attempts to hide their role in shaping the material, their concealment of the mediality inherent to their project. Through my analysis of Mettler's film I demonstrate that immersive reflexivity is a way around the problem of thinking about technological mediation as necessarily distanciating, an approach to image and soundmaking that can operate outside of the skepticism that so often governs the reflexive instinct.

Picture of Light happens to have been made right around the time that the second wave of acoustic ecology was coming together under the aegis of the World Forum for Acoustic Ecology at their first meeting in Banff in 1993 and subsequent 1996 release of the follow-up CD to the original 1973 *Vancouver Soundscape* (which will guide my case study of the Vancouver soundscape on film in the last chapter of this book). This was a moment when documentary filmmakers and soundscape composers alike began to embrace the role that their interventions played in the environments they sought to document and engage with. As I will discuss in the next chapter, the WSP discovered the value of reflexivity for promoting audience engagement for themselves with their development of the art of soundscape composition and its forthright acknowledgment of the role of the sound recordist and composer in shaping the material. My purpose in this chapter is to offer a path to the discovery of reflexivity's immersive power as it is illustrated in Peter Mettler's film, which sets out to expose the processes by which mediality brings audiences closer to the material being documented.

Mettler's deployment of immersive reflexivity depends upon the filmmaker's approach to illustrating the problem of how to document the inaudibility of the aurora borealis, and how this problem is embedded within his exploration of the capacity for sound and image to play off each other to reveal the line that separates them while moving to dissolve it once and for all. The key to this dissolution lies in what Michel Chion terms the *transsensorial* qualities of the cinema, the potential for something seen on the image track to be experienced as sound, and vice versa (1994, 137). Mettler addresses the idea of transsensoriality by suggesting that the aurora borealis move "like thoughts," an external manifestation of an internal experience, a guiding concept for the film that is eventually tied to a later question about whether or not the lights can be heard. Mettler's answer to this question inevitably comes by way of the power of the lights to evoke transsensorial awareness of sound in the absence of anything tangibly audible. This connection between the "movement" of thought and the transsensorial potential of the aurora is suggested by Peter Weber in his description of the film:

> Mettler lets people living under the skies of the aurora borealis tell their story about them by simply letting their hands speak. They seem to be conducting mysterious music. We learn that whoever observes the aurora borealis for a long time loses the sense of distance—suddenly one has this feeling that the play of lights is happening in one's own head. Like thoughts (quoted in McSorley 1995, 112)

The idea that the hand gestures of interviewees link the motion of the aurora to the conducting of music points to the transsensorial potential of the lights as a function of gestural movement, negating the distance between the lights as external phenomenon and one's internal experience of them.

Transsensoriality is the basis for reading *Picture of Light* as an attempt to transcend the second-order nature of the cinema, an attempt to provide the audience with a more direct experience of the aurora than the simple record of their filmed representation can offer on its own.

To excavate Mettler's approach to handling the line that separates sound from image, I will situate his aesthetic strategies in the context of opposing ideologies about audiovisual synchronization that emerged as filmmakers transitioned from the silent era to the technological reality of synchronization. In particular, I will compare the visual music movement with the Soviet Montage school's call for asynchronicity (or *counterpoint*), the former aiming for cinematic expressions of the inseparability of sound and image, the latter founded upon the belief that they can only ever be separate and attempt to conceal this fact is to deny cinema's true power to engage the audience with its subject matter. I will demonstrate how Mettler positions his allusions to transsensoriality within decidedly contrapuntal strategies, joining disparate thinking about sound's relationship to the image through the suggestion that the movement of the aurora borealis is akin to the movement of thought. In turn, this analogy can be productively read through avant-garde filmmaker Stan Brakhage's quest to create the cinematic equivalent of *moving visual thinking*, silent films that explore the "musical" qualities of visual movement as a way of illustrating the transsensoriality at the base of all experience. While *Picture of Light* doesn't look like one of Brakhage's works of visual music, Mettler's film is geared toward very similar ideas about the potential for cinema to challenge the line that separates the film from its audience. So in this chapter I ask, what is the acoustic profile of the lights? How far can they extend past the diving line between sound and image, and what can tracking this profile tell us about the problems of field recording for documentary veracity? In answering these questions, I dive into the heart of Mettler's interest in exploring the dividing line between sound and image, which can be felt most keenly as he plays the inaudibility of the lights into the potential for hearing to be made a function of seeing, dissolving the technical separation between the two. This is his main medial move, and the heart of his immersive reflexivity. The experience of the northern lights in this film, while at an aesthetic remove from the real thing, can trigger the mind in a way that is no different from being there in person. This mental triggering is an attempt to transcend the negative qualities of schizophonia and reveal the positive potential in the subjective experience of external mediation. Ultimately, *Picture of Light* offers an answer to the aging problem of fidelity in the use of recording technology to provide access to particular places and events.

Performing Documentary Convention

Picture of Light makes use of dramatic shifts in approaches to documentary representation, creating a profound connection between the film's immersive power and its reflexive design. There are times when the boundaries between sound and image are ill-defined, creating a wash where abstract electroacoustic music by Jim O'Rourke blends seamlessly with location sound and images that are at once fantastical and grounded in realism. This mixture allows us to question where one element of the soundtrack stops and the other begins, and where the image and soundtrack touch through conventions of realism, asynchronicity, or transsensoriality. Other times the distinction between these various elements is very well defined indeed, creating abrupt moments of disjunction, or shifts between modes of audio-visual synchronization, that provide a more direct example of reflexivity.

An early example of how the film shifts between different strategies of reflexivity comes as a series of traveling shots follow a snowmobile convoy through the tundra in the black of night, lit only by their headlights. As we watch the snow passing quickly by in a POV shot from on board one of the vehicles, Mettler's voiceover explains the nuances that the Inuit language has for describing snow. As is usually the case, the narration is mixed with Jim O'Rourke's electroacoustic music, creating an ethereal quality to the sequence that suits the hypnotic effect of the images. Jerry White finds these stylistic details to be a mark of reflexivity in and of themselves (2006, 26). Yet Mettler ups the ante significantly as this sequence ends abruptly with a cut to a sound recordist next to a stand of trees with microphone in hand. He taps the microphone, and as soon as the hand makes contact we hear the corresponding thump bringing a sudden end to the music track, tearing us dramatically out of the ambient drones that permeated the snowmobile ride. In this way the film cuts from dreamlike floating to the crisp and harsh reality of direct sound. We then watch from a fixed vantage point as crewmember Gerald Packer marches through ever deepening snow, and Mettler tells him from behind the camera that the rest of the crew cannot follow. The sounds of the crunching snow are so prominent as to seem exaggerated, the direct sound recording yielding a stark contrast of reality to the preceding sequence's soundscape treatments. Though the sequence ends with a powerful example of synchronization through direct sound, the transition between the snowmobile ride and the deep snow walking reminds us that even realism through synchronization is only a convention that can start and stop at any given moment. With this transition between modes Mettler is contrasting an observational approach with a highly participatory one, illustrating two extremes that often involve heavily defended philosophies about what constitutes an ethical approach to documentary filmmaking.

This example encapsulates the spirit of *Picture of Light* as first and foremost a meditation on the relationship between the world, its experience by human beings, and the role of technologies of audiovisual representation in mediating this experience. Every step of the way Mettler inserts himself, his team and their equipment into the film, prompting Nathan Clarkson to dub the film's recording devices as "actors" in and of themselves, with their own idiosyncrasies on display (2013, 79). In this way, *Picture of Light* is as much about the making of the film as it is about its stated goal: to capture moving images of the aurora. Yet as with all of Mettler's work, he has a poeticism that prompts Bruce McDonald, Martin Schaub, and Tom McSorely to compare him to esteemed Russian aestheticist Andrei Tarkovsky (Pitschen and Schönholzer 1995, 18, 52, 104). The film's simultaneous lyricism and reflexivity works against the usual role that performativity plays in contemporary documentary theory: in *Picture of Light*, the self-conscious disruption of cinematic illusionism takes nothing away from its powers of immersion. As Jerry White argues, "Mettler exists between the conventional and the experimental, never entirely at home in either and yet fully engaged with each" (2006, 2). Traveling the continuum between convention and experimentation allows for the film to point toward the permeable boundaries between immersion and reflexivity as well, creating the immersive reflexivity that is the fundamental driving force behind the film. This immersive reflexivity is structured around the film's approach to sound/image synchronization: conventions of sonic realism are contrasted with moments of lyricism and asynchronicity that keep us aware of the artificiality of audiovisual relationships while pointing toward their inextricable links within the totality of the film.

Mettler's interest in blending documentary and experimental modes of address is tied to his interest in providing his audience with access to the world that exists in front of his camera and microphones, while simultaneously emphasizing that the audience's experience of this world is necessarily a product of cinematic mediation. Tom McSorley stresses that Mettler's films constitute "a cinema which constantly investigates its own images, its own ways of representing what it sees" (1995, 90) in which "the conflict between the 'way you see and what you see' is exposed and explored" (94). In McSorley's description, the "what" that we see is connected to documentary and the "way" that we see to the avant-garde, thereby suggesting that the essence of Mettler's hybrid style lies in the investigation of the world itself and its mediation by both our senses as well as the technology of cinema.

Mettler's sustained revelation of the filmmaking process on screen makes *Picture of Light* a perfect candidate for use as an example of the now well-entrenched notion of performativity in documentary film theory. Stella Bruzzi sees the "performative" documentary as one that "uses performance within a non-fiction context to draw attention to the impossibilities of authentic documentary representation," a feature that is "an alienating, distancing device, not one which actively promotes identification and a straightforward response to a film's content" (2006, 185–186). She contrasts this definition with that of the "performative mode" identified by Bill Nichols as consisting of films that "stress subjective aspects of a classically objective discourse" (Nichols 1994, 95). For Bruzzi, the idea of performance, "Whether built around the intrusive presence of the filmmaker or self-conscious performances by its subjects—is the enactment of the notion that a documentary only comes into being as it is performed" (2006, 186). In essence Bruzzi is discussing reflexivity in a positive light as it breaks with the canonical association between documentary filmmaking and the idea of the "real." However, Mettler's performativity does not hinge on his skepticism about film's ability to document and communicate the world before his cameras and microphones, but rather the opposite.

Importantly, Bruzzi discusses performativity not only in terms of overt reflexivity, as when filmmakers are present as subjects of the film, but also in terms of stylistic qualities associated with *auteurism*. She points to the films of major figures like Errol Morris in which "the slipperiness and indeterminacy of 'the truth' is principally signaled by how this overwrought visual style becomes linked to a skepticism concerning the capability of the documentary to represent such a truth" (2006, 195). She refutes claims that the idea of the *auteur* has no place in documentary, "for one of the corollaries of accepting that documentary cannot but perform the interaction between reality and its representation is the acknowledgement that documentary, like fiction, is authored" (197). Bruzzi doesn't discuss Mettler's work, but much of what she might identify as performative in these films would be tied to his highly idiosyncratic audiovisual style that allows for comparisons to other acknowledged *auteurs* like Tarkovsky.

Jerry White agrees with the connection made between some aspects of Mettler's style and European art cinema, but he wants to move Mettler past this narrow definition and toward a more global perspective, recognizing that his films are "engaged in a truly global search for the particulars (lights, dance, rhythm) that provide us with a sense of wonder" (2006, 34). This sense of "wonder" is the slippery nexus point around which Mettler equates technological mediation with that of the human sensorium. At the heart of White's assessment is the idea that Mettler's "pursuit of wonder" is grounded in skepticism about the medium of film's role in this pursuit, but that he achieves the goal of sharing wonder with the audience in spite of technology's limitations. So White finds it appropriate that "the sequence where the aurora borealis are finally put front and center is also the most detailed about the technology of the camera," suggesting that "one can only capture the purity of vision through an intense, highly-prepared manipulation" (30). In McSorley's words, "The trick of physics and the 'lies' of the camera that have made the images possible create wonder and awe: the paradox is complete, and the conflict between the way we see and what we see is revealed in all its rich possibility" (1995, 112, 118). It is within this apparent conflict that Mettler finds the most productive way to transcend the barrier between audience and subject: "This is how technology can help us get closer to understanding the truth of our world—so long as we acknowledge the limits of our senses and those of technology itself" (White 2006, 31). The technology of the cinema and the "technology" of our senses both have limits, revealing the fact that all our experience is mediated. So Mettler's desire to explore the relationships between internal experience and the external world is tied to his keen awareness of mediality as a necessary part of how we engage the world.

For Catherine Russell, "The failure of realism to present evidence of the real is the radical possibility of experimental ethnography" (1999, 25), a quality that she would later attribute to Mettler as a filmmaker working within this conflation of genres. Russell praises Mettler's work for its recognition that the cinema necessarily entails a second-degree form of access to reality, offering "valuable clues to the potential of cinematic practice in a fallen world" (2006, para. 17). Russell argues that a film like *Gambling, Gods and LSD* (2002), which is his closest work to *Picture of Light*, is about "a quest for an experience that is ultimately incommunicable," a state of being "somewhere the camera cannot follow" (paras. 4, 12). Just as the camera cannot follow through to the subjective experience of trance states in *Gambling*, it cannot follow to the experience of the aurora borealis in *Picture of Light*. Russell emphasizes Mettler's interest in maintaining a distance from the subject matter in order to call attention to the limitations of the technology, limitations that she ties to the "fall from experience" inherent in Walter Benjamin's account of the cinema whose "illusory nature is that of the second-degree" (1968, 233), a way of being in the world "which is first and foremost, a mode of being among images, in the second nature of the cinema" (Russell 2006, paras. 13, 17).

Indeed, the preoccupations of Mettler's voiceover in *Picture of Light* corroborates Russell's account to a large extent, musing as he does over the nature of experience as mediated by the photographic image while we watch him and his crew fiddling with their equipment. I argue, however, that Mettler's reflexive approach is not solely in the service of acknowledging the "second nature of the cinema" as a way to break from traditions of documentary grounded in photography's indexical potential. Rather, in the film he tries to move past the idea of the world of reproduction as "fallen" and get at something deeper. Here, the camera as extension of the body has different implications—not the surrogate "pleasure machine" that Russell describes as the object of cinephelia (2006, para. 13), but neither the analog for consciousness, the "metaphor for vision" that Russell acknowledges in the work of experimental filmmakers like Stan Brakhage (1999, 15). Rather, I argue that there is profound desire in Mettler's films to create a cinema that offers a true experiential equivalent to the world that existed before his camera, what Jerry White identifies as "the way that interior or mental complexity can echo the complexities of the physical world," (2006, 24). For Mettler, the cinematic equivalent of the pro-filmic world does not lie in realist notions of documentary's indexical relationship to the world, or in trying to simulate internal experience through cinematic special effects. Rather, Mettler is interested in how calling attention to cinema's mediation of the world can help alert us to the way that *all* of our experience is mediated by the senses, thereby creating a cinema that invites the audience to become immersed by way of reflexive strategies. Returning to Jonathan Sterne's description of mediality discussed in the introduction to this book, "communication technologies are a fundamental part of what it means to speak, to hear, or to do anything with sound [or image]. Mediality simply points to a collectively embodied process of cross-reference," without assuming that one form of experiencing the world is automatically less mediated than another (2012, 10).

Though Mettler's style in general might seem the pitch-perfect embodiment of the performative documentary style that Bruzzi describes, I argue that the performative reflexivity in *Picture of Light* is not about skepticism and distrust of the medium. Instead I would describe Mettler's reflexivity as post-skeptical, seeking to move past a filmmaking strategy that emphasizes the distance between subject, film, and audience, and move toward an approach that uses performative strategies to expose the profound connection that our experience of a film can have to our experience to the world outside the walls of the cinema. In other words, in *Picture of Light* Mettler performs mediality. By cuing the audience into the processes of cinematic mediation, Mettler wants us also to understand how the experience of the aurora themselves is mediated by our subjectivity, a mediation that can be transcended by his approach to navigating the line that separates sound from image. Let us now consider one of his key strategies for conducting this navigation: a very particular approach to voiceover narration that defies convention in search of immersive reflexivity.

Mettler's Voice

The relationship between voice and environment is established from the film's very first shots of various crew members testing some customized camera equipment in a cold chamber. From behind the camera Mettler asks the film's producer Andreas Züst to explain what they're doing, and Züst answers loudly, competing with the harsh ambience of the cooling system. Mettler then interviews Charles Bagnall, the camera technician in charge of winterizing the equipment and designing the time lapse electronics that they'll use to attempt recording of the aurora borealis. In this segment, the sound recordist is fully in frame, pointing the shotgun microphone back and forth between Mettler and Bagnall as they converse. The voices fluctuate in volume depending on their position in relation to the microphone, indicating the precarious nature of dialogue recording in noisy environments. We watch this visualization of sound documentation as the filmmakers explain the camera technology, establishing the film's dedication to conspicuous exploration of sound/image relationships from the very start.

Finally, after almost two minutes with the relentless environmental sound competing with speech intelligibility, the film cuts to absolute silence as we watch a series of panning shots over macro-photographed images of ice crystals that resemble aerial shots of the barren tundra. An ambient drone emerges on the soundtrack, and the film's titles appear. Then we cut to the film's first shots of the night sky with a glimmer of movement resembling clouds glowing with the last of the setting sun, moving in time lapse and echoing the images of the aurora we see later on. Here Mettler's voiceover narration begins, telling us of the origins of the journey:

> In the ether one swims and meets complements. I met a man at a dinner who loves to watch the sky. He'd spent as much time watching the sky as I had trying to point cameras and microphones out into the world. It seemed that both of us were trying to find an answer to a question we didn't yet know. As the night closed we agreed to share a path we had in common: the pursuit of wonder.

With this opening volley of narration Mettler suggests one of the key issues raised by the film: the common experience that can arise from nature—looking at the sky—and its technological mediation—pointing cameras and microphones out into the world. For Mettler, both of these activities are in search of an answer to a common question, a path of common pursuit: wonder. This opening narration comes amidst an ethereal sound composition created by Jim O'Rourke that has been sharply contrasted with the film's opening sequence of direct sound in the meat locker. As the film progresses it becomes evident that it will alternate regularly between the brash qualities of direct sound, usually associated with the appearance of the filmmakers on camera, and the lyrical passages that mingle O'Rourke's work with Mettler's sound design, as with the example of the microphone tapping discussed at the start of this chapter. Both strategies are reflexive, either by calling attention to the filmmaking process itself or by highlighting Mettler's personal audiovisual approach to this process. Importantly, Mettler's voiceover narration is invariably set within the context of the latter strategy, situating his questioning voice as part of the most direct assertions of the idiosyncratic style he developed in his earlier and more experimental works.

As the voiceover narration is a major part of the film's soundtrack, let us consider its implications for the argument I am making about Mettler's desire for the film to use reflexivity as a strategy for bringing the audience closer to its subject. From the opening lines of narration quoted above, Mettler demonstrates his interest in blurring the lines between poetry, prose, and the basic delivery of information. The content of Mettler's narration, along with his tone of delivery, are far from the conventional voice of authority associated with what Bill Nichols calls the "expository mode" (1991, 32). Rather than providing a steady stream of factual information (though there is certainly some of that), Mettler is more interested in posing questions about the nature of experience and its relationship to the medium of cinema. He speaks in a gentle, hypnotic manner that, with the help of Jim O'Rourke's sound compositions, creates a dreamlike quality rather than an atmosphere of objective mastery over the film's subject matter. Overtly reflexive in content, the voice also envelops the listeners, hoping to draw us in and keep us immersed. The voiceover, then, is one of the principal ways that Mettler achieves immersive reflexivity.

Jerry White identifies Mettler's use of voiceover narration as a key component of his reflexive style: "Mettler lays his cards on the table through his deeply subjective voiceover; by doing this he makes it clear that he is not hiding an attempt to master the landscape behind faux-neutral observation" (2006, 30). This style of voiceover is part of what White and others argue is Mettler's skepticism about film's ability to connect with reality; Mettler's voiceover eschews the direct connection between the voice of authority that asserts control over the image, opting instead for a looser connection, a voice that hovers in the ether, an equal player with the other elements of a highly nuanced soundtrack that frequently slips free of any realist connection to the image. With this style, Mettler demonstrates his stated belief that all elements of a film's soundtrack should work together as a musical composition (1992, 41). Frequent collaborator Fred Frith says that this respect for the equality of the different components of the soundtrack is something that Mettler demonstrates more than any other filmmaker he has worked with (quoted in Schaub 1995, 42). Indeed, Mettler's approach to voiceover narration can be read as a direct response to criticisms of other forms of narration that seek to dominate both the sound and image tracks.

Stella Bruzzi situates debates about the use of voiceover in documentary within more general debates about sound/image synchronization in film. Bruzzi tells us that "the negative portrayal of voiceover is largely the result of the development of a theoretical orthodoxy that condemns it for being inevitably and inherently didactic" (2006, 47). Bruzzi critiques the way that histories of documentary have created the voiceover as what she calls an "unnecessary evil" in their constant emphasis on documentary films as "an endless pursuit of the most effective way of representing the 'purity' of the real," a purity of visual representation that is displaced, and therefore threatened, by the "voice-of-God" style authority of the voiceover that dominates our understanding of the image (47–48).

Bruzzi situates the negative connotations of documentary voiceover in the context of general concerns over the coming of synchronized sound to film in the 1920s. In particular was the concern over this idea of the "purity" of the image being somehow damaged by an attached and invariable soundtrack. Here she cites Nichols' assertion that synchronized sound aids in establishing the realism of the image—the very fear of the Soviet Montagists who argued for contrapuntal strategies in the pairing of sound and image—whereas voiceover narration "is an intrusion which interferes with this automatic prioritization of the image" (2006, 49). Bruzzi also notes how later sound theorists like Kaja Silverman have contributed to the negative connotations of voiceover by tying it to hegemonic practices of classical Hollywood cinema (58) (which I discuss in more detail in Chapter 4).

These critiques of voiceover are all premised upon the problem of voiceover dominating other sound design elements, just as many commentators feared that through voiceover narration sound could dominate the image in an unwelcome reversal of the primacy of the image established prior to the coming of synchronized sound. Because of these critiques, Bruzzi notes the increasing popularity of the ironic voiceover in performative documentaries used as the narration equivalent of asynchronous sound that deliberately sets itself apart from the image. Many documentary filmmakers have also opted to eschew the use of voiceover altogether, as Mettler himself did in a later film, *Petropolis* (2009), believing that its presence "obscured the perceptual force of the film's images" (Browne 2020, 132). Yet this approach, too, has been criticized. Addressing Mary Ann Doane's argument that the "silencing" of the voice of authority "promotes... an illusion that reality speaks and is not spoken, that the film is not a constructed discourse," Britta Sjogren laments that, "One can only feel somewhat sympathetic toward documentarists, who apparently just cannot win, one way or the other" (2006, 222).

Picture of Light aims to win by presenting neither the voice of authority nor its silencing. Mettler's voiceover doesn't adopt an ironic tone, either. Rather, it is a voice that speaks to the problems of narration by emphasizing its own position in meditating the content of the film while forming an equal partnership with the other elements within the audiovisual totality of the film. As

I will demonstrate now, Mettler's use of voiceover is profoundly connected to the film's goal of using reflexivity to transcend the acknowledged limitations of media technologies and bring the audience closer to the reality of the aurora borealis than skeptics would think possible.

A Surrogate for Real Experience?

Following the film's opening title, we watch and listen as Mettler and his crew make the journey north by train. As the train pulls out of the station we get a shot from the back of the caboose, watching the terminal recede into a night filled with thick steam and mist. The sound of the train is front and center, and at one point we see the sound recordist with his microphone hanging out the window. As the sequence continues, O'Rourke's ambient soundscapes rise in the mix, and the sound of the train becomes part of a more fantastical sound environment. Here Mettler's voiceover continues, establishing the philosophical tension that exists between the wilderness he's interested in capturing on film, and the technology that will allow this capturing to take place, a process of commodification he describes as the extraction of "business and numbers out of life force and wonder." As these words are being spoken, a view of the passing landscape from the moving train zooms jerkily back to reveal the window that frames the view, emphasizing the window's mediating role in the experience, one layer of glass among many in the process of making a film. There is a cut to a shot of the cameraman, Mettler himself, caught in the bathroom mirror, a reflective pane of representation that also emphasizes the mediated nature of this enterprise. The narration continues:

> Maybe this wacky process of harnessing money and technology is just an extension of thinking, of trying to understand. These images and sounds are articulations of experience. We look at them, and try to decipher the reality that gave birth to them. It may well be that the northern lights cannot be filmed, that nature cannot be filmed, that film or media is in conflict with nature. Is it just a surrogate for the real thing? Is film a surrogate for real experience?

Here Mettler positions cinematic mediation of the pro-filmic world as an "extension of thinking," then questions the extent to which film allows access to that which it represents. As these final words are spoken, we are presented with a shot through the window in shallow focus. Andreas Züst is revealed screen right looking out the window through his glasses, and what we see through these glasses is in sharper focus than the window itself. Here Mettler places further emphasis on how the framing of views and the lenses we put between the world outside and the world inside are examples of the mediating agents that we experience on a daily basis. But to what extent do these mediators impede the flow across the division between internal consciousness and the external world?

This question can be answered, in part, by the way that Mettler chooses to describe his own previous experiences of the aurora borealis. "I'd seen the lights before a few times in my life, and I remember mostly how they move: like thoughts." In equating the movement of the aurora borealis with the movement of thoughts Mettler is associating the phenomena of the lights outside in the world and his experience of them inside his mind. It is telling that he situates this equation within his musings on the relationship between the pro-filmic event and its representation. Later in the film, as we see the filmmakers examining some 35mm footage by hand, Mettler connects these ideas more concretely:

> We live in a time where things do not seem to exist if they are not contained as an image. But if you look into this darkness you may see the lights of your own retina. Not unlike the northern lights, not unlike the movements of thought. Like a shapeless accumulation of everything we have ever seen. Before science explained, the lights were interpreted as visions, prophecies, spirits, a trigger for the imagination. Images provided by nature, framed by no less than the universe itself.

With the final sentence in this narration Mettler suggests an equivalency between experiencing images on film, framed by the dictates of the lens and screen, and experiencing images in the sky, framed by the peripheries of our vision and the boundaries of the horizon. Experience of the world is always mediated by framing of some kind, whether imposed by technologies of representation or by the limitations of vision and our perspectival position with respect to what we're looking at. Even more importantly, Mettler is suggesting a kinship between the way the aurora borealis look, and the way we experience the process of our own thinking. Mettler is moving toward the idea that there is a profound kinship possible between his experience of the lights in Churchill and our experience of the lights on film. Toward the end of the film, Mettler puts this articulation into a single sentence: "And we tell ourselves that seeing it on TV just isn't the same as being there," as though this were an idea that humans came up with to keep the boundary between reality and representation perfectly clear. But the boundary is not clear, and it never has been. We may tell ourselves that there is a difference between the external world and its mediation by way of recording technologies, but Mettler is suggesting otherwise.

The idea of the lights being a trigger for the imagination is key here, because it speaks directly to Mettler's questions about whether or not film is a surrogate for experience, or if there is a deeper connection between the two. At one point in the film, as we watch the camera gently moving across barren frozen landscapes, Mettler recounts the legend of the Lumière brothers screening *Arrival of a Train at La Ciotat* (1896) for a public audience in which people were said to have run screaming for the exits for fear of being run over by the train. Mettler then asks: "Are you cold yet?" Though he presents these events as though a matter of fact, his question could be construed as a cynical jab at a story that most contemporary historians see as apocryphal. Even audiences of the late nineteenth century were media-savvy enough to understand the difference between reality and representation in film, but modern commentators need a primitive antithesis to mystify the experiential transparency of film (see Vaughan 1999, 1).

In Mettler's version of the Lumière story, the fear of being run over did not stem from believing the train was real, but rather from *feeling* the same in the face of the representation as one would in the face of reality. If we were to feel cold while watching images of a frozen landscape, it is not because film steps in as surrogate for reality, but that it triggers the imagination, sets our thoughts moving in a particular direction that yields genuine experience of the cold based on whatever past experiences we've had with it. When Mettler refers to the northern lights as images provided by nature and framed by the universe, he's drawing a connection between the kinds of mental triggering that film can effect upon us, and the lights themselves that are no less images that we watch within a kind of frame. Each situation is mediated, and each has the capacity to set our minds moving in the same way. Thus the lights can transcend any thought of experiential surrogacy and speak to us directly, even through their mediation by way of film.

The very particular use of voiceover, hovering between authoritative mastery and its absence, is used to frame Mettler's questions about how the lights occupy that space between the night sky and the internal consciousness of those who look at them. The presence of his voice acts as a conduit through which the other sounds and images in the film can be understood, a line of mediation that calls attention to the very act of mediation itself. Further, both the content of his words and the presentation style of his voice perform mediality itself, demonstrating not simply how the film and sound recording alters or stands in the way of our experience of the natural world but how it is only ever through mediation that we access this world anyway. As such, Mettler's brand of performativity both aligns with and deviates from Bruzzi's figuration of performativity in documentary filmmaking. Mettler's emphasis on reflexive approaches to representing Churchill demonstrates that the world he's attempting to document comes into being as a function of being recorded. The world he shows us is the world in the process of being filmed. At the same time, Mettler breaks from the attachment of this performativity to an emphasis on technology's distanciating effect. For Mettler, there is no other way to experience the world than by way of mediality, so to lay that mediality plain is to offer the audience the same access to the aurora borealis that he and his crew had, bringing us closer to that world rather than keeping us at arm's length from it.

Image, Sound, Synchronization

I will now demonstrate how Mettler's version of performativity plays out by way of his simultaneous engagement with two historically opposite approaches to sound on film: the Soviet Montage school's call for non-redundancy across the sound and image tracks, and the visual music movement that strives for sound and image to be experienced as inseparable. Mettler folds these ways of thinking onto one another through his evocation of the potential audibility of the aurora borealis and the association of their motion with the "movement of thoughts." These associations can be fruitfully explored through the work of experimental filmmaker Stan Brakhage, whose interest in documenting deeply interior experiences of vision without the eyes can help us to understand similarities across Soviet Montage approaches to sound/image synchronization and the goals of visual music.

Mettler's interest in the movement of the aurora borealis and its kinship to the movement of thoughts is positioned within a discussion of phenomena that evoke the transsensorial potential of the lights, their ability to enter the human sensorium through the visual channel but be experienced by the mind as sound. Toward the end of *Picture of Light*, Mettler considers the possibility of hearing the lights:

> Ed says you can hear them, but Bill says all you could theoretically hear is static discharge as though your head being the highest point around this flat terrain acted like some kind of conductor to the currents of the night sky. Or maybe it's our breath freezing into tiny ice crystals and falling upon our nylon parkas.

The sequence ends with O'Rourke's ambient treatments fading out as the visuals fade to white. The sound of breathing emerges, floating for a moment over the blank screen until we cut to a shot of Inuk elder Joseph Natakok. He speaks in his native tongue as the camera cuts from him to panning shots of the frozen tundra. Mettler delays offering translation for a minute and a half, finally stating that, "The old Inuk said that most of all he likes to hunt," just as we watch local motel owner Steve Bosnjak setting up his video camera on the land during a heavy wind. "Perhaps we are modern-day hunters," Mettler continues. Perhaps what they hear while filming the lights is the sound of their own breath in the act of hunting the lights down, the material result of their attempts to use film as a way of accessing the connection between the lights and the movement of thoughts.

With Mettler's attempts to film the lights comes the question of what is heard while so doing. Can the lights themselves be heard? Or only the environment in which the viewing takes place? Perhaps the sound one might hear is just the minutiae of the environment. Perhaps the lights are a trigger for the imagination, putting one in tune with the smallest details of the surroundings, just as Mettler's cameras and microphones do. If Mettler was interested only in the possibility that attention to the lights calls similar attention to the nuances of the environment in which they are viewed, then one could imagine an approach to sound design that emphasizes direct location recording above all else, providing us with access to the auditory minutia of Churchill, Manitoba. Yet as is clear by now, Mettler is far from approaching sound design with strict realist or observational principles in mind. Mettler's sound design is geared much more toward the idea of the lights as trigger for the imagination, of setting the mind moving.

It is significant that Mettler positions the idea of setting the mind moving within references to the potential for the inaudible lights to be heard. This connection aligns Mettler's thinking with the discourse of visual music, which, in turn, he explores in the context of various approaches to the audiovisual asynchronicity espoused by the Soviet Montage school in the late 1920s. At first thought it may seem that these two movements offered incompatible responses to the question of sound's role in cinema with the coming of synchronization. As I will demonstrate now, however, Mettler threads each through the other on his quest to understand how film can access the world, and this approach is essential to understanding how immersive reflexivity works as a response to contemporary skepticism about documentary veracity.

As Judith Zilczer explains, the idea of visual music began with painting: "No longer content simply to reproduce the visible world, painters instead sought to endow their canvases with the emotional intensity, structural integrity, and aesthetic purity that they attributed to music" (2005, 25). From cinema's very beginning, there have been many strains of visual music filmmaking. Some attempted to visualize existing pieces of music by way of literal transpositions of musical elements like pitch, timbre, and rhythm into corresponding visual patterns. Others explored the ways in which image might create sound and vice versa, as in Norman McLaren's *Synchromy* (1971) in which he used images laid into the optical soundtrack portion of 35mm film stock to physically generate the sounds we hear while watching them on the image track. In the digital age there are countless strategies for extending this basic principle to create sound from visual material or generate both from the same computational foundation. At the heart of these approaches to visual music is the idea that sound and image are conceived as being of a piece, inseparable, not a function of deliberate synchronization but rather each an organic manifestation of the other.

The most literal approach to a visual form of music comes with a renewed interest in making silent films in the age of synchronized sound, a practice that often attempts to get at those transsensorial qualities of the image that can transcend the lines of division between sensory modalities. Michel Chion describes transsensorial experience this way: "In the transsensorial model . . . there is no sensory given that is demarcated and isolated from the outset. Rather, the senses are channels, highways more than territories or domains" (1994, 137). He is careful to explain that transsensoriality is not the same as synaesthesia with the latter's direct correspondences between the senses. Rather, he's interested in how certain categories of perceptual phenomena are not specific to any one sense. Chion gives rhythm as an example of an element found in cinema that is neither specifically auditory nor visual:

> When a rhythmic phenomenon reaches us via a given sensory path, this path, eye or ear, is perhaps nothing more than the channel through which rhythm reaches us. Once it has entered the ear or eye, the phenomenon strikes us in some region of the brain connected to the motor functions, and it is solely at this level that it is decoded as rhythm. (1994, 136)

Whether or not Chion's description is fully accurate from a neurophysiological standpoint, the upshot of this transsensorial model for understanding cinematic experience suggests that there are more fundamental levels of the cinema than simply sight and sound, levels that do not differentiate between the auditory and the visual but that cut through both to a deeper and more holistic understanding of experience.

Gesture is another key concept that transcends specific sensory demarcations, tying the general category of movement to qualities of both images and sounds that are embedded within each other. Rolfe Inge Godøy argues that works of abstract sound composition, like the acousmatic music of Pierre Schaeffer (a tradition from which O'Rourke's own music emerged), cannot be experienced as entirely removed from the realm of imagery. Godøy describes this relationship between acousmatic sound and visuality as being linked to "*embodied cognition*, meaning that virtually all domains of human perception and thinking, even seemingly abstract domains, are related to images of movement" in the mind (2006, 150).

Godøy's conclusions here extend from a field of inquiry into the idea of *musical imagery*. Music theorists have long been interested in how the idea of the "image" plays into the creation and reception of music. As Rosemary Mountain illustrates in her discussion of musical imagery in the compositional process, the concept of *image* has various connotations in this field. Of particular interest here are kinesthetic images—our visual understanding of motion—that our minds often turn to when hearing sound alone. Mountain's survey of the concept of musical imagery demonstrates that composers often compose music with a visual intent, the desire to create "effective illusions of imaginary sonic objects moving through time" (2001, 286).

On the other end of the spectrum of thought concerning film as a form of "music" is the contrapuntal approach to audiovisual synchronization espoused by the Soviet Montage filmmakers of the late 1920s through their "Statement" concerning the sound film first published in 1928. Sergei Eisenstein and a few of his contemporaries wanted the cinema to continue developing along the lines of montage, and considered sound as another potential layer of meaning construction. Creating meaning through montage requires a measure of juxtaposition that, for these filmmakers, is impossible if sound is used naturalistically. So they called for a film sound practice based on "nonsynchronization with the visual images" as the key to developing the cinematic equivalent of "orchestral counterpoint" (84). Not long after, Alexander Pudovkin would write, "The role which sound is to play in film is much more significant than a slavish imitation of naturalism" in which, for example, the sound of a car is added to the image of a car (1929, 86). As René Clair put it that same year, "We do not need to *hear* the sound of clapping if we can *see* the clapping hands," (1929, 94), a sentiment later echoed by Robert Bresson in his famous "Notes on Sound" (1977): "What is for the eye must not duplicate what is for the ear" (149). For Bresson, "Image and sound must not support each other, but must work each in turn through *a sort of relay*" (149), an idea that Clair also expressed: "It is the *alternate*, not the simultaneous, use of the visual subject and of the sound produced by it that creates the best effects" (1929, 94).

It is for this reason that the Soviet Montagists, notably Eisenstein and Pudovkin, argued for a different kind of musicality in the approach to sound/image synchronization: counterpoint. A term borrowed from Western music theory, *counterpoint* for the Soviet Montage school suggests that sound operates as another element of juxtaposition within the dialectic approach to montage so espoused by Eisenstein. This ideology resulted in a variety of approaches to the formal implementation of audiovisual counterpoint (Thompson, 1980). Importantly, counterpoint for the Soviets was not necessarily a question of asynchronicity, but rather an approach to synchronization that eschewed conventions of realism. Because of this, Chion has elucidated the confusion surrounding the correct meaning of *counterpoint* since the days of Eisenstein, insisting that the use of this term to refer to jarring juxtaposition has not done justice to its musical origins. Chion notes that the term *dissonance* is much better suited to describe the kinds of audiovisual clashes that are often referred to as *counterpoint*. In music, the term *counterpoint* describes relationships between elements in sequence (horizontal) rather than simultaneous (vertical). Chion uses the term *free counterpoint* for instances where the sound and image tracks operate free of precise cause/effect relationships governed by vertical synchronization, but with a relationship of simultaneity that creates a new layer of meaning that wouldn't exist if the sound and image tracks were presented separately (36–37). Counterpoint, then, treats the sound and image tracks of film as part of a coherent system that needn't be governed by precise points of audiovisual synchronization. What *is* necessary for counterpoint is the simultaneous juxtaposition of sound and image that results in a new layer of meaning through their combination.

Whether advocating for synthesis through counterpoint, or simply hoping to avoid informational redundancy, calls for asynchronicity have one thing in common: the desire to expose the artifice of audiovisual pairing in order to promote audience engagement as they navigate the line that separates sound and image on film. The technology of the synchronized sound film ensures that sound and image will always be locked together, so eschewing naturalism and redundancy allows for this fixed simultaneity to be used to keep the audience aware that sound and image are separate entities, brought together for specific reasons. In other words, you can't spell *asynchronous* without *synchronous*; as a concept, the former is bound up within the latter. The term *counterpoint* operates the same way, building the idea of juxtaposition into the term itself. Counterpoint is one way of acknowledging the separate nature of sound and image, but this acknowledgment is only possible through the fact of audiovisual simultaneity. The task of those opposed to the premise of the talking picture was to think of ways to use synchronized sound that would keep the technical reality of the apparatus exposed: sound and image are separate first, and then brought together. Visual music, on the other hand, approaches audiovisuality from the other end: sound and image are one and the same, and this inseparability must be expressed through the separate sound and image tracks of film.

Although Eisenstein's interest in film sound is generally tied to the "Statement," he was also interested in the transsensorial potential of images alone. In *Nonindifferent Nature* (1987) he speaks of "plastic music," that music which is contained and expressed by the visual aspects of cinema, particularly in the silent era. He says that the idea of expressing music visually fell mostly to images of landscape, "and a similar emotional landscape, functioning as a musical component, is what I call 'nonindifferent nature'" (216). Interestingly, as David Bordwell has noted, Eisenstein moved away from the asynchronous sound manifesto as well as any interest in silent evocations of music to embrace musical score as a powerful element within his filmmaking. In later films like *Ivan the Terrible* (1944) the images are designed in correlation to the music, an "organic" approach that aligns with much visual music rather than the "dialectical" one he insisted upon at the dawn of synchronization (Bordwell 1980, 147). So Eisenstein has run the gamut of possibility for the relationships between sound and image, and ended somewhat far from where he began.[1] Yet his path illustrates an often neglected ideological connection between these different ways of conceiving of film as music, from the "musical" qualities inherent in images, through contrapuntal approaches to audiovisual synchronization, and on into explorations of how sound and image can be thought of as inseparable facets of each other.

What is most at odds between these varying approaches to synchronization is the question of whether or not film should be made reflexive about its two channels of transmission: sound and image. For K. J. Donnelly, sound/image synchronization in film is, by its very nature, an "occult" situation, in the sense that its processes and aesthetics are largely "unapparent," obfuscated from the consciousness of viewers (2014, 70). We can see in the trajectory of theoretical approaches to synchronization that there are conflicting desires in whether or not to bring occult synchronization out of the shadows and into the light of the projection on screen. Contrapuntal practice says yes, while visual music says no. However, these apparently opposing ideologies can be understood as part of the same underlying desire to immerse the audience in the world represented by the film through aesthetic strategies that call attention to the mediality involved in this process. In *Picture of Light*, Mettler explores all points along the continuum from the musicality of silent images (the lights themselves), across both the realist and contrapuntal potential of synchronization, and through to evocations of inseparable audiovisuality. In so doing, Mettler might be termed an anti-occultist, exposing the affinities between these approaches to thinking about sound's role in the cinema, to render visible that which has been inaudible. As I will discuss now, what binds these various audiovisual modalities together is the idea that film can emulate the "movement of thoughts," which I will elucidate through the work of avant-garde filmmaker Stan Brakhage and the various ways in which his work aligns with Mettler's interests in *Picture of Light*.

The Movement of Thought

Stan Brakhage has expressed his own interest in exploring the cinematic equivalent of the movement of thought through the "musical" quality of moving images alone.[2] Jerry White connects Mettler's interest in exposing the materiality of film with a similar interest shown by Brakhage. White suggests that sequences like those that present the lights in time-lapse photography "recall the rough, turbulent work of Stan Brakhage" who "thought carefully" about "the lengths to which you had to take the image, the kinds of abuse you had to inflict on the celluloid in order to make it speak" (2006, 32). Yet what interests me here goes beyond the mutual concern Brakhage and Mettler show for rendering the surface of celluloid apparent to the audience. Even more important are the ideological underpinnings of their shared desire to find a way to get at the transsensorial potential of the cinema that can result in immersive reflexivity.

Though he isn't usually discussed as a visual music filmmaker, Stan Brakhage has explored the realm perhaps more fully than any. His 1990s hand-painted films like *Stellar* (1993) and *Black Ice* (1994) often end with a credit stating that they are to be understood as pieces of visual music wherein Brakhage is the "composer" and the person operating the optical printer is the "visual musician." But he has a long history preceding this overt reference to visual music suggesting a powerful interest in exploring hearing without the ear, and indeed seeing without the eye, through the notion of the movement of thought. For Brakhage, getting at the movement of thought involved some very particular ideas about sound/image synchronization in the cinema and how these ideas led him to the extreme end of visual music in his pursuit of prompting auditory experience through the presentation of images alone.

During his 2001 retrospective at the Cinémathèque Québequoise in Montreal, Brakhage exclaimed, "you sync something and it is sunk, as far as I'm concerned!" (2003, para. 5). He was referring to the banality of treating sound/image relations in mainstream film as elements to be unified through representational cause/effect synchronization, and in so doing aligns himself, at least a little, with the Soviet Montage school. In a letter to Ronna Page on the subject of music, he speaks of his intense dissatisfaction with "conventional uses of music for 'mood' and so-called 'realistic sounds' as mere referendum to image in movies" (1978, 134), echoing the concerns of Eisenstein et al. in their "Statement." So, he studied with John Cage and Edgar Varèse, "at first with the idea of searching out a new relationship between image and sound and of, thus, creating a new dimension for the sound track" (134). He continues:

> The more informed I became with aesthetics of sound, the less I began to feel any need for an audio accompaniment to the visuals I was making.... The more silently oriented my creative philosophies have become, the more inspired-by-music have my photographic aesthetics and my actual editing orders become, both engendering a coming-into-being of the physiological relationship between seeing and hearing in the making of a work of art in film. (135)

Here, as Fred Camper notes, Brakhage is interested in appealing to what he calls the "sound sense," sounds that can be evoked by movement and editing patterns (1985, 373) without the need for an actual soundtrack. With this kind of approach, Brakhage was moving in the direction of exploring the highly soluble boundaries between our demarcations of sound and image to show that a work perceived with the eyes does not mean that we experience it solely as visual information. To this end, Brakhage says he wanted to "get deeper into my concept of music as sound equivalent of the mind's moving" (1978, 135). Here Brakhage associates music with sound, but by tying it to the idea of the "mind's moving," music can transcend the strict delineation of auditory perception and become a marker of holistic perception. This is the realm of "moving visual thinking," which Brakhage describes as "a streaming of shapes that are not nameable—a vast visual 'song' of the cells expressing their internal life" (quoted in Ganguly 1993, 21).

When Brakhage refers to music as the "sound equivalent of the mind's moving" he suggests that the way the mind processes the world is best understood as the movement of thought rather than as a collection of specific sensory phenomena. This movement is not confined to isolated channels of hearing or seeing, but can be represented and expressed by both sight and sound equally well (not to mention the rest of our senses). This is exemplified by the idea that Brakhage's films need no soundtrack for their musical qualities to come through: the brain understands the music even if the ears do not hear it. The transsensorial qualities of experience reflect what Brakhage calls the "totality of thought" (Wees 1992, 77), the post-sensory experience of the world that pays no heed to whether sensory information comes in through the eyes or the ears. It is simply the totality of experience that cannot be broken down the way our technologies of representation make us believe they can. This idea of the totality of thought exists as a kind of movement that Brakhage attempts to get at through his cinematic explorations of moving visual thinking.

Picture of Light, and Mettler's work in general, is aligned with the goals of visual music and the work of Stan Brakhage on several levels. Mettler has stated his personal commitment to the idea that film is a form of music. In his essay "Music in Film: Film as Music," he says,

> Film has the same potential immediacy as music. What I mean by this is that film has many aspects in common with music, especially in its ability to tap into an unconscious or subconscious mode of experience, and in its ability to create meaning through rhythms and emotional colours and tones. (1992, 35)

With this description of film Mettler points toward the potential of the cinema to create an immediacy of experience in the audience that he equates with the idea of music. His description also evokes the transsensorial potential of the cinema in establishing rhythm as a grounding element, a point he emphasizes further when he suggests that, "like music, it could be that the essential element of a film is its rhythm" (36). Here Mettler engages with a long history of filmmaking concerned with the cinematic exploration of rhythm. As I have discussed, rhythm is part of the larger category of movement that lies at the heart of transsensorial experience.

Mettler's question about whether or not the aurora borealis can be heard is a question about the transsensorial quality of the lights that might bind their external manifestation to our internal experience of them through an equivalency of movement. Of course, *Picture of Light* is not a silent film, so Mettler's interest in the lights as a manifestation of what Brakhage would call moving visual thinking is not explored through the same strategies as Brakhage's silent hand-painted abstractions. Rather, Mettler sets the time-lapse images of the lights to amorphous auditory treatments, so that we can experience the movement of the lights in their own right with minimal influence from externally imposed rhythmic and gestural structures. At the same time, however, *Picture of Light* is committed to the aesthetics of free counterpoint, emphasizing the audiovisual nature of sound cinema by exploring the line that separates sound and image in order to arrive at unconventional ways of establishing connections between these two modes of transmission. Mettler explores this transsensorial potential of images alone through an approach to audiovisual synchronization that, at times, aligns perfectly with both the dissonance and free counterpoint that Chion identifies as core aesthetic strategies of the Soviets' call for asynchronicity. By calling attention to the technical separation of sound and image as part of the film's reflexive strategy, Mettler also reveals the distance between his audience and the lights that he filmed in Churchill. Yet by asking whether or not we might be able to hear the lights, he is suggesting their transsensorial potential to enable a common level of experience of the lights between the audience and the filmmakers. So it is essential that we understand Mettler's reflexive approach not as one borne of total skepticism, but rather an optimism for the potential of cinema not only to teach us about life amidst images—a second-order reality—but the cinema as a conduit for experience that extends from the screen through physical space to our interior consciousness. The remaining analyses will focus on the film's deliberate disruption of conventions of audiovisual synchronization in order to demonstrate how these disruptions function as agents of the transsensorial potential of the aurora borealis and their cinematic representation.

Conducting Mysterious Music

One sequence in *Picture of Light* draws all these threads around synchronization together, aligning Brakhage and Eisenstein to invite the audience to partake fully in the wonder that the lights inspired in Mettler and his crew on location. In an interview segment Brian Ladoon, a local dog-team trainer, explains the concept of "blood bathing" wherein a hunter becomes unscrupulous about what prey to shoot and indulges blood lust to an extreme degree. As we listen to him speak, the film shows us images of other dog handlers feeding a team outside in a blustery wind, axing chunks of meat off large frozen blocks and throwing it to the animals amidst blowing snow. The sound remains grounded within the interior space of the interview with just a little bit of external ambient sound leaking through: axe thuds, wind blowing, and dogs barking in the distance to underscore the Ladoon's commentary. The interview continues as we watch one of Mettler's crew setting up a camera in the deep snow. Again, direct sound from the exterior space is layered with the sound of the interview as the dog trainer contemplates the responsibility of the hunter to respect the value of all life. The image track, however, never returns to the dog trainer. Once the interview ends, an offscreen Mettler begins a conversation with the onscreen cameraperson. They discuss the settings for the time-lapse electronics being used to try and capture the lights on film. Once the equipment is set we hear the sound of the camera going off once every few seconds, along with the steady breathing of the cameraperson, providing a rhythmic base to an emerging soundscape featuring O'Rourke's music once again. Mettler's narration begins anew, explaining that after much time spent waiting out bad weather, the skies are finally clear and they can turn the camera upward. As we watch the film's first significant sequence of the aurora in time-lapse, the location sound of the camera and breathing fade out while the sounds of barking dogs fade in, the ambient drone continuing all the while.

This time-lapse sequence of the lights illustrates Mettler's signature approach to auditory accompaniment of the visual phenomena. The lights are a visual phenomenon, and the technique of time-lapse is a particularly silent form of filmmaking. Time-lapse sequences are rarely accompanied by their auditory equivalent: the sound of the pro-filmic environment sped up dramatically. Instead of such a literal approach to the sound of the time-lapse environment, Mettler emphasizes the sound of the mechanism responsible for creating the time-lapse imagery. The sound of the camera and breathing, presented in real-time, are incongruous with the temporal compression visible on the screen, yet their connection has been made clear. This is an example of how an overtly reflexive disruption in conventions of realist synchronization can nevertheless evoke a profound connection between sound and image grounded in the reality of place.

Then, when the camera sound is replaced by the sound of barking dogs, the dog trainer's story about the relationship between hunter and prey is evoked. We have already heard Mettler explain that the lights are often interpreted as spirits by the Indigenous population; here the sounds of the dogs, earlier associated with the spirit of the hunted animals coming out in their last breath, are now associated with the lights as visual representation of the spirit world. Mettler thus takes direct sound recording from one sequence of the film and uses it to create a rich and meaningful moment of free counterpoint for another sequence. The abstract visual phenomena of the lights are thus contextualized within a reflexive strategy laced with an ecological message. Mettler's style is impressive, in part, because of its balance between all these elements to create a reflexive meditation on the act of filming the lights while engaging deeply with the cultural environment in which this filming takes place.

Relationships of audiovisual counterpoint are at their peak during a series of interviews with local residents about their experience of the northern lights. As people talk, they are first presented using the convention of lip-synchronization, the standard for the interview format. Then, however, images begin to slip away from the talking heads whose voices we hear, and instead we are presented with images of *other* interviewees in the process of talking. While it is common for documentaries to insert related imagery while listening to interviewees talk on the soundtrack—as in the images of the dogs over Brian Ladoon's bathing story—it is almost unheard of to layer the sound of one person talking over the image of another speaker whose voice is absent. This strategy serves as a definitive break from the norms of the talking head documentary, and indeed of talking cinema in general. Yet as we are disrupted from the lack of lip synchronization, new synchronizations emerge. As we watch people talk, they gesture with their hands, and these gestures are presented as reflections of the descriptions of the aurora being spoken in voiceover. These are the images of citizens "conducting mysterious music" that Peter Weber describes (see above), and his analogy could not be more apt for this discussion of how the film's reflexive approach to sound/image relationships ties into the theme of film as visual music.

The nexus point of the whole film comes at the end of this sequence when we see Andreas Züst gesturing while we hear the dog trainer describing seasonal differences in the lights that are detectable through the levels of definition around their edges. Züst makes an inverted V shape with his hands just as we hear the dog trainer mention "defined edges." However, at this point in the film, viewers realize that this shot of Züst is from an earlier interview in which he describes not the lights, but the artificially defined edges of a snowdrift that he shaped in his hotel room as an experiment inspired by the boredom inherent in waiting out the weather in Churchill.

While confined to their motel rooms, the crew and some local residents decide to pass the time by shooting a hole in the wall of the hotel room to allow a stream of snow to enter and, hopefully, create a natural drift across the room. This is one of many moments in the film where the boundary between nature and human-made artificiality is brought up. The results of the experiment leave something to be desired, prompting Züst to shape a nicer looking drift than the one created by the experiment itself. His disappointment about the lack of grandeur of the interior drift stems partly from their lack of attention to the other side of the wall, their failure to see how the weather was behaving in relation to the hole they punched to let the outside in. This is one of the constant references in the film to a permeable boundary between inside and outside while questioning what differences there are, if any, between interior and exterior manifestations of the same thing. In this case it's a snowdrift, but this applies also to Mettler's question about media as surrogate for real experience, and his equation of the interior machinations of consciousness with the exterior manifestation of the lights.

The snowdrift sequence ends with a close-up of the drift partially covering the room's television set, making a direct connection once again between the natural and the artificial, the artificial snow drift playing at natural forms while it partially obscures the television's attempt at the same. This connection is brought home when we see Züst gesturing about the edges of a snowdrift while we hear Brian Ladoon describe the levels of definition visible on the edges of the lights at different times of the year. Here we find a convergence of the landscape of the earth—the snowdrift—and the form of the aurora, both of which have been subject to mediation by human hands. We have heard Mettler describe the aurora as moving like thoughts, evoking a connection between the lights in the sky and the "lights" of consciousness. We have read about Brakhage and Eisenstein's interest in visual representations of landscape as "musical" in nature, something Brakhage also equates with the moving mind. With this simple juxtaposition between Züst's hand gesture and Ladoon's description of the lights, the film zeros in on the triangular relationship between psychological space, geographical space, and their connection by way of cinema.

In this interview sequence Mettler uses images from one interviewee as harmonic counterpoint to the sound from another. It is important that the disjunction in this interview sequence takes place on the point of hand gestures. Like rhythm, gesture transcends sensory modalities—physical movement that can be experienced in the absence of both sound and image. The idea of gesture as being tied to moving visual thinking is connected to what Rolf Inge Godøy refers to as embodied cognition, images of movement within the mind, that tie all processing of even the most abstract sound into gestural sensibilities within the brain. The break in lip-sync disrupts the convention of sound/image relationships, yet the gesturing brings these images back into alignment with the sound offering new potentials for making meaning. Here the film ties one of the most basic ideas we have about gesture—hand movements acting as a visual aid while speaking—to the disruption of conventional approaches to sound/image synchronization in order to demonstrate other modes of connecting sound with image. Gesture is the concept that threads these sound/image disjunctions together, just as the gesturing motion of the aurora borealis threads representation with reality, interior consciousness with exterior space. The "mysterious music" being conducted in these shots of gestural hand movements is the "music" of the silent aurora, a transsensorial gesture by Mettler to suggest the potential of cinema to engender a common experience of the northern lights with the people we see and hear on the screen.

In the end it's not that Mettler wants us to feel as though we're actually standing with him in Churchill beneath the northern lights. Rather, the film demonstrates that through exposing the audience to the filmmaking process, while drawing explicit relationships between this process and the machinations of our individual consciousnesses, we can get closer to the experience of the aurora than many would think possible when mediated through the technology of film. "And we tell ourselves that seeing it on TV just isn't the same as being there..."

Manufacturing the Pill

The greatest strength of *Picture of Light* is its quality of immersive reflexivity, to expose the processes of its own construction in order to engage the audience as participants in performing the world that the film brings into being. The result of this immersion is not that the film becomes a realist window out into the world, bringing the audience to Churchill. Rather, it is an immersion in the machinations by which the aurora are captured and brought to the audience, emphasizing mediality as a fundamental mode of engagement with place.

The issue of what is represented in the film is key. Just as the film does not try to limit its representation of pro-filmic reality to realist convention, neither does it try to represent experience itself through the creation of an analog of consciousness. Rather, the film articulates how our experience of the world, whether on film or not, is a function of the technologies through which we engage with the world. Mettler's film is about the difficulties in achieving the technical aspects of filming something in the world under adverse conditions, and questioning the relationship between the world and its representation. *Picture of Light* suggests that the medium of film allows for a transcendence of its own mediation to draw the spheres of interior consciousness and exterior space together.

Here, Mettler might be said to take a cue from filmmaker Alejandro Jodorowsky, who once proclaimed:

> I ask of film what most North Americans ask of psychedelic drugs. The difference being that when one creates a psychedelic film, he need not create a film that shows the visions of a person who has taken a pill; rather he needs to manufacture the pill. (Jodorowsky in Samuels 1983, 33)

Mettler's film seeks to dissolve the boundary between audience and subject in embodying the paradox of allowing the mediator to vanish by foregrounding the process of mediation. Though film provides second-order access onto the world, the connection of the northern lights with the movement of thought has the power to dissolve this second order, to make the mediator vanish. But as mediation can never vanish, the film positions its own mediation of reality front and center so that we can be made aware of the fact that *all* experience is mediated in one form or another. When we realize that, we can move past the problems of indexicality, or reproduction, and focus on those aspects of experience that are common between our experience of film and our experience of the world outside of film.

The conundrum of vanishing mediation in *Picture of Light* is brought home during the above-described interview segment, where local residents discuss their experience of the lights. The local priest, Kees Verspeek, talks about the difficulties in assessing distance when viewing the lights. Mettler talks about the possibility of hearing the lights. These two issues are raised again in the film when Inuit resident Alex Ouskun describes his own experience with the lights. As a child he was told by his grandfather not to look at the lights or else he would hear a wind and the lights would swoop down on him. His experience of the lights is that when turning attention toward them they seem to come closer, and to create a sound. Again Peter Weber's evocation of "conducting mysterious music" (see above) is apt in suggesting that the negation of distance between the lights and their viewers might reveal something audible. To look at the lights is to bring them close, so close that we experience them as internal sound, as the movement of our own thoughts. And this, in the end, is an experience that can transcend cinematic mediation—not through strict representation, but through the immersive reflexivity that Mettler builds through his approach to the formal treatment of sound/image relationships.

The silent image's potential to evoke sound, and indeed to instill the experience of sound within the mind of the viewer, suggests the impossibility of sound ever really being separate from the image. In exposing the technical line between sound and image in his filmmaking, Mettler is moving toward their unification. This is a move from the skeptical to the hopeful, from resistance to wonder. He is following the path of many that have come before, and is offering a way out of the endless debates about cinema's power to authentically represent the experience of place. Mettler's performativity is not about acknowledging that the world he films only comes into being as a result of his filming. Rather, he is showing us the ways in which technologies of mediation help us perform in the world and to understand it, performing the theoretical connection between two separate poles in film sound theory between the goals of pure visual music and the principles of asynchronism. In the end, both were in search of promoting audience engagement rather than distanciation, and Mettler wants to get out of the culture of skepticism that pervades performative documentary and open new avenues to wonder.

Acoustic ecologists ask how attention to sound can help us understand relationships between human beings and their environments. *Picture of Light* offers a way of thinking about the separation of human beings and the natural world through technologies of mediation, the core issues that gave rise to Schafer's concept of schizophonia discussed at length in the previous chapter. Mettler's film illustrates how technological mediation need not be an agent of separation between human beings and their environment. If handled a certain way—as in Mettler's immersive reflexivity—we can situate mediated experience as an important part of the ecological balance between human beings and nature in the modern world. By creating awareness of the split between sound and image, bringing the "occult" nature of synchronization into the light, Mettler demonstrates how a line can extend across this split to create new relationships between these separate entities. This is the acoustic profile I have charted in this chapter, the extension of light into sound, and vice versa, mirroring extensions from the profilmic world into media representation and between external reality and interior consciousness. Mettler emphasizes these boundary lines in order to reveal how these separations can be overcome through transsensorial awareness, a way of thinking about one sense modality that can speak to the totality of human thought and experience. Mettler's performance of mediality emphasizes the fact that this mediality is simply a fact of existence, and can be documented in its own right. In so doing he reclaims technologies of sound and image recording for the purpose of providing access to the world. The lesson we can take away from his work is that the problem with observational approaches like those of the early World Soundscape Project is in their denial of mediality. Put the mediality on display, and the world is there to be revealed along with it.

Mettler's style allows us simultaneous access to the wonders of its subject and the means through which this subject is turned into the film itself. Mettler shows us that reflexivity does not have to jolt the audience out of rapture. Science does not have to negate magic. The occult can exist in plain sight of day. They are each part of the other, as inseparable as the multiple levels upon which the film explores its themes of transcending the line between interior experience and exterior space. When the lights trigger our minds moving in the film's environment of immersive reflexivity, we can hear them loud and clear—even though their sound does not reach our ears. As I will demonstrate in the next chapter, this is the lesson that members of the World Soundscape Project would bring forward from their initial work in the 1970s into the development of soundscape composition as a way of studying the sonic environment through acts of reflexive recomposition. The second wave of acoustic ecology embraced reflexive sound composition as one of its key modes of communicating what it means to engage with geographic specificity through sound, part of a general movement that Mettler also contributed to that found enormous potential in the technologies of recording and transmission to engage the world just as theorists of documentary and film sound were growing increasingly skeptical about this possibility.

References

Benjamin, Walter. 1968. "The Work of Art in the Age of Mechanical Reproduction." In *Illuminations*, edited by Hannah Arendt, translated by Harry Zohn, 217–252. New York: Schocken Books.

Bordwell, David. 1980. "The Musical Analogy." In "Cinema/Sound," edited by Rick Altman. Special issue, *Yale French Studies*, no. 60: 141–156.

Brakhage, Stan. 1978. "Letter to Ronna Page (On Music)." In *The Avant-Garde Film: A Reader of Theory and Criticism*, edited by P. Adams Sitney, 134–138. New York: New York University Press.

Brakhage, Stan. 2003. "Stan Brakhage: Death is a Meaningless Word (Part 1)." *Offscreen* 7, no. 2 (February), http://offscreen.com/view/stan_brakhage

Bresson, Robert. 1977. "Notes on Sound." Reprinted in *Film Sound: Theory and Practice*, edited by John Belton and Elizabeth Weis, 149. New York: Columbia University Press.

Browne, Dan. 2020. *Mediated Landscapes: Technology and Environment in Recent Canadian Cinema*. PhD dissertation, Joint Program of Communication and Culture, Ryerson University and York University.

Bruzzi, Stella. 2006. *New Documentary*. 2nd edition. New York: Routledge.

Camper, Fred. 1985. "Sound and Silence in Narrative and Nonnarrative Cinema." In *Film Sound: Theory and Practice*, edited by Elizabeth Weis and John Belton, 369–381. New York: Columbia University Press.

Chion, Michel. 1994. *Audio-Vision: Sound on Screen*. Translated by Claudia Gorbman. New York: Columbia University Press.

Claire, René. 1929. "The Art of Sound." Translated by Vera Traill. Reprinted in *Film Sound: Theory and Practice*, edited by Elizabeth Weis and John Belton, 92–95. New York: Columbia University Press, 1985.

Clarkson, Nathan. 2013. "Aura, Aurora and Aurality: The Narrative of Place in Picture of Light." *Brno Studies in English* 39, no. 2: 71–88.

Donnelly, K. J. 2014. *Occult Aesthetics: Synchronization in Sound and Film*. New York: Oxford University Press.

Eisenstein, S., V. I. Pudovkin, and G. V. Alexandrov. 1929. "A Statement." Reprinted in *Film Sound: Theory and Practice*, edited by Elizabeth Weis and John Belton, 83–85. New York: Columbia University Press, 1985.

Eisenstein, Sergei. 1987. *Nonindifferent Nature*. Translated by Herbert Marshall. Cambridge: Cambridge University Press.

Ganguly, Suranjan. 1993. "All That is Light: Brakhage at 60." *Sight and Sound* 3, no. 10: 20–23.

Schaub, Marin. 1995. "Music and Travel: Sensing the World." In *Peter Mettler: Making the Invisible Visible*, edited by Salome Pitschen and Annette Schönholzer, 42. Zurich: Reihe Andreas Züst/Verlag Ricco Bilger.

Godøy, Rolf Inge. 2006. "Gestural-Sonorous Objects: Embodied Extensions of Schaeffer's Conceptual Apparatus." *Organised Sound* 11, no. 2: 149–157.

Jordan, Randolph. 2003. "Brakhage's Silent Legacy for Sound Cinema." *Offscreen* 7, no. 2 (February), http://www.horschamp.qc.ca/new_offscreen/silent_legacy.html

McSorley, Tom. 1995. "Pilgrimage to Vision: The Cinema of Peter Mettler." In *Peter Mettler: Making the Invisible Visible*, edited by Salome Pitschen and Annette Schönholzer, 88–121. Zurich: Reihe Andreas Züst/Verlag Ricco Bilger.

Mettler, Peter. 1992. "Music in Film: Film as Music." In *Cinémas* 3, no. 1: 35–42.

Mountain, Rosemary. 2001. "Composers and Imagery: Myths and Realities." In *Musical Imagery*, edited by Rolfe Inge Godøy and Harald Jørgensen, 271–288. Lisse: Swets and Zeitlinger.

Nichols, Bill. 1991. *Representing Reality: Issues and Concepts in Documentary*. Bloomington: Indiana University Press.

Nichols, Bill. 1994. *Blurred Boundaries: Questions of Meaning in Contemporary Culture*. Bloomington: Indiana University Press.

Pitschen, Salome, and Annette Schönholzer. 1995. *Peter Mettler: Making the Invisible Visible*, edited by Salome Pitschen and Annette Schönholzer. Zurich: Reihe Andreas Züst/Verlag Ricco Bilger.

Pudovkin, Alexander. 1929. "Asynchronism as a Principle of Sound Film," translated by Marie Seton and Ivor Montagu. Reprinted in *Film Sound: Theory and Practice*, edited by Elizabeth Weis and John Belton, 86–91. New York: Columbia University Press, 1985.

Robertson, Robert. 2009. *Eisenstein on the Audiovisual: The Montage of Music, Image and Sound in Cinema*. London: Taurus Academic Studies.

Russell, Catherine. 1999. *Experimental Ethnography: The Work of Film in the Age of Video*. Durham, NC: Duke University Press.

Russell, Catherine. 2006. "*Gambling, Gods and LSD*: Cinephilia and the Travel Film." *Jump Cut*, no. 46, http://www.ejumpcut.org/archive/jc48.2006/GodsLSD/index.html

Samuels, Stuart. 1983. *Midnight Movies*. New York: Collier Books.

Sjogren, Britta. 2006. *Into the Vortex: Female Voice and Paradox in Film*. Chicago: University of Illinois Press.

Sterne, Jonathan. 2012. *MP3: The Meaning of a Format*. Durham, NC: Duke University Press.

Thompson, Kristin. 1980. "Early Sound Counterpoint." In "Cinema/Sound," edited by Rick Altman. Special issue, *Yale French Studies*, no. 60: 115–140.

Vaughan, Dai. 1999. *For Documentary: Twelve Essays*. Berkeley: University of California Press.

Wees, William C. 1992. *Light Moving in Time: Studies in the Visual Aesthetics of Avant-Garde Film*. Berkeley: University of California Press.

White, Jerry. 2006. *Of This Place and Elsewhere: The Films and Photography of Peter Mettler*. Toronto: Toronto International Film Festival Group.

Zilczer, Judith. 2005. "Music for the Eyes: Abstract Painting and Light Art." In *Visual Music: Synaesthesia in Art and Music Since 1900*, edited by K. Brougher, J. Strick, A. Wiseman, and J. Zilczer, 24–87. New York: Thames and Hudson.

3

Reflective Empathy

Soundscape Composition and the Spatialization of Music in Gus Van Sant's *Last Days*

Gus Van Sant's film *Last Days* (2005) imagines the final retreat of rock superstar Blake (Michael Pitt), loosely based on Kurt Cobain, at his dilapidating estate in the Pacific Northwest region of the United States. The last time we see Blake alive he is shown walking up his lengthy driveway at twilight, approaching and then entering the rear greenhouse in which he will be found dead the next morning, apparently by his own hand. He mumbles incoherently as he treads the gravel path—a nearly constant state of expression throughout the entire film—while we hear the sounds of his footfalls, trickling water, chimes, doors banging, classical symphonic music, someone whistling, and other reverberant footfalls on a hard interior surface. It is an odd assortment of sounds that encompasses nearly the entire range of possible categorization in the current state film sound theory. Most of what we hear comes from Hildegard Westerkamp's soundscape composition "Türen der Wahrnehmung (Doors of Perception)" produced for the 1989 Ars Electronica festival in Linz, Austria. Using field recordings made in Linz as well as Westerkamp's adopted home of Vancouver, BC, the composition sounds incongruous with the image of Blake walking in the leafy suburban environment pictured on screen.[1] Although perhaps not immediately recognizable as sounds that come from an existing piece of recorded music, it seems clear that the bulk of these sounds are meant to extend from somewhere else—whether elements of score, sound effects to signal Blake's subjective consciousness, or otherwise. Yet just before entering the greenhouse he suddenly turns to look over his shoulder as though reacting to something heard from behind—precisely at the moment that we hear a lone whistler complete a phrase begun by a full orchestra just prior. Does Blake hear the whistler? The question isn't answerable, and as such it points to a way of thinking about the relationship between sound and image in the film that necessitates breaking free of established models for the analysis of music and sound in film and opening up to interdisciplinary and intertextual approaches. In this case, to properly contextualize the sound/image relationships here we need to draw on the discourse of soundscape composition as a facet of acoustic ecology to address how the presence of Westerkamp's piece in the film invites us to rethink the relationship between music and sound effects, and between sound and image more generally, to situate the deployment of music as a spatial device.

Let us think, for a moment, of the serial killer in Fritz Lang's *M* (1931), whose haunting whistle—a precursor to each murder—that Daniel Goldmark et al. have described as a limit case for assessing the position of music in film (2007, 1). Concerning one instance of the whistling's disembodiment from the murderer, the authors ask: "Just what is the source of this music? Who is whistling it? Does it actually occur within the story at all? Or has it become a framing device, imposing itself from outside?" (1). These are all questions put in the service of assessing the limits of contemporary theorizing about film music, and to chart areas for expanded investigation. The whistler in Westerkamp's piece, as presented in Gus Van Sant's film, does the same. But since Westerkamp's whistler is from a pre-existing composition, the usage here in *Last Days* invites us to rethink theories of the compilation soundtrack and the modes of engagement it can engender with the audience. Along with most of the other sounds from her composition that the filmmakers map onto their film, Westerkamp's work in *Last Days* opens up an ecological dimension to Blake's last days and the relationships he has with his entourage: the ecology of human relationships as defined by architectural space. After we hear the whistler, Blake makes his way into the greenhouse, the sound of his pull on the door handle and entrance into the space timed precisely with corresponding door sounds and a shift to a different spatial register within "Doors of Perception." This is a clearly intentional synchronization of sound elements to position Westerkamp's piece as a guide to Blake's navigation of the architectural space in which he lives his final moments. At points like these, Westerkamp's sounds frustrate conventional understandings of the boundaries between the industrial division of the soundtrack into voice, music, and sound effects. Yet her sounds push beyond questions about the permeability of these boundaries and ask us to consider how the genre of soundscape composition, the main artistic offshoot of acoustic ecology, can inform the way we understand Van Sant's interest in the cinema as a form of audiovisual cartography, mapping the main character's journey through the architectural space of his estate and the emotional space of his relationships.

In this chapter I argue that assessing the role of "Doors of Perception" in *Last Days* by way of Westerkamp's practice, as informed by acoustic ecology, reveals the film's highly methodical exploration of the nuances of spatial representation in the cinema that has been largely missed by the film's critics. I will demonstrate how Westerkamp's piece activates awareness of the ways in which other music in the film is deployed spatially, offering an alternative approach to considering the function of the compilation soundtrack. Goldmark et al. argue that film music can work as an active agent with the ability to "move or 'transport' the audience into recognitions, subject-positions, and reflective understanding that could be accessed in no other way" (2007, 7). In *Last Days*, the presence of soundscape composition as an element that hovers between conventional understanding of compilation music and sound effects prompts the need to situate each within the other in order to access the film's broader goal: to position the theme of empathy, absent between Blake and the people around him, as a function of spatial relationships between these characters within the spaces they occupy in the film.

At the heart of *Last Days*, as in most of Van Sant's oeuvre, lies the theme of friendship. Blake is surrounded by people who consider themselves to be close to him, yet the film portrays their relationships as fundamentally one-sided. The film positions this one-sidedness as an effect of superstardom on a single individual, the paradox of being known by everyone while knowing very few in return. Blake seems neither able nor willing to communicate effectively with any of the people around him; he retreats further into himself until he is finally found dead under mysterious circumstances. The film is about the basic problem of empathy in human relationships: the limits on the access that any of us have to the emotional and psychological space of others. The film uses the framing device of the doorway to illustrate these limits of interpersonal access, traceable through how the characters interact with the spaces of the house by way of the doorways through which they all must pass. Westerkamp's piece intersects with this framing device through its own structured use of the sounds of doors to mediate spaces at once separate and conflated.

To bring Westerkamp's piece into dialogue with Van Sant's film, I use the term *reflective empathy* to examine the theme of friendship and its development through sound design. My formulation of reflective empathy follows

Katharine Norman's notion of *reflective listening* (mentioned in the introduction to this book and further developed later in this chapter). For Norman, reflectivity in soundscape composition is when the field recordings used as the building blocks for composition are referential to the world in front of the microphones while also reflecting how they have been shaped by the composer (1996, 5). In other words, reflective listening is a form of mediality that charts acoustic profiles back and forth along the line of mediation, to hear how external sounds extend into compositional strategies, and how these strategies shape our perception of the external world in the process. In human relationships, reflective empathy indicates the mediality between people who can extend their engagements with each other across the line that divides their status as individuals, shaping their experiences of each other as a result. The problem of empathy, here, is the same as that of sound fidelity discussed in the previous chapters: the limited capacity for people to share empathetic space without losing their status as individuals completely, just as mediation can never vanish in the face of sound technology. Reflective empathy is like a window that can just as easily allow light to pass as bounce it back toward the viewer, providing illusions of transparency while maintaining its isolationist properties.

After opening this book with two chapters in which I apply acoustic ecology's ideas to film analysis, *Last Days* now offers a rare instance in which the worlds of film sound design and acoustic ecology intersect directly through the use of Hildegard Westerkamp's work, continuing Van Sant's practice from his previous film *Elephant* (2003). Understanding the role that these pieces play in these films requires a hybrid analytical model that extends the study of soundscape composition into the realm of film sound design, one that can approach the formal strategies employed by Van Sant through a framework established by the study of Westerkamp's own creative practice. *Last Days* is a master class in running through the established conventions for positioning film sound, and the role of Westerkamp's work is to break down some of these divisions, get us listening a different way, and then apply this listening across the film as a whole. It is all the more appropriate that *Last Days* is a film about a musician featuring several potent evocations of compilation soundtrack material, along with two live performances recorded with direct sound, integrated unusually tightly into the narrative fabric of the film.

Understanding the film itself as an extension of soundscape composition allows us to map questions about the effectiveness of soundscape composition in engaging audiences with real-world spaces, and whether or not films can do the same. Westerkamp's piece teaches us how to think of the film as an exploration of ecological issues of engagement with place, to think of music spatially, and to consider how the characters engage with their spaces—both architectural and emotional—through the use of sound technologies and music. Acoustic ecology has asked us to think about how environmental sound can be thought of musically; film's positioning of compositions developed from acoustic ecology teaches us how to think about music spatially. In *Last Days*, this means addressing the spatialization of music as a function of how space delineates the relationships between the characters in the film, and how they use music—and its technologies of production and reproduction—as tools for engagement and/or alienation. Mediality in this film is a direct function of how Westerkamp's piece teaches us to hear the acoustic profiles charted by acts of playing and listening to music between people whose lines of communication have become opaque.

Running the Gamut

The use of sound in *Last Days* is structured upon a systemic deployment of the various modes that film music can embody as it investigates the spatial and emotional relationships between Blake and his entourage. We can chart a rather tidy bell curve through the different possibilities for musical register in film: it begins with a clear distinction between music positioned as score and environmental sound effects positioned as source; these registers are then conflated through the mingling of Westerkamp's piece with location sound recording for the film; then a series of musical performances within the diegesis, some prerecorded and played through media technologies by the characters, some performed by Blake on his instruments in the house; then a return of Westerkamp's piece co-mingling with location recording and other source effects; and ending with the same clear separation between the inside and outside of the diegesis as at the film's beginning. As such the film can be used as a textbook case for well entrenched conventions and their dissolution through decidedly avant-garde experimentation. I argue that in drawing the line through these various auditory deployments, *Last Days* opens up new ways of thinking about music in film by way of the role of Westerkamp's piece within the sound design. In this section I will delineate the broad outlines of the film's sonic structure before moving in for closer analysis of its various elements.

The film opens and closes with the same piece of pre-existing music, Clement Janequin's popular renaissance *chanson* "La Guerre" as sung by the King's Singers. The song's position on the level of score is as clear as can be, beginning over a black screen as the HBO logo comes up, carrying over into the first shots of Blake stumbling and mumbling through the forest without changing the sonic particularities of its studio production. There is no mistaking the music here for part of the environmental sound; it is recorded with attention toward minimizing what Michel Chion calls *materializing sound indices*: sonic indicators of the objects producing the sounds we hear and the space in which these sounds are produced (1994, 114). This can be tied to the notion of "pure" voice idealized in the pre- and post-Romantic periods, times when, as Sherry Simon explains, "voice was marvelous for its own sake, when its role was to unfold in a display of pure surface," allowing for a "break with naturalism" which "frees the listener to hear the voice as separate from the body" (Simon, 110). So it is significant that this music returns over images of Blake's dead body at the end of the film. Also significant is how the film goes on to explore a variety of other sonic registers that stand in various states of contrast to this disembodied vocal track that opens and closes the film.

As "La Guerre" continues, environmental sound effects cut in directly as the first shot of the forest appears, an editing strategy that suggests that source sound and image are locked together while music on the level of score can float across. "La Guerre" then ends, and we are left with the sounds of Blake's mumbling, the birds, and the crunching of leaves and twigs below Blake's feet. At the end of the film the situation is reversed, "La Guerre" re-entering after a period of environmental sound as we watch the police investigation unfold around Blake's body in the greenhouse, the King's Singers continuing over a cut to black as the image and environmental sound disappear entirely. The two instances of "La Guerre," leading into and out of environmental sound, creates a perfect pair of auditory bookends to the film.

Once the choral music stops the film spends its first section developing a strong formal synchronicity between sound and image, both grounded in location recording to create a rigorously realist aesthetic as Blake passes through various different environments. He goes for a swim in the river, and later camps next to a fire where he sings loud into the night, his voice reverberating through the wooded environment and prompting a response from a dog in the distance. Blake is able to engage with the space by using his voice to activate its echoic qualities and connect with other beings in the distance. The dog also provides the first evidence of Blake's proximity to civilization, which increases when a train passes as he makes his way back home. Importantly, the train is heard well before it is seen, an audible presence that begins without visual motivation. Not long after this we hear the first strains of Westerkamp's "Doors of Perception" as Blake approaches the house. Here the piece includes incongruous sounds of public transportation bells, motors, and doors opening and closing. These elements blend with the sounds of the wind, footsteps, and Blake's ever-present mumbling as produced for the film.

The passing train in the previous example sets up Blake's environment as one in which offscreen sound might become visualized. So the presence of these sounds from Westerkamp's piece operate as what Chion calls *active offscreen sounds*: they prompt us to wonder where they come from and if we will see their implied sources on screen (1994, 85). This is one of the ways that soundscape composition in the film gets us to reflect upon spatial representation and the line between realist and expressionist techniques. When sources are not revealed and remain somewhat inexplicable, we begin to understand their presence as a function of music rather than environmental sound along with associated connotations of compositional intent rather than the random capturing of field recording.

Westerkamp's piece continues to mingle with various location sounds from inside the house, functioning sometimes as diegetic sound effects, other times like subjective internal diegetic sound, and still other times like score. The most complex interaction comes when it plays along with another piece of pre-existing music, "On Bended Knee" by Boyz II Men, and then disappears from the film for a while as we move through an emphasis on pre-existing music performed within the diegesis, either as recording with the Velvet Underground's "Venus in Furs" or live performance as with Blake's electric improvisation and final acoustic performance of "Death to Birth." As I will argue in the pages to follow, the earlier use of Westerkamp's composition invites new ways of hearing these pieces of source music not simply as music but also markers of spatial orientation. Then we return to "Doors of Perception" for the sequence described at the beginning of this chapter, hearing it with new ears after the film's spatial deployment of the earlier songs. Finally, the film ends with a long stretch of environmental sound following Blake's death, capped with a return to "La Guerre" for the closing credits. And so we find a neat curve tracking a clear distinction between the simplistic demarcation between the inside and outside of the diegesis, then deliberate complications of this distinction and through to a firm abandonment of any elements of score, back through new complications, and then outward once again to where we started.

Mapping Personal Noise

Chris Chang identifies the importance of the underlying principles behind Westerkamp's compositions for understanding the thread that runs through Van Sant's work in the mid-2000s. He quotes the "Soundwalking" article, addressed in my introduction to this book, in which Westerkamp lays the foundations for beginning the process of soundscape awareness:

> Start by listening to the sounds of your body while moving. They are closest to you and establish the first dialogue between you and the environment. If you can hear the quietest of these sounds you are moving through an environment that is scaled to human proportions. In other words, with your voice or your footsteps you are "talking" to your environment, which in turn responds by giving your sounds a specific acoustic quality. (Westerkamp in Chang 2005, 16)

Westerkamp is interested in the relationship between distinct individuals and their environments, and understands environmental engagement as a reciprocal process defined by the relationship between a sound's origin and its propagation through space. Chang suggests that "the idea of a symbiotic play between personal noise and the contextual ambience of location is a type of interaction—I would argue it is the defining component—experienced in Van Sant's trilogy" (16).[2]

I agree with Chang that the interaction between the self and the environment is the defining component of these films. However, despite his attention to the spirit of Westerkamp's work, Chang ultimately relegates the status of Westerkamp's sounds to the realm of the psychological in *Last Days*, marking Blake's subjective experience of his environment filtered through the mental stress that leads him toward death. Chang suggests that the presence of Westerkamp's work is "a visceral enhancement to uneasy states of mind," and describes the kinds of odd and out of place sounds heard in the film as "aspects of a constantly invasive sound environment" that Blake is trying to escape from (2005, 16).

Ascribing Westerkamp's work to the role of subjective sound in Van Sant's films is a common response among critics, whether they recognize the source material or not. Speaking of *Last Days*, Amy Taubin goes so far as to say that "Leslie Shatz's sound design is at least an equal partner to [cinematographer Harry] Savides's haunting images. It's primarily the sound design that conveys Blake's blurring of inside and out—of the sound in his head with the sound around him" (2005, 19). Of course, a good portion of the sound design makes use of Westerkamp's work, which Stephen Dalton describes as adding "a subtle air of dislocation to the rustic wandering of Pitt's hero, Blake" (2005, 65), acknowledging how the soundtrack can help us understand the character's feelings of alienation. Similarly, Danijela Kulezic-Wilson examines the use of Frances White's work in *Elephant* and *Paranoid Park* (2007), where she finds significance in the fact that scenes were designed with this pre-existing soundscape composition in mind, again tying the suggestive qualities of the sound to psychological space (2008, 129).

One of the reasons why the use of Westerkamp's work has been associated with Blake's subjective experience is because of certain moments in which "Doors of Perception" (the title itself evoking altered states of consciousness by way of reference to Aldous Huxley and William Blake) functions brilliantly well as a marker of interiority in the film (Falsetto 2015, 101). The most obvious example of such a moment comes just after Blake (apparently) digs up a box in the back yard containing heroin and prepares himself a fix. I say "apparently" because the film skirts around the particulars, showing us simply a montage that reverses the usual function of such a sequence. Instead of showing us all the action, the sequence shows us the in-between moments: we see Blake with a shovel but not what he digs up; we see him walking into the kitchen with a box wrapped in a plastic bag, but not opening the box to reveal its contents; we hear Blake talking to himself about the need for a spoon, but this could just as easily be for the breakfast cereal he is preparing as for cooking up a fix. After this montage, however, sound steps in to suggest Blake's drug-addled mind: as he climbs the stairs to his bedroom, we hear the sounds of a chiming clock offscreen.[3] This could easily be a standard source sound, for this kind of clock would certainly fit within this environment, and it bears the spatial signature of a location recording in a mildly reverberant space rather than the dry quality of a studio fabrication. For these reasons the sound of the clock is not likely to be perceived as out of place and thus pointing to its origin in a work composed separately from the film. However, as Blake slows his gate and falls backward onto the bed, the sounds of the clock begin to distort, multiplying in different pitches and displaying other obvious technological manipulations that give it a hallucinatory quality. These manipulations are at once signs of Westerkamp's interest in exposing the technological mediation through which her compositional process is filtered, while also working perfectly to add a psychological sound dimension to the observational quality of the images.

Tempting though it is to default to the subjectivity thesis, I argue that there is a much more rewarding way in which to understand how Chang's notion of "personal noise" figures into Westerkamp's work within the context of *Last Days*. To begin with, the equation of "personal" with "subjective" isn't quite in the spirit of acoustic ecology's interest in the relationship between an individual's soundamaking and the contextual environment. Nor does ascribing an expressionistic tendency to Van Sant's representation of Blake do justice to the importance of his starkly realist approach across much of the film. Both Westerkamp and Van Sant are interested in how we navigate physical space, and what role sound can play in our understanding of our spatial environments. It is on this front that these two artists' work intersect most productively. To understand this intersection, we need a better account of what personal noise might mean in this context.

Westerkamp's prescription for soundwalking is premised upon a sense of ecological balance, when one can hear the sounds they are making interact with the acoustic properties of the environment through which they pass, an awareness of one's own role in mediating space that she also argues is the key to understanding soundscape composition as a form of acoustic ecology (see Westerkakmp 2002). This notion is intimately bound up with acoustic ecology's construction of "human scale" (1977, 207). As discussed in the introduction to this book, critics like Jonathan Sterne take issue with "human scale" as being premised upon "the spatiality of the unamplified voice" (2003, 342). The idea here, a guiding tenet in early acoustic ecology, is that sound environments are ecologically balanced when they do not interfere with unassisted verbal communication. This is a reflection of R. Murray Schafer's preindustrial biases, and has been critiqued for its failure to account for all the ways in which technologies of sound recording and transmission function at the level of human engagement. Later developments in acoustic ecology have moved away from this bent, with composers like Westerkamp demonstrating their commitment to medial presentations in her compositions that allow a more nuanced approach to human scale that includes technology as part of its range, and Westerkamp acknowledges architectural space as part of this mediality (as is clear from the premise of "Doors of Perception"). So if we acknowledge that personal noise is about human engagement with place, while accepting that human scale can extend into the realm of technological expansion beyond unamplified acoustics, then we have arrived at the basis for the soundscape compositions of Hildegard Westerkamp, whose approach to making sound work is frequently reflexive about the technology she uses to heighten engagement with our sonic environments.

In the analyses that follow I will consider the implications for the concepts of personal noise and human scale as they relate to the position of Westerkamp's soundscape composition within the overall sound design of the film. In so doing I will demonstrate the importance of understanding how Blake's isolation and alienation functions within the physical spaces he occupies, to reveal the material conditions of his last days alive and reflect upon the role of music as the guiding force in this life about to end. Personal noise becomes a way of conceptualizing human scale around relationships of communication rather than their technological means, and the relationships of interaction between characters that define the friendships and distances here. It is tempting to make a schizophonic reading of the film that posits Blake's success, enabled by technologies of sound reproduction and transmission, as the key factor in putting him beyond human scale and causing his downfall. But it's not about schizophonic technology here, as the breakdown in community that Blake experiences is happening in close quarters well within the means of human scale, the spatiality of the unamplified voice. Westerkamp's work shifts our attention away from the idea of technology as the enemy, and toward a nuanced understanding of how music, when understood spatially, can reveal the problem of empathy in human communication.

I will concentrate on a key stylistic similarity between the structure of *Last Days* and "Doors of Perception": the use of doors as mediating agents, calling attention to how people move between separate spaces, drawing them together while also keeping them apart. "Doors of Perception" is the principal soundscape composition used in *Last Days*, and is patterned around the use of door sounds to mediate transitions between spaces that would not ordinarily coexist. Tracing how this composition is mapped onto the film can tell us much about how space is used to express the fundamental issues of their narratives: the processes of empathy in human friendship, expressed through the varying levels of extension that music is granted between spaces separated by doors. We hear the sounds of doors opening and closing to bring spaces together that would ordinarily be incompatible, creating an overtly reflexive journey through impossibly overlapping spaces that call attention to the role of technology in constructing our understanding of these spaces in the first place. Sometimes the doors draw a rigid line between soundscapes, a limited acoustic profile with no bridges across the sound of a door opening or closing. This is what we hear as Blake approaches the house at the beginning of the film. As the piece progresses, things become increasingly fluid and abstract, the sounds of doors mingling with extended ambiences rather than keeping them separate, sections that Van Sant uses later in the film to complicate spatial representation in the film. Doors in the real world mediate sonic spaces, keeping them separate when closed and bringing them together when open. So it is also with the sounds of Westerkamp's doors opening and closing here, bringing spaces together and then breaking them apart. Van Sant and his sound designer Leslie Shatz import this formal strategy into the film, exploring how the divided spaces of Blake's house function as registers of the emotional spaces between him and his friends.

Delayed Coverage: Spatial Coherence through Non-Linear Narrative

As many critics have noted, *Last Days* tends to eschew elaborate character development for an approach to narrative that emphasizes dead time, most notably through sequences dominated by a long take aesthetic in which characters are filmed from behind as they walk between spaces, usually separated by doorways, repeated at different points in the film from different perspectives in a non-linear approach to narrative progression. Speaking of *Elephant*, which employs very similar strategies to *Last Days*, Amy Taubin observes that this non-linearity is positioned within a dialectic between "documentary-style immediacy and formalist distance" (2005, 18). The "documentary-style immediacy" comes, in part, from a highly realist approach to visual representation combined with an unusual emphasis on location sound recording, the latter going against the grain of contemporary mainstream American filmmaking. A key element of the "formalist distance" that most critics latch onto is the looping narrative the continually revisits scenes presented earlier to either complete them or present them from a different perspective. A striking feature of *Elephant* as well, Taubin ties this non-linearity to the way the films position themselves in relation to the real-world events upon which they are based:

> The effect is to transform what seems like "real" time into recorded time and the time of memory, which is the mode in which the "reality" of Columbine now exists. The reversals also suggest a longing to stop time, to prevent the inevitable tragedy from ever taking place. (2005, 18)

One could make the same point about *Last Days*, in which Taubin suggests that this feeling of looping time is also tied to the drug-addled subjectivity of Blake who appears to be a heroin addict on relapse. "The disconnections in the narrative, such as it is, reinforce the feeling of emotional disconnection among the characters" (2005, 19), a feature of *Elephant* that prompted Kent Jones to refer to Van Sant as "the prince of calculated disaffection," (2003, 28). As I will show, however, the disconnection and disaffection at work in the structural non-linearity ultimately serve to demonstrate how music in the film is deployed spatially around the function of doors within the mansion. Yes, the narrative disconnections emphasize the distance between characters, but they break up around specific instances of architectural separation of spaces, emphasized by how music operates in relation to these separated spaces. As such, the narrative structure is tied to the way in which music functions as an aspect of space, allowing Blake's space to be considered ecologically around questions of human scale and the processes of empathy between he and his people.

The film's three most pronounced structural loops revolve around the presence of songs being played in the house: first is "On Bended Knee" (1994) by Boyz II Men, presented as a music video on a TV in the den; second is "Venus in Furs" (1967) by The Velvet Underground, presented as an LP played on the turntable in the living room; and third is "Death to Birth" (2005) written by Michael Pitt and performed by him as Blake on solo guitar and voice in the studio corner of the living room. Each of these songs is presented twice as the scenes in which they first appear are revisited from a different perspective as the film progresses. And each song bears a different relationship to the use of "Doors of Perception" throughout the film. In this section I will analyze the scenes involving "On Bended Knee" and then demonstrate the song's value in offering ways to think about the rest of the film's use of pre-existing music.

The first strains of "On Bended Knee" by Boyz II Men comes a short while after Blake's aforementioned collapse on the bed upstairs to the sound of distorting clocks. He awakes and moves downstairs where he deals with two intrusions from the outside: first a phone call from his bandmates to see if he will make their upcoming tour, to which he responds simply by hanging up;

then, an in-person discussion with a representative from the Yellow Pages who shows up at the front door and takes Blake for the proprietor of a locomotive parts shop. Blake plays along with the mistaken identity, a narrative detail emphasizing that his interactions with others tend to be based on who they want him to be rather than who he really is inside. Each of these sequences is marked by location recording in which the mildly reverberant nature of the mansion's hardwood interior is evident, an auditory strategy that continues as he then moves into the den and closes the door.

From here the film cuts to a shot of Asia (Asia Argento) walking down the stairs and stopping in the hallway, "On Bended Knee" quietly audible as though coming from the other room. Asia walks over to the den and opens the door. Blake is passed out on the other side, and falls over as the door opens, blocking the entryway. The volume of "On Bended Knee" is raised in conjunction with the door opening, suggesting its source from inside the room but without much change in spatial signature. We cut to Asia walking back upstairs, only to be interrupted by another doorbell. She calls Scott (Scott Patrick Green) down to go and answer it, and he finds the Friberg twins (Adam and Andy Friberg) here to provide information about the Church of Jesus Christ and the Latter Day Saints. Scott invites them in, and their proceeding discussion is intercut with shots of Blake in the den, shots that are soon revealed to be from a prior point in the narrative when Blake passes out against the door where Asia later finds him.

In these shots of Blake in the den, he turns on the TV and finds a Boyz II Men video of "On Bended Knee." We cut to the Fribergs discussing their ability to communicate directly with God, and then cut back to Blake. Along with this cut back to Blake comes the sudden emergence of an excerpt from "Doors of Perception" consisting of a steady drone of processed bell and choir recordings punctuated with the sounds of doors and woody thumping with a similar timbral quality to the location sounds we've heard throughout the house.[4] The refrain from the television reiterates, "Can't somebody tell me how to get things back the way they used to be?" This is a sentiment easily relatable to the sadness of Blake's current situation. While we hear these lyrics, Blake stoops forward and drops to his knees in a protracted moment of self-imposed slow-motion, the Boyz II Men song fading out and leaving only the ethereal qualities of Westerkamp's piece along with some light ambience from location recording. Eventually Blake ends up on all fours, his fist hitting the floor with a sound that could easily have come from "Doors of Perception," and crawls toward the door. As Blake crawls, the Boyz II Men track returns, while the sounds of doors and creaking wood from Westerkamp's piece continue to emphasize the sound of the door against which he finally passes out.

Aside from light room tone and the sound of Blake's fist hitting the floor, the rest of the soundscape is provided by "Doors of Perception" and "On Bended Knee." Here the door sounds from Westerkamp's piece echo the sounds of the doors we heard Blake opening and closing earlier, similar in timbre, texture and spatial signature creating a synchronicity between her piece and the space represented on screen. Meanwhile her additional treatments point to a space entirely outside this realm, reverberant bells and choral sounds creating an otherworldly ambience.

If hearing "On Bended Knee" suggests that this scene is a revisitation of the earlier iteration of the song, the loop is confirmed as Asia suddenly opens the door and finds Blake in front of it, an event that was first presented prior to the arrival of the Fribergs. The sound of the door opening is timed with a major shift in the tone of Westerkamp's piece featuring a lower register drone punctuated by distant foghorns and processed bird calls, the least referential section of the piece. Here Van Sant and Leslie Shatz adopt Westerkamp's own strategy: the sound of a door opening recorded for the film provides a formal opening for a new soundscape to emerge, just as Westerkamp's own shifts in soundscape are mediated by the sounds of doors opening and closing. Timing this shift in "Doors of Perception" to the sound of a door from the film suggests that the new soundscape of foghorns and birds is meant to reflect a vaster level of extension, the open door moving the soundtrack beyond the space of the den. However, the kinds of sounds we hear are not commensurate with the space we see on screen, and a cut to the reverse angle from outside the den reveals no corresponding cut on the soundtrack to suggest its grounding in the diegesis. The open door has opened us up to a register of the soundtrack that simultaneously suggests Blake's altered state of consciousness and the artificiality of the film's constructed diegesis. Asia then steps over Blake to enter the room, props him up against the wall, and exits, closing the door behind her. Cutting back into the room, the excerpt from "Doors of Perception" is gone and the camera lingers on the TV as the rest of the Boyz II Men song plays out.

Like the film's opening presentation of "La Guerre" by the King's Singers, the sound of "On Bended Knee" is presented close to an ideal state as a studio recording, not bearing any materializing sound indices that ground it within the space represented on screen, in this case the markers of its supposed emanation from the small speakers of the TV set or the spatial signature of the room in which it is being played. Importantly, "Doors of Perception" provides the bulk of the "environmental" sound heard in conjunction with the music track. The correspondence of "Doors of Perception" with the class of film sounds usually associated with sound effects is enhanced by its co-presence with "On Bended Knee." Indeed, this is a rare instance of two distinct pieces of music being played simultaneously in a film, and it is made possible by the extreme difference between the two tracks—and that the audience is unlikely to recognize one even as "music," much less bring awareness of it from prior exposure (although this segment's inclusion in the prior film *Elephant* enhances this possibility). This opens up a similar tension to that embodied by the presence of "Doors of Perception": sounds that seem like they could be part of the environment are revealed not to be, where the music from the TV sounds like it comes from outside the diegesis while being grounded within by way of the visible source of the sound.

This is a complex sequence. The interaction between Blake and Asia is a classic example of how people relate to Blake in the film: the doors of communication are blocked, making empathy almost impossible. The non-linear cross-cutting, combined with the structural loop, serves the distanciation and disjunctive experience of time associated with Blake's subjectivity, while also emphasizing the distance between characters: the first angle on the scene gives us Asia's perspective while the second situates us with Blake—and never the two shall meet. But the non-linear strategies also build important thematic associations between different elements of the sequence. We hear Boyz II Men singing about praying "on bended knee" for a way back to the past, intercut with the Fribergs relating a story about how the founder of their religion came to find Christ, and the impact this event has on their present practice of prayer. Both threads deal with spiritual issues and questions of faith, supported by the sounds of bells and choir in "Doors of Perception" that, as noted earlier, come back in the final shot of Blake alive.

Significantly, "On Bended Knee" was a number one hit in the United States in 1994, the year that Kurt Cobain died. As such the song also foreshadows Blake's death when read as an intertextual marker of Cobain's real-life story, adding another layer of complexity to the identifications this song engenders for the audience of the film. Further, the studio quality presentation of the song here, abstracted from the spatial signature of the den, highlights how different this style of pop music is from the "dirtier" sounds of the grunge that Cobain popularized and which Blake is associated with in the film. This song literally comes from a different world of popular representation than

Cobain's grunge scene, and yet Cobain was reluctantly but inevitably moving toward this glossy world with his increasing popularity, another factor in the disillusionment we can attribute to both Cobain and Blake. This music is not of Blake's community space, but its thematic call to "get things back the way they used to be" speaks to Blake's dissatisfaction as his increasing popularity moves him closer to the world of pop, and he reacts by retreating further from it. So the plays on varying extension present in the scene become loaded with questions of Blake's distance from those he shares his environment with, both within the house and the larger world of the music industry.

This scene, as spread across two nonconsecutive sequences, marks a high point of intersection between different spatial registers in the film's sound design: the on-the-air sound from the TV is at once visually grounded within the space we see on screen, while its sound points to a dimension only realizable in the recording studio. This duality reflects the tension implicit in Blake's retreat from his own music production. The location sound recording grounds him firmly within the space of the den, while Westerkamp's piece teases that grounding outward into abstraction, alluding simultaneously to a vast extension into the distance and a full retreat into Blake's psychological space. The scene is thus infused with the ecological implications of schizophonia. A Schaferian reading of the scene would surely suggest that Blake's distress is a direct result of his schizophonic profession. It is as though the representation of the televised music here reflects the ability of recording technology to bring us to another plane of experience, a schizophonic potential that threatens to disrupt the here-and-now-for the there-and-then. Yet the way that Westerkamp's piece interacts with different registers of music and location recording provides the audience with the opportunity to reflect upon this space as a highly mediated environment despite its grounding in representational material. Importantly, the reflection inspired by soundscape composition here can also be carried into other moments that do not involve such complex interactions between varying sound elements.

The key here is how Westerkamp's composition serves to spatialize the other, more conventionally defined music in this scene, a function that depends in part on attending to its aesthetic deployment while situating that deployment within the context of the music's origin outside the text. This is standard practice in scholarly assessments of the compilation film soundtrack, but I argue that accounting for the role of soundscape composition as compilation soundtrack material requires some modification to existing models. I turn now to some suggestions for a new model of the compilation soundtrack that I will then apply to two other prominent instances of preexisting music in the film, informed by soundscape composition while, in these cases, presented separately from Westerkamp's work.

Musical Identification and the Space of Empathy

While it is quite rare for an entire film to be designed around an existing musical work, the use of existing music in film soundtracks is ubiquitous. When treated with a mind toward audiovisual integration, a compilation soundtrack has the power to make the existing pieces of music seem as though they were made specifically for the film. Yet as Anahid Kassabian explores in her book *Hearing Film: Tracking Identifications in Contemporary Hollywood Film Music* (2001), audience members who recognize an existing piece of music in a film can't help but bring very specific identifications to it, regardless of how integrated the music becomes. She suggests that this process of identification with a film's soundtrack is different from what we experience with a commissioned score that an audience hears for the first time in conjunction with the movie.

For Kassabian, what is most important is that the filmmaker's intention for a piece of music is the realm of *assimilation*: with no prior experience with the film's music, the film is free to create a set of identifications with the audience from scratch (2). This "assimilating identification" takes on another dimension when *affiliation* comes into play, the domain of the compilation soundtrack containing pieces of music that spectators may recognize from contexts other than their situation within the film (3). With this distinction Kassabian is expressing the tension inherent in intertextual relationships, where a given film text cannot function as a closed system because it points outward to the existence of other texts. This prompts the question: what happens when a film makes use of existing music that uses field recordings rather than instruments as the basis for composition, thereby resembling the traditional category of "sound effects" more closely than "music"? In other words, how does the distinction between assimilating identifications and affiliating identifications work in the realm of sound effects?

Here the proximity between film sound designers and soundscape composers becomes especially important to consider. Take the example of any given door sound from Westerkamp's "Doors of Perception": it is instantly recognizable as a door sound, something we recognize from our experience outside the world of the film, and we bring affiliations to that sound based on that experience. This is a kind of affiliation that is central to all representational work, and is one facet of Katharine Norman's concept of reflective listening: we recognize a sound as having a source in the world, while also recognizing how it has been organized within the form of the composition (1996, 5). This is the source of the "context-based" approach to soundscape composition described by Truax (2008). Yet if we recognize that particular door sound as coming from Westerkamp's piece, the kind of affiliation that Kassabian describes also comes into effect. This dual-affiliation makes the process of identification with the domain of sound effects more complex than usual with pieces of pre-existing music more conventionally defined. The use of soundscape composition as part of a film's sound design, then, adds layers of dimension to Kassabian's models of identification.

For Kassabian, the status of music as either coming from an implied source in the story world or from somewhere outside has to do with increases in volume, appropriateness of kind, and a temporal continuity over cuts that indicate a temporal ellipsis on the image track (43–44, 57, 77, 92). This model works well when addressing an example like "La Guerre" during the opening moments of *Last Days*: this is a well-known piece of music that is understood as non-diegetic because its volume level remains stable as it starts in conjunction with a black screen and the absence of any other sound, then continues unabated as we cut to the shot of Blake walking through the forest, complete with attendant location sound recording. Similarly, we assign it the category of non-diegetic sound because it is not the *kind* of music we would expect to hear in this forest environment. Yet, as discussed, it is also an important marker of the limits of such clear distinction between the inside and the outside of the diegesis, a distinction troubled by the emergence of "Doors of Perception" shortly thereafter. Using Kassabian's model, "Doors of Perception" has to occupy contradictory registers simultaneously, some sounds fitting expectations for diegetic source while others do not; some sounds functioning empathetically while others do not. This is one reason that Kassabian limits her examples to particular kinds of music, easily recognizable as such.

On the plus side, Kassabian's distinction between assimilation and affiliation offers a useful critique of the way that film sound theorists tend to situate music by using the labels *diegetic* and *non-diegetic*, too simplistic when trying to account for the way that film music is always implicated within the narrative. Here Kassabian separates the uses to which a filmmaker puts a piece of music, and the "uses" that an audience member brings to the music: "the more identifiably within the narrative the music is produced, the less liable it is to take its cues from the events of the narrative" (2001, 49). The basic point here is that if sound is thought to be diegetic, it is less likely to act as support for the narrative than if the music is understood to have been added by the filmmaker for just such purposes. This is a problem that dates back to the origins of song use in sound films. As Katherine Spring points out, in the early sound era, conspicuous diegetic musical interludes in "non-musical" films posed a "threat to narrative plausibility" if the song being performed in the film spoke too closely to narrative details (2013, 95), an example of how distinctions between diegetic and non-diegetic affected audience perception right from the beginning. For Michel Chion, this theoretical problem stems from the conventions of practitioners. He uses the terms *empathetic* and *anempathetic* sound to identify the idea that diegetic sound should be perceived as somehow less contrived than non-diegetic sound: empathetic sound "can directly express its participation in the feeling of the scene, by taking on the scene's rhythm, tone, and phrasing" (1994, 8); anempathetic sound exhibits a "conspicuous indifference to the situation, by progressing in a steady, undaunted, and ineluctable manner" (8). Chion notes that anempathetic sound is much more likely to be diegetic, just as sounds in the real world don't usually follow the pacing or emotional tone of any given individual on the street. Meanwhile Robyn Stillwell adapts Claudia Gorbman's term *metadiegetic* to refer to music or sound that opens up a space "beyond empathy" in which a character's subjectivity becomes the locus of audience identification, bridging the gap between audience and diegesis (2007, 196). And here the functions of assimilation and affiliation can take on particular importance when addressing the nebulous position of a piece like "Doors of Perception" as soundtrack material. Rather than simply operating as empathetic or anempathetic to Blake's psychology, Westerkamp's sounds bind together the various registers on the continuum between the inside and outside of the diegesis, which, as Mario Falsetto suggests, can "force the viewer to enter into a different kind of relationship with the material on the screen" (2015, 101). This "different kind of relationship" aligns with the "different psychology of cinema" that James Batcho attributes to the workings of "sensory empathy," in which creative approaches to audiovisual relationships in film can prompt audience participation in the construction of their identification, evoking "a harmonious relation of feeling what resides within the reality of the film's fiction" (2022, 27).

Thinking of Westerkamp's work in *Last Days* as reaching for alternative understandings of cinematic empathy can help us undo the problems inherent to the terminological impasse of the *diegetic/non-diegetic* distinction, while also correcting the problem of failing to attend to the spatial dimension of film music when addressing compilation soundtrack material. The key here is to add a new dimension to Kassabian's affiliating mode that accounts for processes of extratextual identification that don't necessarily depend on recognition of a pre-existing piece of music. I argue that the affiliating mode of listening can be extended through situations like Westerkamp's work in Van Sant's film by reading this mode through Katharine Norman's concept of reflective listening. Norman refers the kinds of soundscape composition at issue here as *real-world music*: compositions that blend a documentary approach in their use of field recordings with the compositional sense found in more traditional models for music. In her words, "real-world music leaves a door ajar on the reality in which we are situated" while seeking a "journey which takes us away from our preconceptions," ultimately offering us a new appreciation of reality as a result (1996, 19). Reflective listening is a mode of identification in which understanding the source of a sound (i.e., a door, bird or running water) is positioned in the context of the use of this sound within the piece (i.e., the conflation of incompatible spaces in "Doors of Perception"). This negotiation on the part of the listener creates a constant interplay between reality and its creative manipulation, and is the substance of the reflective space opened up by real-world music. The incorporation of this kind of music into a cinematic context adds further levels of negotiation which create an even greater potential for reflection. I contend that Norman's discussion of real-world music establishes a category for potential compilation soundtrack material that requires new ways of thinking about the relationship between film sound and musical composition, extending Kassabian's definition of the affiliating mode into new areas. Westerkamp's work asks us to apply this affiliating mode of musical experience to more conventional compilation materials across the rest of the film.

Westerkamp's work in *Last Days* invites us to understand empathy as a structural process for designing audiovisual relationships on film, and to read the processes of empathy as fundamentally ecological in nature. To help illustrate, I turn briefly to Mikhail Bakhtin's formulation of empathy. In *Toward a Philosophy of the Act* (1993), Bakhtin refers to the impossibility of a "pure empathy" in which one person's subjectivity is subsumed by another. He says: "After looking at ourselves through the eyes of another, we always return—in life—into ourselves again" (17). This return into ourselves is at the heart of what makes empathy possible, for we must be within ourselves in order to experience something as ourselves. If we were to lose ourselves completely into our experience of the other, then there would be no room left for the empathetic act of feeling someone else through our own experience—we would simply become the experience of the other. This is one aspect of his concept of *dialogic* relationships where the life of a society lies in the interactions between individuals, acknowledging that these interactions are only possible because they exist between separate entities.[5] Dialogism can be understood as another form of mediality, calling attention to the way that two entities work together to enact an engagement, rather than one mediating—and thus standing in the way of—the other. In turn, we might refer to sound/image relationships themselves as an articulation of dialogic space, separate tracks with a limited capacity to extend into each other. The acoustic profile of the soundtrack stands at varying degrees of extension into the image track, and vice versa.

Bakhtin's formulation adds nuance to the idea of reflective empathy, a simultaneous entering into and bouncing off of a surface that allows entrance while marking a distinction between inside and out. Bakhtin's formulation of empathy allows us to move past questions of identification with characters on the part of the audience, and any need we might have to pin down whether or not a particular sound is diegetic or otherwise. Instead, we can address how the film as a whole is structured around the very idea of empathy, and how our affiliating identification with the sounds of doors can map onto the way in which the filmmakers assimilate the functioning of these door sounds within the film. In *Last Days*, Blake's acoustic profile is charted in terms of both architectural and emotional processes of empathy that emphasize this dual quality of assimilation and distance, particularly through the framing device of the door, a conceptual tool and architectural feature that allows spaces to enter into each other while also demarcating their separation. The sounds of doors in Westerkamp's piece offer the affiliating quality of those sounds that allows for the assimilation of the listener into differing environments. The same is true in Van Sant's film, here operating around doorways that separate the listener's understanding of the space of Blake's house and his relationship with his friends. The conflation of spaces made possible by an open door is analogous to the empathetic relationships between people.

Last Days uses Westerkamp's work as a guide around separate spaces mediated by doorways, the setting in which the film explores the processes of empathy, and lack thereof, between Blake and his entourage. Hearing Westerkamp's work in the film as an expression of the problem of empathy, both human and architectural, trains us to engage with other instances of music differently by way of attending to their deployment in space. I turn now to two particular cases: a playback on the Velvet Underground's "Venus in Furs," and Blake's performance of "Death to Birth," an original song written for the film. While one is heavily loaded with affiliating potential and the other necessarily assimilative, both function identically in how they illustrate the spatial and emotional disconnection between Blake and his entourage within the space of the house and the non-linearity of the film's narrative.

The Song Loops

One of the film's most prominent song-based set-pieces revolves around a party scene in which Asia, Luke (Lukas Haas), Nicole (Nicole Vicius), and Scott stumble intoxicated into the house one evening and cue up the Velvet Underground's "Venus in Furs" on the living room turntable. Westerkamp's piece is not present here, and there is no ambiguity about the sources of the sounds we hear: the entire scene is presented in direct sound, the song partially garbled by the spatial signature of the living room, and by Scott singing along with the recorded voice of Lou Reed. In the middle of the song, Scott gets up and walks out of the room into the kitchen through the open hallway that separates the two, the camera panning to keep him in frame but stopping short of following him through the doorway, thus remaining fixed within the boundaries of the living room walls. We see Scott through the doorway from the back talking to someone in the kitchen who we later learn is Blake. Then Scott returns to his spot in the living room and resumes singing along. The scene ends just after the lyric "on bended knee," drawing an explicit parallel between this song and the Boyz II Men track heard earlier.

Later in the film we find Blake making macaroni in the kitchen. "Venus in Furs" begins to play offscreen, bearing the spatial signature one would expect from a song played on the stereo in another room, indicating that we have looped back to a previous point in the narrative. This time we stay in the kitchen with Blake until Scott enters through the doorway, and here we learn that their conversation consisted of Scott's attempt to borrow some cash for apples (he's hungry), a jet heater (he's cold), and a ticket to Utah (he needs to get out of town). When the conversation ends we cut to a shot from the living room as Scott re-enters, the sound of the music cutting to a closer perspective in conjunction, marked by an increase in volume and decrease in the ratio of direct to reflected sound, thus emphasizing the distance between the living room and the kitchen.

The simple treatment of the sound in these sequences works well to establish the spatial qualities of the living room and kitchen, as well as emphasizing their separation from each other. Hearing "Venus in Furs" from the kitchen is an example of how two spaces can meld while remaining distant, a function of an open doorway rather than a closed one. While highly realist in convention, this is also a metaphorical use of sound to underscore the communication between Blake and Scott: each has only partial access to the other, an ultimately superficial relationship where Scott is positioned essentially as a mooch and not a real friend with whom a greater degree of spatial conflation—empathy—would be possible. Blake is essentially alone in the house, even as he is surrounded by people he knows.

Aside from the spatial qualities of the song's presentation, the choice of "Venus in Furs" also involves complex affiliations both within the narrative and by audience members listening to the film. The Velvet Underground, of course, is iconic of a particular scene in the late '60s wrapped up in the emergence of new forms of rock music and social rebellion helmed by Lou Reed whom Patti Smith, upon his death, referred to as her generation's New York poet, "championing its misfits as Whitman had championed its working class and Lorca its persecuted" (2013). The Velvet Underground is also wrapped up in the hype surrounding Andy Warhol's factory where they performed in their earliest days, notorious for being simultaneously subversive and superficial, famously characteristic of Warhol's own social maladjustments. As such the band acted as a major influence on the grunge scene in the 90s for which Kurt Cobain stood as reluctant representative. Scott's identification with the song by singing along indicates both an engagement with the music while illustrating the impossibility of really being part of a scene long gone and associated with the opposite side of the country.

The connection between Lou Reed singing the line "on bended knee" and the Boyz II Men song of that name can be read through the idea of longing for the past, of getting things "back the way they used to be." But that's an impossibility, and Blake's distance from this schizophonic engagement with the past is telling: he is too young to have been part of the original Velvet scene, nor is he a part of its attempted recapture by Scott and his posse. Hearing this song as a record played within a listening space becomes loaded in emphasizing its status as recorded object as opposed to the studio perfection of the Boyz II Men track with its absence of materializing sound indices. Blake might live on through the recordings he has made throughout his career, but the interactions this engenders with his audience run the risk of being as empty as the one we witness here between Scott and the Velvet Underground. They also promise to be as loaded for generations to come.

Blake's distance from the people around him is made most clear immediately following the first iteration of the "Venus in Furs" scene. Just after we hear the lyric "on bended knee," we cut to a shot of Blake seated at a drum kit listening to Luke discuss a song he is working on. Luke says he's having trouble with the bridge section, and would like Blake's creative input. Scott enters and interrupts, whispering in Luke's ear: "Why don't you leave him the fuck alone and come upstairs with me?" Luke complies, apologizing to Blake for talking his ear off. We cut to a shot of Scott and Luke on the stairwell as the former tries to convince the latter that Blake doesn't really want to have anything to do with them. As this conversation takes place, we hear Blake begin to sing and play guitar offscreen, performing "Death to Birth," a song positioned as a Blake original in the story and, in fact, written by actor Michael Pitt for the film. Like "Venus in Furs," this song is presented in a realist fashion that emphasizes the sound of the space that separates the music room from the stairwell. We follow Luke and Scott as they go up to the bedroom and remove their clothes, Luke stating that he doesn't believe Scott's claim that Blake isn't really their friend. So we find a desire on Luke's part to engage meaningfully with Blake, while Scott's selfish sexual interests in Luke stand in the way. All the while Blake is heard singing alone downstairs, prevented from the one kind of communication he might actually enjoy: a discussion about music to which he is clearly still committed.

The second iteration of "Death to Birth" comes just after the second iteration of "Venus in Furs." This time we enter the conversation between Luke and Blake earlier, and learn that the song Luke wants help with was inspired by a situation in which the best sex Luke ever had was with a woman that he didn't want to follow up with afterward, resulting in a cognitive dissonance that bothers him to this day. In giving us this back-story, Luke is demonstrating his own problems of communication in the world, problems that lead him to try and express the feeling of isolation through song, ultimately seeking to communicate meaningfully with Blake in the process. After Scott enters and takes Luke out of the room, this time we stay with Blake as he picks up his guitar and performs "Death to Birth" in its entirety, the refrain "It's a long, lonely journey from death to birth" emphasizing his position in the world while foreshadowing his death. As such, this song takes on some of the characteristics of a theme song, dating back to the transitional era when distinct musical performance sequences in films outside the musical genre could take on narrative justification when integrated well into the overall aesthetics and structure of the film (Spring 2013, 97–99). Here, in its second iteration, the onscreen performance of "Death to Birth" reveals depths of Blake's character that have been slowly layering up to this moment, largely through the prior instances of musical integration discussed across this chapter. Presented in direct sound with its attendant spatial signature, the song projects out into the space where we know from the earlier iteration that Luke and Scott can hear it as they go upstairs. Again, the treatment of sound here emphasizes the fact that Blake is there, in the house, his music interacting concretely with the space, while those who share the house with him choose not to interact with him. It is significant that Scott would rather interact with a recording of a band long gone than with Blake performing live right in front of him, and this could be interpreted as one of the dangers of schizophonic experience in Schafer's original sense of the term: technologies of recording and transmission disrupt our sense of engagement with the here-and-now, and Blake suffers from this as a recording artist whose representation has become separate from his in-person identity. Here, however, Blake plays acoustically, on a traditionally human scale that operates according to the spatiality of the unamplified voice, and he is alone and ignored.

As Luke and Scott share a moment of intimacy, Blake is left alone downstairs where his singing grows from the kind of incoherent mumbling we've heard throughout the film to a decidedly articulate and assured chorus with the words, "It's a long, lonely journey from death to birth," briefly reaching a volume that activates the house's latent reverberant qualities. Like the sound of Blake singing beside the campfire, the sound of his voice here is grounded within the space of his immediate surroundings, speaking back to him through spatial signature in a feedback process that Westerkamp would describe as "speaking from inside the soundscape" (2001), an essential part of how we can engage actively with our auditory environments. Such feedback is not present in his human relationships, and so it is essential that this moment of clarity come when he is alone. The earlier presence of soundscape composition in the film invites the audience to become active in assessing the spatial qualities of what we hear, and to reflect upon the significance of small nuances of spatial detail like the sound of Blake's voice here. In another film this final example might seem banal in its direct-sound approach to realism, but here it is much more interesting when situated within the film's overall strategy of using soundscape composition to reflect on the spatial qualities of music as a key factor in understanding its thematic content.

To render a bit of room reverberation significant with the weight of the empathetic imbalance that the film explores is something that Westerkamp's soundscape composition can bring to an overall hearing of *Last Days*. Sound theory has taught us that such a seemingly innocuous handling of audio-visual relationships is deceptively realist. Even though presenting a long static take recording a performance in real-time, this synchronization is heavily mediated to present this very particular organization of space that speaks powerfully to Blake's position within it. As such this scene is no less composed than the previous example of the song's iteration. If the audience walks away from the film with a heightened sensitivity to the potential social, political, and industrial significance of something as simple as the sound of a room's reflective qualities, then the work of Hildegard Westerkamp in *Last Days* is done, and what we learn from Van Sant's appropriation of soundscape composition here can help us to hear all films differently when in the mindset of acoustic ecology's media practice.

Through a Closed Door

After the level of subtlety achieved in the scene of Blake's final musical performance, Westerkamp's piece returns for the final walk up the driveway, described at the beginning of this chapter. The audience is now sensitized to the minutiae of the sound environment and the role of music in revealing its spatial details, and Blake is seemingly sensitized also as he looks back after the whistler blows, and the sounds of the doors from Westerkamp's piece are synchronized to his entry into the greenhouse, and his stare into the distance timed with the sound of distant bells.

A short while later Blake is shown one last time, with one final use of a door as mediating device. In the climactic shot—significantly the only superimposition found in the film—his transparent naked body is seen rising from his corpse. The shot involves a complex mise-en-scène in which the camera peers through the glass door at the front of the greenhouse, across Blake's dead body, with another French door at the back. In the foreground the groundskeeper stands just outside the door, blocking a portion of the front door's window grid and leaving the shape of a cross in what remains. The grid of the windowpanes on the back door provides the illusion of a ladder rising from the floor to a point beyond the top of the frame. As Blake rises from his corpse, he latches onto the ladder-like grid and proceeds to climb up it and out of the frame, viewed across the shape of the cross in the foreground. The religious symbolism is not subtle, but not at all forced given the film's recurring themes of spirituality discussed throughout my analysis here.

In this shot Blake is at once transcendent and grounded, a fact reflected by his existence on two planes of the film's surface being presented as one, their separation distinguishable only due to his ghostly translucence while rising from the body on the floor. Interestingly, the ghostliness of this translucence is offset by the reflective surface of the window through which we are seeing him; his transparency could just as easily be the result of the play of reflections off the glass as it could be an indicator of the supernatural. The presence of a door once again acts as the marker of mediality, this time between the world of the living and the world of the dead, perhaps the world of the diegesis and the world that lies outside. Blake's translucence mediated by the reflective door mirrors Westerkamp's auditory equivalent: sounds that merge with Van Sant's environments, at once seeming a part of these worlds while remaining quite distinct, and the attenuation her work brings to our experience of reflections like the reverberation on Blake's voice as he sings his final song. It is as though Westerkamp's sounds are housed within the spaces we see on screen, while continually offering a ladder out of the frame to lands that lie beyond.

This final shot of Blake thus presents a visual analogy for the way in which Westerkamp's work charts spaces of empathy in the film: two distinct planes have been positioned in the same space forging a connection between two worlds that seem simultaneously incongruous and at peace with one another. Our experience of the journey to this moment is, among other things, a soundwalk through shifting planes of attention guided by Hildegard Westerkamp. Her soundscape compositions help us enact the changing awareness necessary to enabling an engagement with the film, a process of engagement that has been well respected by Van Sant and Shatz in their appropriation of her work here. They create an audiovisual enactment of the state of film reception they hope to engender, in which the audience is aware of the mediated nature of the world they experience onscreen rather than continually engaging in a state of suspended disbelief. This awareness is the goal of reflective listening in soundscape composition, and here it becomes a function of reflective empathy when we consider how soundscape composition functions within the ecology of *Last Days*.

The use of soundscape composition as part of the sound design of the film creates the opportunity for the audience to negotiate the spaces between their points of audiovisual synchronization and engage with the material in a way that would be otherwise impossible. It is this opportunity that allows for access to the deeper levels of each film's engagement with its subject matter without recourse to complex character psychology or overt cause/effect narrative structure. In the end, the position of Westerkamp's work in *Last Days* is an enactment of the movement from the documentary impulse to soundscape composition within acoustic ecology itself, implying the argument that the compositional process, from recording to mixing, can be a productive mode of engagement with place, and that much of the goal of soundscape composition is to sensitize listeners to the role of hearing space in understanding our environments. Westerkamp's work, tied to the relevant theme of human empathy and the formal strategy of spatial mediation by way of the door, brings us to a point in the film where human scale as traditionally defined can be understood as potentially equivalent to the scale of electronic reproduction. Blake ends up just as lonely in his acoustic performance of "Death to Birth" within a small space as he does in his widely distributed material. The lesson here is an inversion of Schafer's original formulation of human scale but also an acknowledgment of the shift in dynamics within acoustic ecology to account for the positive role of technology in engagement with place.

References

Bakhtin, Mikhail. 1981. *The Dialogic Imagination*. Edited by Michael Holquist. Translated by Caryl Emerson and Michael Holquist. Austin: University of Texas Press.
Bakhtin, Mikhail. 1984. *Problems of Dostoevsky's Poetics*. Edited and translated by Caryl Emerson. Manchester: Manchester University Press.
Bakhtin, Mikhail. 1993. *Toward a Philosophy of the Act*. Edited by Michael Holquist and Vadim Liapunov. Translated by Vadim Liapunov. Austin: Texas University Press.
Batcho, James. 2022. "Living Time: Re-Evaluating Cinematic Empathy through Li Zehou." *Cinema: Journal of Philosophy and the Moving Image* 14: 26–40.
Chang, Chris. 2005. "Guided by Voices." *Film Comment* 41, no. 4 (July/August): 16.
Chion, Michel. 1994. *Audio-Vision: Sound on Screen*. Translated by Claudia Gorbman. New York: Columbia University Press.
Dalton, Stephen. 2005. "*Last Days*." *Sight and Sound* 15, no. 9: 65–66.
Falsetto, Mario. 2015. *Conversations with Gus Van Sant*. London: Rowan and Littlefield.

Goldmark, Daniel, Lawrence Kramer, and Richard Leppert, eds. 2007. *Beyond the Soundtrack*. Berkeley: University of California Press.

Jones, Kent. 2003. "Corridors of Powerlessness." *Film Comment* 39, no. 5: 28.

Kassabian, Anahid. 2001. *Hearing Film: Tracking Identifications in Contemporary Hollywood Film Music*. New York: Routledge.

Kulezic-Wilson, Danijela. 2008. "Sound Design is the New Score." *Music, Sound and the Moving Image* 2, no. 2 (Autumn): 127–131.

Norman, Katharine. 1996. "Real-World Music as Composed Listening." *Contemporary Music Review* 15, nos. 1–2: 1–27.

Schafer, R. Murray. 1977. *The Tuning of the World*. Toronto: McClelland and Stewart.

Simon, Sherry. 2004. "Accidental Voices: The Return of the Countertenor." In *Aural Cultures*, edited by Jim Drobnick, 111–119. Toronto: YYZ Press/Walter Phillips Gallery Editions.

Smith, Patty. 2013. "Lou Reed." *New Yorker* (November 11). https://www.newyorker.com/magazine/2013/11/11/lou-reed

Sterne, Jonathan. 2003. *The Audible Past: Cultural Origins of Sound Reproduction*. Durham, NC: Duke University Press.

Spring, Katherine. 2013. *Saying It with Songs: Popular Music and the Coming of Sound to Hollywood Cinema*. New York: Oxford University Press.

Stillwell, Robyn. 2007. "The Fantastical Gap Between Diegetic and Nondiegetic." In *Beyond the Soundtrack*, edited by Daniel Goldmark, Lawrence Kramer, and Richard Leppert, 184–202. Berkeley: University of California Press.

Taubin, Amy. 2005. "Blurred Exit." *Sight and Sound* 15, no. 9: 16–19.

Truax, Barry. 2008. "Soundscape Composition as Global Music." *Organised Sound* 13, no. 2: 103–109.

Westerkamp, Hildegard. 2001. "Speaking from Inside the Soundscape." *The Book of Music and Nature*, edited by David Rothenberg and Marta Ulvaeus, 143–152. Middletown, CT: Wesleyan University Press.

Westerkamp, Hildegard. 2002. "Linking Soundscape Composition and Acoustic Ecology." *Organised Sound* 7, no. 1: 52–56.

4

The Schizophonographic Imagination

Visualizing the Myth of Sonic Fidelity in David Lynch's *Twin Peaks*

It is inevitable that a discussion of sound in *Twin Peaks* Season 3 (2017) begins with the first new footage presented at the opening of Part 1, following a flashback to events that closed the original series in 1991.[1] The first of any *Twin Peaks* material to be presented in black and white, we find Special Agent Dale Cooper of the FBI (Kyle MacLachlan) seated opposite the entity once known as The Giant (Carel Struycken), to be rebranded as The Fireman later in this season. The Fireman's first words have become ground zero for academics and fan communities engaging with the acoustic qualities of the Twin Peaks universe: "Agent Cooper, listen to the sounds."[2] Cooper obeys, turning his head toward what appears to be a gramophone, and we cut to a shot pushing in on the horn as we hear some rather indescribable acoustic events. After delivering a few more cryptic messages, which was The Giant's function in the original series as well, he finishes by telling Cooper, "You are far away." Cooper then vanishes from his seat with a distinctive visual effect, suddenly appearing as though printed on paper and cut into several pieces, each of them flashing on and off independently for a moment until they all disappear into thin air, like a two-dimensional collage now digitally deconstructing. The sonic counterpart to this deconstruction is a light electrical crackling such as you can hear beneath high tension power lines, one of a wide variety of electrical sound effects that permeate the series, largely constructed by Lynch's long-time sonic collaborator Dean Hurley. End Scene One.

The original series opened with a compelling mystery in 1990: the first scene in the pilot episode reveals the body of a small-town high school senior wrapped in plastic and washed up on the beach, leading to the question that would hang off the lips of viewers for the next year: who killed Laura Palmer (Sheryl Lee)? This is the question that brought Agent Cooper out to the backwater berg of Twin Peaks in Washington State. Twenty-seven years later, Season 3 might be criticized for the lack of an equivalent central question to drive the narrative forward. But I'd like to suggest that here, in the opening scene, we have more than meets the ear. The questions aren't stated explicitly, but of course we must know: what are these sounds that Cooper is asked to listen to, and where did he go after hearing them?

Instinct dictates that listeners approach the first question causally: what auditory event in the world might have been recorded to produce these sounds? It wasn't long before one Redditor attempted to ease this dissonance, noticing that the repeating rhythm of the sounds matched up with the sound of slot machine levers that Cooper pulls repeatedly in Part 3 upon his arrival in Las Vegas (see Getman 2021), his first stop in the human world after passing through various fantastical transitional stages following his disappearance from The Fireman's refuge. Even more compelling is a YouTube video that compared the gramophone sounds to a brief clip of Laura Palmer unlocking her diary in a deleted scene from the feature film prequel to the original series, *Twin Peaks: Fire Walk with Me* (1992).[3] As Getman concludes, this kind of sleuthing is good fun and offers the fan community a deepened capacity for engagement with the material in the digital age (42–43), while opening interesting formal questions about why the show might draw parallels between the sounds from The Fireman's gramophone, the sounds of the slot machine lever, and/or the sounds of the lock on Laura's diary. It is certainly provocative that the mystery of the gramophone sound is laid parallel to the mysteries contained within Laura Palmer's most personal document, some missing pages of which are important clues within the narrative arcs of both the original series and Season 3 (and also the substance of some narrative discontinuity across these two iterations of the series). Even if this connection was deliberate on the part of the filmmakers, I agree with Getman that there are limits to the understanding that can be produced by revealing direct causal connections between these instances of a particular sound effect (43).

In this chapter, I frame the mystery of the gramophone sounds differently: why might it be important that the source of these sounds is never revealed? The most significant detail here is that there is no phonographic disc visible in the machine. Lynch has a long and storied history of visualizing record players (along with a wide variety of other sound technologies) within the diegetic spaces of his films. This is the very first time in that long history that we don't see a record on one of Lynch's players. And along with this visual absence there is a sonic absence, too: no evidence of materializing sound indices (Chion 1994, 99) to indicate a record as the medium for these sounds.

This is also something new for Lynch, who has long stressed the material quality of the records that play in his films. We could thus shift the question about the source of these sounds to a question about the medium through which they are transmitted. In that spirit my principal question is this: why is the record absent? To put it another way: why has the media vanished? To answer this question I will assess the recurring role of phonography in the *Twin Peaks* universe, allowing for us to chart a shift between Lynch's pre-digital and digital eras to better examine a particular problem of fidelity that has dominated discussions in the critical reception to Season 3: the faithfulness of the new *Twin Peaks* material to the old, and the relationship of all this material to Lynch's broader body of work in general.

I will demonstrate how the mystery of the missing record offers a parallel line of inquiry to the original series' question about the murder of Laura Palmer, two threads that are explicitly related in Season 3. The question of the missing media in The Fireman's gramophone provides a way of assessing how Season 3 reshapes the image of Laura Palmer as an increasingly embodied figure, just as the series itself engages with the increasingly disembodied characteristics of the cloud-based streaming dissemination of our present moment. With this comes the need to engage in the debates around the materiality of digital technologies, and how they extend and/or break from the non-digital media that dominated moving images and sound recording, reproduction, and transmission for one hundred years. In turn, questions of the shifting status of medium-specific materiality in Lynch's work open up pathways to rethinking the issue of sonic fidelity, challenged in various ways in the previous chapters of this book, and central to understanding how mediality functions through the portrayal of sound technologies across Lynch's body of work. To what extent does the third season of *Twin Peaks* illustrate the conundrums of media convergence? For Henry Jenkins, focusing on the black boxes that deliver content is a fallacy; content itself is media, and what is important is how it flows through its networks, not the apparatuses that make the flow possible (2006). Jenkins' black box fallacy is the antithesis of the medium-specificity that once dominated discussions of media and their effects, and certainly works against any preciousness that we vinyl enthusiasts hold for our preferred playback format. Does The Fireman's gramophone comment on the new status of *Twin Peaks* as digitally produced streaming content, breaking free from its roots in broadcast television and theatrical film? What might this freedom tell us about the role of one specific technology, the phonograph, in Lynch's work?

The answers to these questions lie in the changing status of the figure of Laura Palmer herself. In the original series, Laura was all media. Found dead in the opening scene of the pilot, she appeared throughout the show in her iconic photographic portrait as homecoming queen, on audiocassette tapes she recorded for her psychiatrist, on a videocassette of a picnic with friends, and in the crime scene photograph of her lifeless visage enshrouded by plastic. In the opening credit sequence to *Fire Walk with Me* a TV set is smashed to pieces, which many critics read as a clear statement that the film will break with expectations and "explode past the limits of the series" (Nochimson 1997, 192). The prequel film certainly did break from expectations, presenting a living Laura Palmer at the center of the narrative as we watched her last seven days play out, displaying a stark reality that was continually obfuscated in the series: that she was repeatedly raped by her father for years before he finally killed her. And so the film "revealed both the physical and spiritual trauma of childhood sexual abuse" with a "realism that continues to resonate with many, including survivors" (Stallings 2020, 8). The smashed TV could also be read as a gesture to set Laura free of her containment within specific media objects and allow her to live as a fully embodied human being, a gesture that continues into Season 3 by removing the determination of the original narrative arc and setting Laura on an entirely new path. At the end of Season 3, Agent Cooper is inserted into a scene from *Fire Walk with Me* to intervene into its narrative certainty, preventing Laura from engaging in the activities that led to her death on the night of February 23, 1989. Shortly after, we discover that a woman named Carrie Page, who looks almost exactly like Laura Palmer, has been living in Odessa, Texas. When Cooper finds her there he believes she is Laura and attempts to bring her home to Twin Peaks. This trajectory for Laura Palmer's corporealization is the medial move that reveals the myth of vanishing mediation at the heart of the discourse of fidelity. As I will demonstrate, in the original series the materiality of the record player at the Palmer residence was explicitly linked with the activities of her murderer. In Season 3, the missing disc in The Fireman's gramophone replaces the missing person premise of the original series, just as Laura Palmer herself disappears from the story and re-materializes as Carrie Page. The vanishing of the media thus underscores the return of Laura as Carrie, challenging the very status of the original as source for the series' return. As such, Season 3 mobilizes the disembodied sound of The Fireman's gramophone to thematize the problems inherent in tracking its origin.

To ground my discussion of how *Twin Peaks* Season 3 mobilizes questions about the materiality of the digital realm through the figure of Laura Palmer, I will harness the troubling implications of R. Murray Schafer's notion of schizophonia, discussed at length across this book, in the form of a modification: *schizophonographics*, a term that I have defined as "evocations of the schizophonic condition through the graphic representation of materials and/or processes pertaining to phonography" (2012). Schizophonographics call attention to the relationships between the "split" between sound and source, the potential for psychological disturbance that guided Schafer's original use of the term, and how films mobilize the onscreen presence of phonographic technology. For Isabella van Elferen, the cognitive dissonance created by "the obfuscation of causal relationships between source, sound, and signification," is a key marker of Lynch's sonic style, which she positions as explicitly schizophonic (2012, 180). In this spirit I situate the missing phonographic disc in The Fireman's gramophone within Lynch's history of schizophonographics, discuss how this history engages with anxieties around the digital turn in the technologies of moving images and sound, and demonstrate how rewriting Laura Palmer's canonical history provides a grounded solution to the problems embodied by the term schizophonia itself. I connect anxieties around the digital shift to core anxieties around the divide between sound and image at the heart of the cinema, best embodied by Michel Chion's theorization of the *acousmêtre*. I will demonstrate how the potential visualization of this classically invisible character type, who draws its supernatural power from the disembodied voice, is central to Laura Palmer's own embodiment as answer to the question of the missing media in The Fireman's phonograph. Laura's shifting corporeality suggests the presence defined by the absence of the missing disc, offering a new perspective on the role of phonographic media across *Twin Peaks* and Lynch's work more broadly.

The acoustic profile under consideration here, then, is the very range of extension from the original series, subsequent film, and return of *Twin Peaks* charted by the vanishing media of The Fireman's gramophone. Season 3 renders earlier *Twin Peaks* material malleable and unreliable, questioning its status as *original* to challenge the thesis that posits the problem of fidelity as the relationship between source and copy. Season 3 narrativizes this challenge to the source/copy dichotomy by changing Laura Palmer's path, and this change in path is rooted in the anxieties that have surrounded sound media across all its material iterations.

Phonographic Bodies

The void opened up by The Fireman's missing phonographic disc is filled by the renewed embodiment of Laura Palmer at the end of the series. The connection between the two is made explicit in Part 17, when the gramophone sounds return for the first time since Part 1, a good sixteen hours into the running time for Season 3. In a surprising turn of events, Cooper materializes inside a scene from *Fire Walk with Me* with the same collage flickering and electrical crackling effects with which he disappeared from The Fireman's place in Part 1. Also connecting the opening scene of Season 3 and this return to the 1992 film is the fact that the *Fire Walk with Me* footage is rendered in black and white instead of the original color, establishing a continuum between The Fireman's refuge and the narrative of the original series while hinting that the past is not what it once was. Here we catch up with Laura as she sneaks out of the house to go on a motorcycle ride with her boyfriend James (James Marshall), whom she will abandon for another group of friends who will set the conditions for her murder later that night. Cooper watches from the woods across the street as Laura and James stop on the side of the road to talk in lines familiar to fans. The conversation draws to a close as she tells James that, "your Laura disappeared; it's just me now," a repurposing of original dialogue to suggest her coming shift in identity to Carrie Page. Soon after, James speeds off into the night as Laura disappears into the woods. Cooper finds her there, and Laura recognizes him from a dream (portrayed earlier in *Fire Walk with Me* and the original series). Cooper takes her hand and tells her he is going to bring her home, thereby shifting the direction of her story. The change in plan is underscored by a shot of her friends on the other side of the woods, waiting for her to join them. Now she never will, as we cut to a familiar shot from the pilot episode with her body washed up on the shore, wrapped in plastic, which now disappears in the same collage fizzle that brought Cooper into the scene. But Cooper's plan is also thwarted. As they walk through the woods, all environmental sound disappears and the distinctive sounds of The Fireman's gramophone re-emerge. Cooper turns to look behind him, and Laura is gone. The gramophone sounds, still without concrete source of transmission, act as the score for this disappearance, now doubling the layers of missing bodies: no record in the player, no dead body on the shore, and no Laura Palmer in Twin Peaks at all. The Fireman's gramophone sounds, free of any visible media, now evoke Laura's own disappearance, who began the series as a media object herself, then became flesh and blood, and is now gone altogether.

The de-emphasis on phonographic corporeality, here, is something of a change for Lynch, whose record players have long tied their specific material qualities to the portals that open up for their listeners. Although Lynch demonstrates a fascination for sound technologies of all kinds, record players have a special place within his oeuvre. While Danijela Kulezic-Wilson notes the myriad instances in which music itself, regardless of source, serves as the conduit across Lynch's frequent spatiotemporal slippages (2015, 110), I will emphasize the ways in which Lynch focuses on the medium rather than its content as a frequent conduit for rendering multiple realities. In *Eraserhead* (1977), for example, Henry's (Jack Nance) turntable—a model already decades old for the 1970s, one factor in the indeterminate time period in which the film takes place—serves on the surface as a tool through which he can enjoy his Fats Waller music after a long day at the printing factory. But the film's slippage between worlds comes at the record's end, when the crackling loop of the end-groove takes over, joining the mechanical chorus of repeating industrial sounds in Henry's apartment to which Henry "cannot help but attune himself" (Batcho 2018, 96). It is in this sonic environment that he gazes into the radiator where he finds a stage, not unlike that in the Roadhouse bar of Twin Peaks, where a singer (Laurel Near) assures him that, "In heaven, everything is fine" (see Janisse 2017). Ultimately the vinyl's repeating end-groove forms one thread of an acoustic fabric in which Henry finally gives in to the maddening taunts of his strange infant child's cackling in the dark. He cuts the bandages in which it is swaddled, allowing its organs to splay across the room as the electricity goes wild, setting Henry free to join the Lady in the Radiator in a blast of triumphant light sucked straight out of the wiring of his building, which promptly goes dark. From Lynch's very first feature film, then, violence to the body is scored by the material sounds of phonography and its electrical sustenance, allowing passage to an alternate plane of existence.

In later years, amidst the digital turn, Lynch's phonograph turntables extend their original function but are presented in a different way. Since the arrival of CDs and then web streaming there has been a general tendency in American films to differentiate vinyl playback as an "other" to the new digital norms, with this "otherness" defined by its sonic particularities (Garwood 2016, 247–248) and its visuality (Anderson 2008). This new prominence given to medium-specific materiality has shifted the record player to the status of a fetish object for nostalgia, a highly visible and audible format in a time when digital musical media take up less visual space and whose sonic particularities are not so easily identifiable. This use of record players in the digital age can be likened to a form of "remediation" as "the formal logic by which new media refashion prior media forms" (Bolter and Grusin 1999, 273). Lynch's early turntables were not set in a period context, though Henry in *Eraserhead* and (as we'll soon see, the Palmers in *Twin Peaks*) owned units that were much older than the settings of the films. Record players disappeared from Lynch's films after the original *Twin Peaks* series until he entered his own digital filmmaking phase with *Inland Empire* (2006), the first of his feature films to be shot on a format other than film. Then they became regular again, and in each successive turntable appearance, from *Lady Blue Shanghai* (2010) to the latest iteration of *Twin Peaks*, Lynch's turntables have been connected to a more specific period context. This is new for Lynch, whose previous films regularly evoked styles from decades past, an aesthetic often regarded as postmodern simulacrum (Jameson 1991, 294–297), but were never explicitly framed as period pieces (with 1980's *The Elephant Man* being the notable exception). In Lynch's later films, record players evoke time periods more explicitly. In *Lady Blue Shanghai*, for example, Marion Cotillard's unnamed character arrives at her present-day Shanghai hotel room to find a vintage 78rpm turntable inexplicably blasting music from the 1920s. She rips the needle out of its groove, an action that opens up a vision of the past where she experiences the memory of a lost lover from before her time.

Inland Empire amplifies Lynch's treatment of spatiotemporal slippage considerably. The film opens with a close-up of a gramophone needle dragging across a spinning disc. Lit with stroboscopic effects, this is Lynch's most elaborate visual treatment of a turntable to date, recalling the pyrotechnic dance of spinning records in Germaine Dulac's gorgeous *Disque 957* (1928). Through the crackle a voice emerges to announce "the longest running radio play in history," which serves as set-up for a scene introducing us to a "lost girl" (Karolina Gruszka) trapped in cycles of physical violence within a Polish prostitution enterprise. Later, when actress Nikki Grace (Laura Dern) gets lost in her own Hollywood film set, she exits into the Poland of an earlier time. The transition is mediated by a return of the gramophone shots seen at the film's opening, now with Nikki's face superimposed over the black shellac disc as she listens to the "lost girl" explain the secret to seeing through the void. "You need to burn a hole through the silk with the cigarette, and look through the hole," she says, just as the cigarette and the gramophone needle are superimposed on the image track in a graphic match. Here the connection between the turntable technology and the portal to another world is made visually specific in an evocation of what Murray Leeder calls "co-registration, the depiction of different spatialities and temporalities simultaneously, seemingly collapsed onto a single plane" through the cinematic process of superimposition (2017, 97). Co-registration was a common visual strategy in early cinema to indicate the overlap of spirit worlds with everyday reality, drawing on the role of spirit photography and X-ray technology in the popular imagination of the late nineteenth century. Lynch's representation of phonography adds a sonic dimension by using phonographic surface noise as a co-registrant that signifies the emerging presence of another dimension, evoking spiritualist beliefs about the nature of communication that "straddled the line between physical transmissions . . . and spiritual ones" (Peters 199, 100).

The relationship between old-world Europe and the violence inherent in its colonization of North America is manifested through Nikki's experience of the incongruity of living across different histories, a spatiotemporal loop that leads to her own cycles of violent death and shining rebirth. As Liz Greene points out, this narrative simultaneity of differing periods and settings is matched by a conflation of old-school technological presence like the gramophone and the new aesthetic qualities of Lynch's experimentation with digital image capture (2012, 102). Caught between worlds, both narrative and aesthetic, Nikki Grace suffers no small psychological distress, and ultimately ends up being stabbed by the jilted wife of her Hollywood scene-partner and bleeding out on the street among the street dwellers of Hollywood boulevard. Nikki serves as yet another of Lynch's characters to suffer bodily transgression connected directly to a slippage between spaces mediated by phonograph technology. Here Lynch ties this violence directly to a critique—both in content and production context—of the Hollywood system through which he struggled for so long and from which *Inland Empire* marked his triumphant escape—for all time, we thought, until the unlikely return of *Twin Peaks* eleven years later.

With the distinction between Lynch's pre-digital and digital eras in mind, it is instructive to see how *Twin Peaks* has passed through both and shifted its own relationship to the presentation of phonography on screen. As Kathryn Kalinak put it following the original series, "is there another fictional town on television with as many record players as this one?" (1995, 86). In the time of the original series, the CD era was yet very new, and the lingering predominance of vinyl as the main mode of home music listening is not clearly distinguished as an "other" to new digital norms. Instead, it functions very much like Henry's turntable in *Eraserhead*, a film made well before the dawn of the digital music era: a medium whose material particularities are exploited in their own right, as mysterious in the present moment of those narratives as they were at the time of their invention around the turn of the century. It is through phonography that on-the-air sound opens up to the parallel worlds that intersect with the town of Twin Peaks, perhaps most explicitly referenced in Episode 5 of the original series. Here Cooper finds the cabin in the woods where Laura Palmer spent time on the night of her death, and inside a record player with an automatic repeat function has apparently been playing Julee Cruise's "Into the Night" on a continuous loop ever since. Cooper lifts the needle up and repeats a line that the Little Man from Another Place (Michael J. Anderson) told him in a dream from Episode 2, "And there is always music in the air." With this connection of Cooper's dream space with the reality of the town through the machinations of phonography, the series displays the mediality at the heart of its mystery. I will now elaborate on how this phonographic mediality plays out most substantially on the Palmers' turntable in Episodes 2 and 14.

In Episode 2, Leland Palmer (Ray Wise) finds himself desperate for a dance partner. Since the death of his daughter Laura he has become obsessed with the idea of dancing and frequently puts on old records to get him moving. Here he plays the Glenn Miller Orchestra's "Pennsylvania 6-5000" and begins dancing as though with a ghost. Looking around for something to reach out to, he picks up Laura's homecoming queen portrait from an end table, holds it out in front of him, and begins to spin around in circles. Lynch intercuts point-of-view shots wherein the room appears to spin around as though the viewer is holding Laura's picture while dancing. His wife, Sarah Palmer (Grace Zabriskie), then rushes into the room and wrestles with Leland over the photo, causing the glass frame to break. Sarah runs over to the turntable and violently whacks the needle off the record, an action accompanied by the expected scratching sound. Leland, having cut his hand on the broken glass, now caresses the photo directly, smearing Laura's image with his own blood in the process.

Several key issues are raised by this sequence. Firstly, it is significant that Leland's need for dance is accompanied by his desire for music on vinyl. The use of the body as a kind of mediation between the production and reception of music can be seen as a function of the physical nature of music as the propagation of soundwaves through space. Just as sound moves through the air, so too do bodies in the act of perceiving it. Dancing is a way of becoming the music that suggests a kinship between musical and human corporeality. Secondly, the lyrics on the record refer to the act of making contact between human beings through telecommunications technology. Here the turntable joins with the telephone as the technological presences involved in Leland's struggle to fill the hole left in his life by the absence of another human being. For Alistair Mactaggart, this absence is made uncannily present through the "strangeness of overproximity" in the close-up on the surface of the record that begins this scene (2010, 129). This close-up also reveals that the record player itself is not of the same vintage as the floor-standing cabinet that houses it; it is a modern turntable housed in a much older casing, an interesting confluence of differing eras of music reproduction in the pre-digital age (a point to which I will return at the end of this chapter). Thirdly, Leland's dancing needs are a factor of his having lost someone close to him, causing him to seek a partner. His engagement with Laura's photograph emphasizes her status as a media object along with the record on the turntable. Lastly, Lynch emphasizes Leland's emotional desperation by filming his dancing movements in ways that mimic the movements of the technology playing the music. It is as though Leland wants to become the technology that fuels his nostalgia in order to travel back to a happier time, bridging the gap between past and present through human/machine interaction. In short, he wants these media to vanish and leave the originals in their place. Here the joining of sound and image through technologies of representation is further emphasized by the violence of the scratching sound, as Sarah drags the needle off the disc, in conjunction with Leland's hand being cut by the broken glass. The materiality of sound, image, and human flesh intersect with psychological distress here in a lavish display of schizophonographic mediality.

The second example, this one from Episode 14, also involves the turntable in the Palmer living room, and again concerns the act of Leland dancing to a vinyl record with a facsimile of his daughter: Maddy Ferguson (also played by Sheryl Lee), the cousin and spitting image of the deceased Laura. Having once been very close with the family, Maddy visits the Palmers in their time of grief. A foreshadowing scene finds Maddy sitting on the couch between the Palmers whereupon she tells them that she'll be driving back home the next day. Louis Armstrong is heard singing "What a Wonderful World," carrying with it the distinctive sound of aging vinyl. The scene is comprised of one long take that begins with a close-up of a side table with photos of Laura and the family, then pans rightward to reveal the couch in the background just as Maddy sits down between the Palmers. As they converse, the camera tracks to the right, passing behind the floor-standing turntable cabinet and coming to rest with the spinning record it plays squarely in the foreground beyond which lies the centrally composed trio on the couch. Here the stage is set for Maddy's murder at the end of the episode, occurring in the same room, with an ambient soundtrack provided by the sound a record on that turntable looping in the end-groove.

The presence of the turntable thus provides the center around which the murder takes place. Materiality is again a primary concern here, along with the idea of repetition as a function of mechanical looping. Just prior to the murder scene, we find Agent Cooper witnessing the appearance of The Giant on stage at the Roadhouse bar; he advises the detective that, "it is happening again," followed by a dissolve that merges The Giant and the Palmer turntable as we transition from the Roadhouse bar to the Palmer residence (prefiguring the relationship between The Fireman and the gramophone in Season 3). Beginning with The Giant's warning setting up the idea of repetition, followed by the manifestation of such repetition through the turntable's looping action, the murder sequence unfolds in a formal pattern of alternation through which the theme of repetition runs. The idea that Laura Palmer's murderer is still on the loose, and that the act of murder will be repeated, has set up the anticipation of the return of Killer Bob (Frank Silva), another denizen of worlds beyond introduced by way of Cooper's dream in Episode 2. Bob's reappearance in Episode 14 begins with his face looking back at Leland as the latter's reflection in a hallway mirror, revealing for the first time that Leland himself is the killer while playing host to the possessing spirit. The reflection is itself an embodiment of repetition—the repetition of light rays as they bounce off the reflective surface, the visual equivalent of an echo. Maddy then enters the room and sees Bob standing in the hallway. Maddy is also a kind of reflection in so far as she is nearly identical to Laura Palmer. So, one reflection looks at another, and the violence begins.

During the attack sequence, the fact that Bob and Leland both inhabit the same flesh is suggested through a system of technical devices resulting in alternate appearances of the two. Once Maddy has been partially subdued, Leland begins to dance with her in a circular motion echoing his dance with Laura's picture in Episode 2. During the dance, Lynch uses quick dissolves to make Bob appear in Leland's place. When Bob is dancing with Maddy, the film runs in slow-motion with complementing slow-motion sound, and the lighting changes to a bright spotlight on the subjects contrasted against a darkening of the rest of the room. When Leland pops back into the picture, the regular speed is resumed, as is the more normative lighting style. This alternation between Bob and Leland happens several times before Maddy is finally killed.

One of the most important things to note about this scene is that, while most of the soundtrack slows down to complement the slow-motion imagery when Bob is present, the sound of the looping record remains unchanged throughout. The material texture of vinyl, with its powers of evoking the past, acts as a kind of timeless grounding to the scene unaffected by the other scene's other formal fluctuations in the flow of time. The sound of the looping record is like a conduit between worlds, charting an acoustic profile that extends between the territory of Leland's world and that of Bob. It also suggests the early days of phonography, laden with the anxiety of separating the senses from each other, and the body, that lay at the heart of cinema (see Gunning 2001). Bob might be a manifestation of the anxiety of being caught between separated worlds; in this scene he exerts his most powerful efforts yet to force his way into the material world through the medium of Leland Palmer.

The fact that it is the sound of vinyl that Lynch uses to "score" this scene alludes to a time when spiritualism was alive and well, with many people believing that the spirit world could be contacted by way of sound reproduction technology (see Sconce 2000). The idea of a medium, or material, through which such contact takes place is crucial here. Lynch not only foregrounds the materiality of the phonograph, but also of cinema through his co-registrations of image and sound speeds along with the lighting styles. Lynch puts the intersection between worlds on material display as an extended loop of the repeating vinyl texture opening up a new space where Leland and Bob exist simultaneously. The brief moments of superimposition that formally indicate the coexistence of Bob and Leland visualize the layering of worlds. The cinematic expression of this flow between worlds is a function of Lynch's exploration of cinema's materiality, a materiality ultimately equated with that of the human body through the scene's startling violence. The theme of mediumship here, in Bob's possession of Leland, is another expression of the mediality at the heart of *Twin Peaks*.

Bodily transgression through the material qualities of phonography are on display once again in Part 8 of the third season of *Twin Peaks*. Part 8 is now legendary for its dramatic break from the style of the rest of the series, presented mostly in black and white, going back in time to the first nuclear test at White Sands, New Mexico, and offering up a series of highly experimental sequences exploring the material qualities of a nuclear explosion and the role of The Fireman in attenuating the effects of this new energy unleashed upon the world. Within the cloud of the nuclear blast, we witness what appears to be the birth of Killer Bob in a bubble belched forth from an unidentified entity. This is paralleled later by the appearance of Laura in a different bubble, this one summoned by The Fireman and handled by Señorita Dido (Joy Nash), who is shown in The Fireman's refuge sitting next to the very gramophone we saw in the series' opening moments. We hear a Lynch/Hurley collaboration entitled "Slow 30s Room," a composition that is rife with the kind of surface noise expected from a 1930s 78 rpm disc, patterned on a looping structure that recalls the sound of a record skipping. And yet, once again, there is no disc visible in the gramophone itself. This scene stands as the center point to the series as a whole, as an alarm goes off and The Fireman enters to address the concern through a series of ambiguous actions that result in the emergence and dispersal of the Laura orb. There is a clue here about the emergence of two bodies—Bob and Laura—that will engage in violent confrontation over the right to inhabit a single corporeal space. "He says he wants to be me or he'll kill me," Laura tells a confidant in *Fire Walk with Me* about her encounters with Bob. In their spherical forms here they are presented as material media on their way to corporealization, where one will try to become the other. The missing media in The Fireman's gramophone now suggests his role as producer, sending media objects out into the world via the film screen upon which he keeps the world under surveillance.

Later in Part 8 we do catch a glimpse of the only phonographic disc to appear in Season 3. The period jumps to 1956, and we arrive at the KPJK radio station where the DJ is spinning "My Prayer" by the Platters. The station is infiltrated by the Woodsman (Robert Broski), descended through the air from parts unknown. His arrival is marked by a particular sound of electrical interference (another of sound designer Dean Hurley's many contributions to the soundtrack, which the closed captioning on the Crave TV stream labeled as "brooding atmospheric music" with "ominous scratching noise"). The "scratching noise" is what sets this treatment of electrical sound apart from the myriad others across the series, later echoed by the sound of crackling vinyl when the Woodsman commandeers the DJ booth, sending the needle skidding across the spinning record—recalling Sarah Palmer's gesture in Episode 2 of the original series—that blends with radio static as we watch confused listeners across town reacting to the interruption of the musical broadcast. After penetrating the DJ's skull with his bare hands, another iteration of corporeal violence underscored by phonographic materiality, the Woodsman then takes to the airwaves with a poetic recitation: "This is the water, and this is the well. Drink full and descend. The horse is the white of the eyes, and dark within." Across several repetitions of this verse we watch as various townspeople drop unconscious in their tracks at the sound of the Woodsman's voice on their radios. One of these is a teenage girl (Tikaeni Faircrest) who, in her forced slumber, opens her mouth to become host to a winged reptilian creature that hatched from an egg in the desert, apparently another spawn (along with Bob) of the monstrous figure during the fallout of the Trinity nuclear blast. This is a violation of her body, a trespass upon corporeal grounds, perfectly in keeping with the themes of rape, incest, and murder that lay at the core of the *Twin Peaks* mythology. And the electrical interference cue that marked the Woodsman's appearance returns over an image of the girl lying asleep, now possessed, as the end credits roll.

There seems little that can be done about the repetitive insistence of violence associated with Bob, for which the turntable's materiality—the interruption of recorded musical content to reveal the sound of the medium itself—acts as both metaphor and gateway. What is most remarkable in these instances of turntable presence in *Twin Peaks* is how the otherworldly quality of the medium is tied specifically to its materiality. This is an intriguing inversion of hi-fi culture's emphasis on the notion of sonic transparency that invites listeners to transcend the space of their living rooms into the performance venues in which the recordings were made. For Lynch, it is the revelation of sound technology's material qualities—those that hi-fi culture attempts to banish from consciousness, the surface noise on vinyl and electrical buzzing from its amplification—that allows passage between worlds, folding spaces onto each other like the Guild Navigators in *Dune* (1984). For Lynch, it is when the medium reveals itself that the barrier between spaces becomes transparent, at least until the media vanishes in the opening to *Twin Peaks* Season 3.

Digital Anxieties

The missing media object in The Fireman's gramophone seems tailor-made as a visualization of the myth of vanishing mediation upon which cultures of fidelity rest. As discussed throughout this book, the discourse of fidelity in hi-fi stereo culture imagines a transparent technology that leaves no trace of itself in its presentation of content, so that playing a recording of a symphony might make the listener feel as though they are right there in the symphony hall where it was recorded. For R. Murray Schafer, the potential confusion over live and recorded sound is a problem, but it's largely an imaginary one invented by the hi-fi industry to sell product. It depends upon what Jonathan Sterne calls "audile technique," ear training that allows listeners to "differentiate between sounds 'of' and sounds 'by' the network, casting the former as 'exterior' and the latter as 'interior' to the process of reproduction" (2003, 283). The trick, then, is to design machines that can minimize the "exterior" effects and maximize the signal to noise ratio (the "hi" in the "fi"). But these exterior effects are always present. As Hillel Schwartz puts it, "Noise is what makes perfect repeatability humanly impossible" (2011, 25). And when you add Rick Altman's argument that there can be no real "original" sound to repeat in the first place, given the role of positionality in receiving any given sound event (1992), the whole foundation for fidelity as perfect equation of source and copy simply crumbles. Schafer deliberately invoked the language of mid-century hi-fi culture to frame his approach to listening to the world, and suggested that the proliferation of electroacoustic sound transmission in modern environments came with the potential for sound technology to confuse the listener about where—and when—we are. Yet Schafer doesn't address the fact that such confusion posits a naïve listener, one lacking in audile technique, unable to hear the technology behind the transmission. In short, his rhetoric buys into the myth of transparency in audio playback designed as a marketing tool by the recording industry. Lynch, on the other hand, seems to work in opposition: it is precisely the material qualities of mediation that invite otherworldly transcendence. It is in hearing the surface noise of the record that Nikki Grace learns to see through the portal to the other side. And Henry's turntable must yield to the surface noise of the disc before he slips into the radiator. Lynch seems bent on training his listeners in the art of audile technique so as to better hear the sounds *of* the network and understand their role in the paths his characters chart.

The primacy that Lynch accords phonographic materiality aligns with what Jay David Bolter and Richard Grusin term *hypermediacy*, an artistic style that foregrounds the medium of the work in question, the opposite of *transparent immediacy* in which the artist attempts to erase all traces of the medium (1999, 272–273). Here we can also distinguish between the transparency that once governed classical approaches to film scoring, the "unheard melodies" that Claudia Gorbman identifies in the use of film music as nearly subliminal underscore (1987), and a new "cinema of the senses" marked by a stylistic excess that "wants to be heard" (Kulezic-Wilson 2021, 368). For Lynch's phonography, however, the sensual score lies in the textures of the musical medium rather than its recorded content. Understanding the significance of what we might call Lynch's sensual hypermediacy, particularly as it transitions from the pre-digital to digital domains, requires a deeper investigation into the logics of transparency itself.

In sound, the idea of transparency works best as a marketing metaphor when referencing acoustic performances bound by the spatiality of the unamplified instrument and voice, like Blake's performance of "From Death to Birth" in *Last Days* discussed in the previous chapter. The minute any studio manipulation is brought in, the very foundation of transparency ceases to make sense: there can only be transparency to an original performance if there is an original performance to begin with, so anything short of a live-to-tape capture fails to satisfy the very conditions required for the idea of an original sound event. Transparent immediacy can be attempted as an artistic style, but in the reality of material sound reproduction the idea is difficult to comprehend: equipment of mediation is a necessary link in the chain between performance and listener, since the listener is listening to the performance through that equipment. Yet it is this equipment that the listener hopes will disappear, leaving only the performance in its wake. As is particularly the case with vinyl fetishists, it is precisely the indexical link made possible by the material processes of phonography that are said to allow these material processes to render themselves inaudible. Transcendence of the equipment, in other words, is dependent upon its material embodiment. Apparent absence of the equipment is made possible by its presence, and the presence of the original performance event is made possible in turn by the equipment's absence.

The insistence on indexicality is a crucial point in understanding the way pre-digital media technologies are said to connect source to audience in ways that digital media cannot. In "Defining Phonography" (1997), Eric Rothenbuhler and John Durham Peters pose a thought experiment based on the common argument that there is an indexical link between source and reproduction inherent in the technology of the phonograph that is absent in its digital counterparts. The argument is that transcendence of the media is made possible only through the "unbroken chain" of indexicality "from the sound in the living room to the original sound as recorded" (252). If the medium can actually erase itself and place the listener in the moment of original performance, it is precisely because the medium is physically attached to this original performance (253). The equipment can bring the presence of the performer into the space of the home listener. This erasure through physical tracing, the authors say, is absent in the digital realm, where the translation to binary code breaks the indexical link and therefore severs the material connection that makes the vanishing mediation possible. In digital media it is the connection that vanishes through the media, rather than the media vanishing through the connection.

The argument against digital indexicality is a clear example of what might be called the gentrification process for anxieties induced by twentieth century technologies of reproduction: early distress over the phonograph's powers of disembodiment is cleaned up through an argument for the medium's grounding in the embodiment offered by indexicality, only to push the original distress into the digital quarter of the media world by arguing that digital media is, by definition, purely symbolic in its reproduction of reality. Rothenbuhler and Peters thus examine a position that has accepted phonography as "natural" in its indexical functioning where earlier audiences found it to be decidedly "unnatural" in its apparent propensity toward disembodiment. Yet this position exhibits an anxiety toward digital technology that is remarkably similar to the anxiety expressed by an earlier public unaware of phonography's foundations in indexicality. They argue that digital media's reproduction of reality involves a gap between original and copy, a sentiment familiar to early phonograph culture. As such, "Defining Phonography" presents a view of digital media couched in the simultaneity of presence and absence that has been the foundation for anxieties surrounding all manner of new sound reproduction technologies throughout the twentieth century, not the least of which being phonography itself.

The case made by Rothebuhler and Peters is the culmination of the consuming public coming to identify with the dreams of the phonograph's creators. Thomas Edison once boasted about the phonograph's ability "to reproduce sound waves 'with all their original characteristics'" but this was not necessarily understood by the public as being a function of a recording's indexical relationship to its source (Rothenbuhler and Peters, 245). As the authors readily admit, phonography was once received with some feelings of distress concerning "its ability to capture voices and sounds no longer tied to the human body or to the organic cycle of birth and death" (245). So it indicates a big step forward that vinyl enthusiasts can now describe the virtues of phonography in terms of the transcendent qualities of its powers of embodiment, when once it was understood as being transcendent precisely because of its powers of disembodiment. If there is now an accepted mythology that phonography is material in ways that the digital is not, then digital media is to the late twentieth century what phonography was to the late nineteenth century, a reproduction technology that involves a mysterious gap between source and copy. So, Rothebuhler and Peters haven't dispelled anxieties about the mysterious processes of sound recording in general. They've simply displaced these anxieties to a new medium more fitting for the present moment. As Peters would later put it, "Every new medium is a machine for the production of ghosts" (1999, 139).

This displacement of anxiety is interesting to consider in light of its difference from anxieties expressed in the nineteenth century. For example, Lisa Gitelman discusses the emergence of the idea of "language machines" in the late 1800s, machines that would improve the speed and accuracy with which the spoken word could be turned into text. She states that "persistent proposals for new, improved means of reproducing, inscribing, and communicating suggest [that] representation was the site of anxiety" (1999, 82). Again, this anxiety is a function of the need to bring source and copy closer together, to heighten the indexical relationship between the represented and its representation. Essentially, what Gitelman describes is a desire to bring acts of representation to the state of reproduction in which a transcription is no longer considered a mediated version of that which has been transcribed: a desire for the equipment to become transparent.

What we can observe between the era that Gitelman describes and the argument against the very validity of the "original" itself (Altman 1992 and Lastra 2000) is a historical arc indicative of changing attitudes toward expectations of fidelity. On the one hand, early anxiety surrounding lack of fidelity in representation is addressed by a desire to create technologies of reproduction. So the dream of the phonograph is to shift the distant copy of textual transcription into the closer copy of the indexically linked recording. On the other hand, anxieties emerge around these reproductions being too close to their originals, apparent disembodiments of the human subject. Hillel Schwartz notes that it was commonplace for early consumers of new sound technologies like the phonograph to be impressed by the verisimilitude their transmissions offered in spite of an abundance of system noise (2011, 333). Interestingly, as fidelity grew the skeptics would take over, arguing that technologies of recording and transmission can never reproduce, regardless of how well they minimize system noise, removing expectations for fidelity altogether. Finally, along comes the digital and, all of a sudden, its appearance of immateriality, owing largely to a lack of frictional surface noise in its transmissions, reinscribes the pre-digital with an authenticity now said to be lacking in binary code transcriptions. All these shifts in perception, however, are indexically linked in an unbroken chain of anxieties about the relationship between flesh and machine that simply move onward into the future, link by link by link.

There is something provocative in the possibility that The Fireman's missing disc thematizes vanishing mediation just as *Twin Peaks* went digital for the first time on all levels: the narrative emphasis on current digital technologies, the digital image capture on the production, and the digital dissemination through streaming platforms. To flesh out the significance of The Fireman's missing disc in the context of the digital turn, I will now elaborate on how the aforementioned examples of turntable presence in Lynch's films mesh with the anxieties around sound reproduction discussed in the present section, coalescing into schizophonography that taps deeper into cultural fears surrounding the relationship between bodies and machines, the postmodern threat of disappearing context from our experience of daily life, and the cinema's propensity toward the presentation of disembodied voices. I will argue for thinking of The Fireman's gramophone sound as an articulation of what Michel Chion calls the *acousmêtre*, and demonstrate how this figure, too, has shifted status in the digital era. In theorizing the connection between the myth of vanishing mediation and the privileged positions granted to invisibly speaking bodies, I will demonstrate how film sound theory's concern with embodiment in relation to cinematic voices is the final link that connects The Fireman's missing media with Laura Palmer. The Fireman's disc, like the *acousmêtre*, exposes the artificiality of embodiment through synchronization of sound and image, the mediality that allows for Laura Palmer's fate to be changed, challenging the indexical link between the source material of the original series and its new digital iteration.

Visualizing the (Gendered) *Acousmêtre*

In "Doing for the Eye what the Phonograph Did for the Ear" (2001), Tom Gunning pins Thomas Edison's titular goal for the kinetoscope on two concerns in early twentieth century life: the separation of the senses popular for studies of perception, and "a desire to heal the breach" resulting from anxiety surrounding this separation (16). Gunning holds that, in the context of the spiritualist traditions alive and well at the time, the technological separation of the human voice from the body was often considered to be unnatural and demanded a restitching of the isolated elements. In this narrative, Edison's stated desire to reunite sound with image by building the phonograph's visual corollary was, in part, a response to early schizophonic separation anxiety. Healing the breach between sound and image was also the goal of a variety of film conventions that sought to minimize attention to the technologies that made the illusion of sound/image synchronization possible. One such convention is what Michel Chion calls the *acousmêtre*, a character consisting of a voice that is not attached to a visible body, a condition that depends as much on image as it does sound, rendering the cinematic *acousmêtre* distinct from disembodied voices found in other media.[4] The *acousmêtre* is accorded a position of privilege, often imbued with supernatural powers, because of its ability to roam free of physical attachment, like a deity or ghost. As Brian Kane puts it, "the *acousmêtre* depends on the *paradox* of the effect without a cause" (2014, 39), a situation that aligns with R. Murray Schafer's "affirmative claim for sonic uniqueness" of embodied source over transmitted copy (142). These powers disappear once the cause is revealed, attaching the voice to a visible body through the convention of lip-synchronization, as when the Wizard in Oz is revealed to be an ordinary man concealed behind a curtain, his technological apparatus laid bare as the source of his mysterious disembodiment (Chion 1999, 28–29). The powers associated with the *acousmêtre* are required to provide a narrative veil to the underlying apparatus, concealing the fact that "it is an inherent consequence of the material organization of cinema that the voice and body are at odds" (127). In other words, the breach between sound and image that so concerned Edison was imperfectly healed by matching image technologies with sound technologies, and bodiless voices threaten to expose this imperfection unless they are given supernatural justification for their mysterious powers.[5]

Enter David Lynch playing FBI Chief Gordon Cole in the opening scene of *Fire Walk with Me*, the partially deaf director of the Blue Rose cases to which the mystery of Laura Palmer's murder belongs. Hearing aids armed and ready, Cole hollers at his secretary who stands not three feet away: "Get me Agent Chester Desmond out in Fargo, North Dakota!" Then, having secured Agent Desmond (Chris Isaak) on the phone, Cole identifies himself by screaming into his receiver, causing Desmond to pull the hand-piece away from his ear as Cole's voice audibly distorts through the tiny speaker. This scene recalls descriptions of Edison hollering into the bell of his phonographic cylinder recorder, both because this early microphone was unamplified and because he was hard of hearing (Kittler 1999, 22). It is almost as if Lynch, through Cole, is positing himself as a reincarnation of Edison, placed in charge of investigating the otherworldly by-products of so many electrical devices that populate his films. Just as Friedrich Kittler notes that Edison's recording device was born out of human impairment, Lynch foregrounds Cole's dependence on hearing aids and the telephone distortion resultant from his compensation for this dependence. Here Lynch also conflates what James Lastra has called the telephonic and phonographic modes of sound representation in film, emphasizing speech intelligibility and perceptual fidelity respectively (2000, 138–139). The joke is that Cole's diminished capacity to experience the sound environment in its totality (perceptual fidelity) also leads to his diminished capacity to communicate through speech (intelligibility). The tools for assisting both are failing, and Cole's disembodied voice on the other end of the telephone emphasizes the material conditions required for separating voice from body. Cole thus highlights the inherent flaws in the system, and by extension, the inherent gap between voice and body in the cinema. Cole fails the test of the classic *acousmêtre* because his attempts at projecting his voice are thwarted by the imperfect mesh of flawed flesh and flawed equipment. But in opening the film this way, Lynch sets the conditions for how access to alternate planes of reality can be opened through this very same mesh.

Cole's role in Season 3 finds him listening through to the depths of the other worlds that intersect with the town of Twin Peaks, largely under the influence of an amorphous entity known as "Judy," first mentioned in passing in *Fire Walk with Me* but referenced more substantially in Season 3 as the foundation for the evils that have beset the small town from earliest days. Steven Wilson (2021) makes a compelling argument for the status of Judy as *acousmêtre*, tracking a variety of sound design treatments, largely from Dean Hurley, as acousmetric expressions of her "voice" whose articulations function like musical motifs that connect narratively with key sequences in the series. Wilson's exegesis offers an example of how the integrated soundtrack, that treats sound design as score, requires attention to all sonic material in order to understand relationships between the traditional functions of film music and the very separate functions of voice, bound together through the art of sound design. For my purposes, it is useful to consider how the materiality expressed by sound effects associated with things like phonography and electricity serve as the material conduits for the more classically defined *acousmêtre*: the speaking voice without a visible body. As I'll demonstrate, Lynch's interest in the figure of the *acousmêtre* lies in its potential to retain the powers associated with disembodiment even as the technological foundations for this disembodiment are laid bare, just as Lynch's version of vanishing mediation depends on the visibly mediate.

The *acousmêtre* is cast as an invisible character in a visible world. Yet more recent thinking about the *acousmêtre* suggest possibilities for its own visibility. In his updated epilogue to the 1999 edition of *The Voice in Cinema*, Chion has identified characters who behave as *acousmêtres* through only partial visual concealment: a mask that obscures the mouth as the site of full embodiment for the voice (1999, 166–167). Chion has also recognized how improvements to the resolution of cinematic sound can allow for voices to be coded as separate from bodies through greater capacities for spatialization around distinct sonic tracks (167–168). The age of discrete digital surround sound formats has the potential to push the *acousmêtre* outside of the boundaries of the screen, and to situate this figure within a heightened diegetic realism that might free it from its threat to the boundary between sound and image. As Mark Kerins has explored in detail in *Beyond Dolby (Stereo)* (2011), enhancements to surround technology have brought even more visible *acousmêtres*, able to be seen onscreen but maintain their powers by extending the voice into an array of discrete channels offscreen. Yet Kerins concludes that the enhanced spatialization made possible by discrete channels can't ultimately solve the problem of the fundamental separation of voice and body that Chion suggests is inherent to the sound cinema (2011, 276). True, amidst the increasingly complex spatialization made possible by digital surround sound there is more potential for the powers of the *acousmêtre* to be exploited through enhanced auditory localization. For Kerins, a main consequence of this new digital reality is that we must at least add the category of spatial-synchronization to that of temporal sync when conducting our analyses of how acousmetric figures play out in a digital sound film (262). Yet along with providing a more three-dimensional model for the cinematic representation of space, multi-channel sound also brings with it even greater potential for the seams holding this space together to come undone. The *acousmêtre* in this scenario has to work harder to function as deflection away from the gap between sound and source.

So it would seem that the figure of the *acousmêtre*, whether presented in monophonic or digital surround sound, visible or invisible, is fundamentally doomed to remain an agent of potential threat to the exposure of the cinematic apparatus. Chion's own discussion of the Wizard of Oz as a quintessential *acousmêtre* is a case in point: this figure is not merely a disembodied voice, but also a disembodied head floating in space. Chion refers to this head as a mask that functionally conceals the true speaking face of the man behind the curtain (1999, 28). Clearly, under Chion's rubric it is possible for these partially visible figures to exist in the monophonic environment just as the Wizard does. The thrust of this revelation is as follows: what is so important about the Wizard of Oz is not simply that his powers disappear when his visibly speaking body is revealed; rather, it is essential that along with the revelation of his body comes the revelation of the technological apparatus that allowed for his acousmetric status. This points to the crux of the *acousmêtre* as a cinematic figure: it exists to offer plausibility to a situation that should expose the cinematic apparatus, but does not.

The Lynchian *acousmêtre* flips this script. The Woodsman from Part 8 of Season 3 is perhaps the clearest example, a figure whose power stems from the disembodied voice, but with heightened attention to the technology that makes this disembodiment possible. The Woodsman has the ability to render all who hear his voice unconscious, an act that exerts his power over an entire town. Yet he is far from invisible, or even masked, and the technology he uses to make his voice heard across a broad geographical area is plain to see. If the Woodsman were the Wizard of Oz, the revelation of his use of the radio broadcast system to cast his spell would have dissolved his power. Instead, it is precisely this technology that enables his power to be realized. It should be noted that this is also a highly gendered expression: a male figure commands technology to impose his will on others. But Lynch also flips this script on occasion by opening spaces for women to embody the powers of the visible *acousmêtre*.

Lynch's *Mulholland Drive* (2001) provides an explicit demonstration of how the revelation of the apparatus is what is most important in understanding the power and limits of the *acousmêtre*, featuring a woman at the controls. In the Club Silencio sequence, house magician (Richard Green) lectures the audience (including us) on the illusory nature of live sound, powerfully illustrated by Rebekah Del Rio as she collapses in the middle of a captivating Spanish rendition of Roy Orbison's "Crying." The sound of her voice continues as she's dragged apparently lifeless off the stage, a scene that sends protagonist Betty (Naomi Watts) into a fit of convulsions as she listens, prefiguring the dramatic reconfiguration of the narrative in the film's final act. It is as though the illusion offered by lip-syncing is so powerful that when its mechanics are laid bare it disrupts the very fabrics of space, time, and identity. In this moment, Del Rio reveals that she has always been an *acousmêtre*, that any expectation of natural voice/body relationships in the cinema are flawed. Importantly, Lynch grants Del Rio's voice its supernatural powers along inverse lines to Chion's theorization: it is at the moment that the illusory power of the apparatus is revealed that the voice breaks free of the body, rather than the other way around. And although we have just been given an explicit demonstration of how sound technology can fool us into mistaking the recorded for the real, Schafer's perfect schizophonic situation, we remain bewildered. It must also be noted that this voice/body split is visualized through Del Rio's onscreen death, her lifeless body a precondition for the mystery of her living voice floating free upon the air.

Rebekah Del Rio returned as a performer in the Roadhouse in Part 10 of Season 3 to sing a beautiful version of her collaboration with Lynch and Badalamenti entitled "No Stars." The online fan communities immediately flared up with expressions of disappointment over her apparent use of Autotune, the pitch correction software that many producers employ as much for its aesthetic side-effects as for attempts to smooth over vocal imperfections.[6] Many couldn't hear the use of Autotune in this case, while others said it was so prominent that they couldn't stand to listen to the song. Thus the debate hung off of differences in audile technique, and this skill was inevitably used as a tool for attempting to diminish our assessment of Del Rio's vocal skills. In a bizarre twist, some actually pointed to Del Rio's performance in *Mulholland Drive* as an example of how wonderfully she can sing without technological enhancement, and that the production choices on her appearance in Season 3 were a betrayal of her natural talent. Of course there seems to be a missed point in this line of argumentation somewhere. More to the point, critiques of her use of Autotune here reinforce gender stereotypes around the technologized voice that have been grounded in the figure of the *acousmêtre* all along. With this revelation of technological illusion, Rebekah Del Rio has been killed twice over: once on screen in *Mulholland Drive*, and once on the subreddit forums for *Twin Peaks*. But for Lynch, these technological revelations are not meant to illustrate disempowerment; to the contrary, it is the power of Del Rio's voice carrying on after her death that thrusts open the portal to the alternate dimension that Betty will inhabit for the rest of the film. And her return in *Twin Peaks* evokes the angelic presences that have populated the universe throughout.

The gendered nature of the discourse around disembodied voices in film finds its quintessential expression in Kaja Silverman's *The Acoustic Mirror* (1988). Her chief interest in the book is the representation of sexual difference through approaches to the relationship between voice and body in a specific range of classical Hollywood films. Drawing examples from Chion's *The Voice in Cinema*, Silverman critiques the general premise that underlies the concept of the *acousmêtre*: that attachment of voice to body is most complete in the context of lip-synchronization, and ultimately that "to embody a voice is to feminize it" (Silverman, 50). Silverman argues that disembodied voices in classical Hollywood cinema have tended to be coded male until the point of visual revelation. Here she develops a methodology that uses Chion's writings as an example of the creation of a negative fantasy of female corporealization that she suggests is the same fantasy used by classical Hollywood to contain women's voices within the inferior position of the body. For Silverman, and the psychoanalytic film theory that she works with, the body marks an absence that is distinctly feminine.

Almost two decades later, Britta Sjogren's *Into the Vortex* (2006) challenges Silverman's argument to suggest that a position of disembodiment is not necessarily a position of privilege, and that the corporeal body is not necessarily an inferior place from which to enunciate. Speaking of Silverman's map of the classical Hollywood approach to difference, she says, "the body can be nothing else in this system—always codified as the weighted signifier of lack" (45). Her way out? "Space, I shall argue, constitutes a way to figure, relative to the voice-off, a place of subjectivity not contingent on the body and its visual restrictions" (36). This idea of the body as a space that exists independent of visualization is the critical point at which Sjogren departs from her predecessors whose approach to film sound, she argues, has been too dependent upon reference to the visual. By shifting the idea of the body from the visual to the spatial, Sjogren wants to reclaim certain aspects of classical Hollywood for positive female subjectivity. She critiques Silverman for mapping Chion's postulations about negative feminine corporeality onto classical Hollywood cinema, and in so doing ends up leaving Chion by the wayside (44). For Sjogren, Chion's work does not share with classical Hollywood cinema an inherent positivity toward feminine subjectivity worth trying to excavate.

The crux of Sjogren's argument lies in her engagement with the work of Mary Anne Doane. In addressing what she finds most valuable in Doane's work on the voice Sjogren focuses on the former's notion of how "voice-off" can work to "deepen" the diegesis beyond the visual realm (38). Sjogren draws this idea of a deepened diegesis from a seemingly innocuous observation by Doane: that a potentially embodied voice, heard from a position within diegetic space but not pictured on the screen, serves to help demarcate space beyond fixation upon the visual. Sjogren acknowledges the original function of Doane's claim as an observation about one of the most common functions of offscreen sound, yet finds in it the potential for something more radical: recovering a space that is heterogeneous to the image, a "lost dimension" that, in fact, cannot be visualized (38–39). This is a "deepening" of the diegesis to create a space beyond the visual realm rather than simply extending the possibly visible through offscreen sound. For Sjogren, the lost dimension is that of the body as space rather than as a visually corporeal object.

Despite Sjogren's dismissal of Chion's theorization of the bodiless voice, her reading of Doane actually points to an agreement with Chion on one essential point: that sound and image on film is always a forced marriage that covers a gap that is little explored in its own right. She calls attention to Doane's assertion that asynchronous sound, and the voice in particular, runs the risk of exposing the cinema's dual nature because of its lack of synchronization (Sjogren 2006, 61). Yet the very idea of synchronized sound is somewhat arbitrary, "for one 'syncs up' 'non-sync' sounds with as much diligence as 'sync' sounds in film production practice" (6). This position is fundamentally connected to Chion's view of the duality of sound and image in the cinema that informs his early work on the voice, and his later conclusion that, because of this duality, all speaking voices in the cinema are necessarily disembodied. "If the voice, even strictly synchronized with an image, *always* suggests someone speaking *behind* the visible source, it is because the human voice has no organ" (Chion 2003, 300, my translation). Drawing on the fact that human speech derives from a multitude of transferable body parts, he concludes that these parts are not the true source of the voice, a source that is ultimately not subject to visualization. Like puppets, many of the forced synchronizations have repackaged the *acousmêtre* to a state of visibility that ultimately suggests one thing: that any visible body in the cinema is but a mask concealing the true nature of the speaking body, one without visible organs—a space unto its own (300–301). And so for Sjogren,

"Thinking about sync as also 'other' and 'off' helps one keep in mind the multiple significations generated by any voice (or sound) during a film viewing" (2006, 6). Any sound in a film can be understood as separate from its synchronous image, a space that constitutes an unseeable body. This, in the end, offers a corrective to the negative fantasy of the feminine body as a site of absence, offering new ways of understanding the unbounded positions from which bodies speak.

The lesson in the debates around the *acousmêtre* and the power of the disembodied voice is in its challenge to prevailing ideas about the nature of the "source" of voices that hold powers associated with disembodiment, whether these powers be those of male privilege or something more supernatural. Questioning the idea of vocal source also speaks to the more fundamental critique of the source/copy binary that underlies Schafer's schizophonia and the myth of vanishing mediation more broadly. The Fireman's gramophone stands as an anomaly in Lynch's work, the only record player without a visible disc. The question about the source of the sounds that the gramophone emits is usually handled on the level of originary sound event, yet could just as easily be asked in terms of the medium of transmission. Does the void apparent in the gramophone's cabinet suggest a portal through to the originary sound event, a literalization of vanishing mediation? Or does the missing disc ask us to think about the nature of the medium of transmission here, the displaced materiality? The answer lies in the notion that space itself can constitute a form of corporeality, and that the materiality of this space is the body of the media that we don't see here. And this interpretation opens the door to reassessing the role of Laura Palmer in the *Twin Peaks* universe, herself having been presented across a variety of mediated and embodied forms that continually shift until the final seconds of the Season 3 finale.

Following Sjogren, we must acknowledge that source does not need to be visual in the cinema, that the inevitability of "de-acousmatization" through visualization is a variation on the myth of vanishing mediation. The uniting of visual body with audible voice only serves this myth, and maintaining the distinctiveness of the voice without a body reveals this myth. Cinematic convention has taken the primacy given to origins in the likes of Schafer's thinking and attached this to the primacy of the visual in its representational strategy. The missing disc in The Fireman's gramophone suggests that we don't need to visualize the source of these sounds, just as we don't need to know what that source is. Rather, it's important that they point backward into a deep end of the diegesis where bodies can live without being seen.

Laura Palmer's Schizophonographic Identity

Let's go back to the beginning, to Laura Palmer, who *is* the beginning. Her absence as living character in the original series necessitated emphasis on the police procedural that grew from her death, placing Agent Cooper as the central character. In *Fire Walk with Me*, on the other hand, "the momentum . . . moves from the hero that much of the audience learned to love toward his origins, that is, to the enigmatic Laura, the secret-bearer" (Nochimson 1997, 173). Nochimson's reading of Laura Palmer as origin is compelling in the context of the debates around the source/copy and voice/body binaries that I have been charting here, and is essential to understanding Laura's relationship to Cooper in Season 3. For Nochimson, *Fire Walk with Me* establishes a simultaneous distance and connection between Laura and Cooper, embodied in the film's final image of the two together in the Red Room, she seated and he standing with his arm on her shoulder, an angel floating nearby (196). This distanced connection, or connective distance, combines the seeker (detective) with the secret (victim) into a unified whole, linking the rational mind with its subconscious (196–197). I will modify this psychoanalytical reading to suggest that the distanced connection on display here is between the secret as origin and the seeker as copy whose success is defined by the level of connection it is able to establish with the source. As with Nochimson's description of the final image of Cooper and Laura in *Fire Walk with Me*, the tension between source and copy in sound theory is one of distance versus connection.

The secret in this case, like the very notion of an original sound event, is unattainable. In the first Red Room sequence of Cooper's dream in Episode 2, Laura Palmer (or someone who looks "almost exactly like Laura Palmer") whispers in Cooper's ear. Upon waking, Cooper explains that Laura's whisper revealed the identity of her killer—which he then promptly forgets. This secret, of course, drives the original series forward. This whisper is also a variation on the *acousmêtre*: here we have a speaking body with a voice audible only to a single character, and then only momentarily. This absent voice holds a power associated with the secret to the mystery, embedded within the alternate reality of the Red Room where things move backward and forward at the same time. In the Red Room, the actors' speech and movements are enacted in reverse while being filmed in reverse so that the effect on playback is an uncanny blend of correct linear progression with an impossibly backward articulation. The Red Room is a timeless place of waiting that both Cooper and

Laura visit in their dreams, a place that lays its mediality bare in the overt evidence of technical manipulation that defines the way the space functions. In this environment, Laura's inaudibly disembodied voice, trapped in the otherworldly stasis of the Red Room, is the origin of the *Twin Peaks* saga. Laura and Cooper are connected through this space, but their distance remains. The voice floats free of its source but is altered beyond recognition in its replication in Cooper's memory.

Just before Laura imparted her secret to Cooper, she told him she would see him again in twenty-five years, a now prophetic pronouncement that was clearly a major motivating factor for Lynch and writer Mark Frost to revisit the show around twenty-five years after the original series conclusion. This motivation is acknowledged when the very first thing we see in Part 1 of Season 3 is a flashback to the original instance of Laura speaking that very line of dialogue from the original series. The reference then expands in Part 2 when Cooper, apparently still trapped in the Red Room after his doppelganger escaped in the original series finale, meets Laura Palmer again, both now visibly aged. She approaches Cooper once more to whisper in his ear, and again the audience is not privy to the message. This time, however, the contents of the secret cause Cooper to show visible distress. Upon completion of the whisper, Laura gets swept up in some kind of interdimensional warp, the image of her face distorting in superimposition with violently undulating curtains, another spectral co-registration that precludes her disappearance. Combined with a sound of tumultuous wind and the flapping of heavy fabric, Laura lets out a terrific scream and flies out of the top of the frame. Cooper looks up to watch, and it is not long before he is also violently ejected from the Red Room, beginning the journey that we follow for the remainder of the series. However, we don't see or hear an embodied Laura again until Part 17, when Cooper beams into the scene from *Fire Walk with Me* and stops her from meeting up with her friends in the woods, thereby interrupting the inevitability of her murder later that night.

As described earlier in this chapter, Laura disappears as Cooper attempts to lead her out of the forest, marked by a return of the sounds of The Fireman's gramophone. These sounds are followed immediately by another return: that of the aforementioned scream with wind and fabric rustling that marked Laura's disappearance from the Red Room. In Part 17, this series of events is followed by flashbacks to footage from the pilot episode in which Laura's body disappears from the beach on which it was discovered in the opening moments of the show. The function, here, is to show how Cooper's intervention has altered the past. In Part 18, we find out how this intervention has altered the future. Laura's disappearance from the woods at Cooper's hand is repeated at the beginning of this final installment for Season 3, along with the same sequence of sounds. Then, there is a sudden cut to Cooper seated in the Red Room next to the One-Armed Man (Al Strobel), who asks, appropriately: "Is it future, or is it past?" Shortly after, Laura is shown once again approaching Cooper to whisper in his ear, followed by her ejection from the space, rendered identically to how the scene plays out in Part 2. Formally, this reiteration serves to remind the audience of the source of that scream, wind, and fabric rustling sound that was presented acousmatically in the woods just prior. In turn, setting Laura's disappearance from the woods to these sounds, as well as those of The Fireman's gramophone, connects everything back to the opening scene of Season 3, The Fireman's command for Cooper, and the rest of us, to "Listen to the sounds." The disembodiment of the sounds from the gramophone are now tied explicitly to the removal of Laura's own body from the scene, and of her dead body from the shore the next morning. The conjunction of these two sound events, both calling attention to the absence of their associated bodies, is the climax of the show's turn around the question of The Fireman's missing disc. These missing bodies, permeating the space with their disembodied sounds, point toward Britta Sjogren's deep end of the diegesis: that space which can't be visualized, but where materiality lives nevertheless. It is into this deep end of the diegesis that Cooper ventures in search of Laura.

In Part 18 Cooper is finally able to exit the Red Room of his own accord, where he begins the final journey to discover Carrie Page in Odessa, Texas. When Page answers her door, Cooper addresses her by the name Laura. While Page says she has no memory of that name, she consents to Cooper's invitation to drive her up to the Palmer home in Twin Peaks, clearly in a bit of trouble and needing to escape from Odessa as quickly as possible (emphasized by the dead man seated on her living room couch). Page is hardly living her best life, and is far from fulfilling a dream of freedom from Laura's own fate. It seems both are doomed to cycles of violence at the hands of men.

After a long drive, Cooper and Page arrive at the Palmer house. Cooper expects Sarah Palmer to answer, but finds one Alice Tremond instead (played by Mary Reber, the current real-life owner of the property), who claims that she has never heard of any Palmers in the recent history of the house. Disappointment turns to disorientation as Cooper and Page walk back down the front steps and Cooper asks: "What year is this?" Sarah Palmer's voice is then heard, hollering, "Laura!" from somewhere deep in the diegesis, recalling the early moments of the *Twin Peaks* pilot as she races through the house frantically looking for her missing daughter the morning after her murder. Here the voice is distorted, as it is in the re-iterations of similar auditory samples later in the series and prequel film where they are used over ominous shots of the infamous ceiling fan associated with the transgression of Laura's body within the pretended safety of domestic space. In this way the closing scene of Season 3 loops back to the genesis of the show through the repetition of a sound cue. But nobody can go home again, no matter how much time has passed (or in which direction). Page screams and the house lights go dark, her voice extending out into the disembodied space of the *acousmêtre*, the possibility of her true identity as Laura Palmer tied to the ambiguity of her voice itself in a final schizophonographic disruption of time and space. In the dark, the show lands in the deep end of the diegesis, where Laura continues to live, invisible, like the missing disc in The Fireman's gramophone that signals her disappearance in Season 3.

In 1992, Lynch ended the *Twin Peaks* saga by giving Laura Palmer the space to speak for herself as a living human being in all her complexity. This was the culmination of her gradual shift from media object to embodied person. She began the original series as a figure locked to media forms like the iconic high school portrait as homecoming queen, the cassette tapes she recorded for her psychiatrist, and the videocassette recording of her picnic with best friend Donna (Lara Flynn Boyle). These media were all presented as distinctly single-channel: she is seen in photographs and video, but not heard; she is heard on the cassette tapes, but not seen. Her voice and her image are kept separate, a narrative device that threatens to expose the fundamental disjunction between the two at the basis of the cinematic apparatus. In true Lynchian fashion, these representations of Laura also emphasize the material specificity of the media through which they appear. In these ways Laura functions something like a ghost, her absence creating a strong presence that structured the series (Stalling 2020, 5), emphasized by the material objects that call attention to the fact that she isn't there. Laura is acousmetric both in her disembodied voice and images, her corporeality now dispersed through the myriad townspeople who hold a part of her in their lives, pieces of the mystery that Cooper was sent to assemble. In *Fire Walk with Me*, Laura is freed of her sound and image portraits and allowed to live within the diegesis. For Martha Nochimson, this allows the film to be "liberated from the limitations of the would-be rescuers" (1997, 174); knowing that her fate is inevitable, we are free of any question surrounding the film's ending and can, instead, focus on the details of Laura's life and the complexities of her personality. But in Season 3, the stability that came with the certainty around Laura's status is disrupted again as her death at the hands of her father shifts to an uncertain fate as Carrie Page, a fate that is still bound to violence. Page emerges just as Laura disappears again, reinstating her ghostly status as absent presence, now signaled by the invisibility of the medium in The Fireman's gramophone. What are we to make of this process of shifting Laura's status as media object across the saga as a whole?

Laura Palmer has been all things to all people, and this multiplicity has been embedded within a long history of *Twin Peaks* criticism bound up in the discourse of postmodern style (see, for example, Reeves et al. 1992 and Richardson 2004). For Linnie Blake, Laura Palmer is emblematic of a general patterning to characters in the original *Twin Peaks* series for which "there is no integrity to the self" (2016, 237). Citing the language of Fredric Jameson on the postmodern condition, Blake argues that "Lynch's depiction reveals her as little more than a disparate collection of parts, a code that needs to be broken, or a repository for the secrets of others," rendering her "the putative subject of postmodernity" (237). There is a brutal critique here of the broader moment of American neo-liberalism in which "postmodern ethics provides justification both for the peddling of raped and murdered women as a primetime entertainment and for the adoption of economic policies that benefit only a tiny minority" (237). From her vantage point writing twenty-five years after the original series ended, but before the airing of Season 3, Blake sees the show's "postmodern innovations" in the light of a quarter century of neoliberal effects on the world at large, questioning the role of the series' references to the supernatural in all this: an allusion to the need to uncover the "unspoken truths of our culture," or participation in "flattening history" through its co-registration of multiple times and spaces that render so effectively the play of surfaces without depth that Jameson warns against (243)?

On the surface, Season 3 certainly doesn't do much to assuage these kinds of critiques. The show is arguably more postmodern than ever, identities even more fragmented than they were before, violence proliferating on all levels. For Ryan Diduck, there are simply no positive female characters here either, all the more problematic in light of cultural shifts around movements like #metoo and the rise of Trumpism that erupted co-temporaneously with our return to *Twin Peaks*. With fake news permeating our media feeds and political divisions entrenching, Diduck argues that "beholding ourselves in this fun-house mirror only reflects how distorted and terrifyingly near everything has become—that we are now wedged in a time when it is more comfortable to be lost in illusion that resolved in certainty" (2017). In this critique, Diduck mirrors the earlier worries over the rise of postmodernism and its simulacra, as well as critiques of the instability around the Laura Palmer character.

Fredric Jameson himself was a critic of Lynch's work as part of his development of a more general condemnation of postmodern society. In *The Cultural Logic of Late Capitalism* (1991), Jameson argues that the fragmentation, isolation, and surface reassemblage of experience characteristic of postmodernism amounts to a loss of historical context, a breakdown in the signifying chain of memory that schizophrenics exhibit in the form of "a series of pure and unrelated presents in time" (27). Jameson actually uses this negative associational formulation to critique *Blue Velvet* (1986) (294–296), a film very close to the original *Twin Peaks* series in terms of Lynch's approach to period melange. Importantly, Jameson's take also reflects (albeit less explicitly articulated) R. Murry Schafer's own critiques of emerging postmodernism in his use of the term schizophonia itself. In particular, Schafer's concern over spatiotemporal confusion, as well as his negative reference to neurodivergence (like the condition of schizophrenia), is also well in line with the emergence of critiques around postmodernity and its effects. Both Schafer and Jameson privilege the idea that time is linear and should be considered on hierarchical terms: anything experienced in the present is built upon a foundation of the past and the two should never conflate. In short, they both exhibit a sort of context worship dependent upon clear lines that connect times and spaces together, not unlike the argument for indexicality in Durham and Peters' explanation of phonography's advantage over digital technologies. It seems no coincidence that the postmodern effects that Jameson critiques arose in the age of the digital turn in music reproduction. I'll wager that both Jameson and Schafer, if forced to make a choice, would have preferred vinyl over digital formats for their music listening.

For others, however, Laura Palmer's representation has been deeply embedded in the cultures of the times, a necessary reflection of reality that enables engagement beyond the superficiality of postmodern formalism. Kate Rennebohm argues that while Lynch's representational politics are often questionable, he nevertheless has always had a strong sense of the cultural moment, as true with Season 3 as ever: "This shift toward the colder and crueller aspects of Lynch's universe is as much a matter of the current cultural climate as it is the tempermental proclivities of the creator.... The earlier *Twin Peaks* mined power from revealing the horror beneath '80s fantasies of an idealized postwar America, even as it venerated the Edenic vision; the new *Twin Peaks* finds its horror in the fact that we can no longer conjure such visions of innocence at all" (63). As for Lynch's treatment of women, Rennebohm points out that his often fetishistic approach "has in the past been accompanied (and, some would argue, justified) by an overt thematizing of how men transform women into ownable, consumable images; the depiction of Laura Palmer in the original *Twin Peaks*, as an image subject to everyone's interpretation but her own, is the supreme example" (64). Here the emphasis on Laura's status as media object serves as a reflection on the process of objectification itself, another aspect of how Lynch's interest in media materiality draws a line to deeper recesses of the worlds these media inhabit. To this I would add that Laura's objectification also reinforced the fact that she did have secrets of her own that could never be revealed through her mediation, and that much of what *was* revealed by this mediation revolved around the secrets of others projected onto her. Fidelity between source and copy, you might say, is as much about the listener as it is about the sound.

Laura Palmer's objectification, too, shifted in *Fire Walk with Me*, a film in which she finally had real agency, despite her fate being governed by the patriarchal power that permeates her world (Janisse 2017). For Sara Swain, "Laura's suffering was never meaningless" and the feature film "gave her pain both significance and scale" (2017). One might argue that the lack of integrity of the self continues in the film with Laura's famously erratic personality on display, shifting dramatically between a variety of moods and modes of self-expression (enabled by Sheryl Lee's stunning performance), qualities that are often associated with schizophrenic tendencies. But for many, this aspect of Laura's character was all too grounded in familiar reality. Courtenay Stallings argues that Laura's characterization in the film clearly depicts symptoms of PTSD common to sexual abuse victims, particularly dissociation (2020, 11). In her book *Laura's Ghost: Women Speak about Twin Peaks*, Stallings chronicles female identification with Laura around her abuse, and the fact that she rings true to reality on this point poses a serious challenge to critiques of her character as the depthless object of postmodern superficiality. For Stallings, the show's supernatural trappings did not gloss over the horror of the reality of incest (the way an *acousmêtre* glosses over the seam between the dual apparatus of the cinema). Rather, the supernatural element made the real horror all the more hard-hitting, because it was tied to Laura's perspective. She experienced horror, and so must we (9). For Sheryl Lee herself, Laura's legacy is that she puts the all-too-common reality of her situation on full display, an important step toward open dialogue about sexual abuse (12).

So what of Carrie Page and the disruption of the narrative line in *Fire Walk with Me*? It is entirely understandable that many would find the conclusion to Season 3 to be deeply unsatisfying. It offered neither the objectified Laura of everyone's personal interpretation, nor the humanized Laura in her own voice with which so many have identified. We don't know Carrie Page, and we don't know where Laura went when Page entered the picture, so the agency that Laura exhibited in *Fire Walk with Me* is stripped in Season 3. While the feature film required the inevitability of her death, a popular reading of the conclusion is that, at the very least, her sacrifice thwarted the malevolent spirit Bob from inhabiting her the way he did her father and, later, Agent Cooper (one of the main threads of Season 3). Further, Carrie Page clearly holds trauma, so she does not stand as evidence that Cooper's intervention allowed Laura to be free of that, either. Cooper as the seeker has failed. In this, however, Laura's power as bearer of her own secret is reinstated. We will never know Carrie Page's story, and that is Laura Palmer's new secret, a return to the power of the original series' mystery, now as conclusion rather than introduction.

Laura persists, and it is on her image—and sound—that Season 3 concludes. "The original series—now in retrospect—was never just about her devastating absence. It was about her persistent presence in the negative space she left behind. . . . As the origin of and impetus for the series, then, it makes sense that [Season 3] would entrust her with the last word" (Swain 2017). This last word, of course, is a scream, and its resonance carries over from the terrifying close-up of Page's face to the Palmer residence going dark and finally to black screen, a final detachment of voice from body that recalls Chion's *acousmêtre*. Courtenay Stallings argues that Page's final scream is her way of acknowledging that Laura's trauma, symbolized by the Palmer house where so much of it originated, speaks to her own unknown trauma from Odessa. Page's story is that "of a lost and traumatized woman who is roused by a dark memory when she hears her mother call out her name" (2020, 282). Page and Palmer create a loop that simultaneously takes us back to the origins of the Twin Peaks saga and points toward its endless extension. Page's story is at once unknowable and already known. Her presence challenges the sanctity of the idea of the "original," based as she is on a rewriting of the original narrative arc for the series. At the same time, Page reinstates the mystery at the heart of the original series as the substance of Season 3's conclusion.

Carrie Page illustrates the conundrum of fidelity itself that has run through the various threads I've have charted in this chapter (and across the book as a whole). Fidelity implies a strong match between source and copy. Schafer's notion of schizophonia suggests the violation of the sanctity of uniqueness in any originary sound event, a violation at the heart of critiques of postmodernity's proliferations of simulacra as well. If we follow Rick Altman and James Lastra, however, there can be no such thing as an original sound event because sound lives in space and space requires positionality. Every sound carries with it the story of its propagation through space and through technologies of transmission. Fidelity to an original sound event cannot exist because the point of comparison between copy and source is subject to the specifics of position, often impossible to pin down. However, it is essential that we recognize that this does not doom representation to the world of the simulacrum, the copy of a copy of a copy for which no original ever existed. The simulacrum is the surface play of an entirely virtual reality that pays no reference to the context of the real world, the critique of the postmodern condition levied at Lynch in general and *Twin Peaks* in particular. What Carrie Page shows us, rather, is that the instability of origin need not hinder a deep rooting in reality's complex depth, just as the digital world's break from the indexical processes of pre-digital recording need not break it entirely free from its capacity to reach back to that reality. The absence inside The Fireman's gramophone is an invitation to think past the idea that an original is impossible and into the invisible space of the deep end of the diegesis, where bodies live in all their grounded materiality, but in ways that demand recognition of our own positionality in experiencing them.

The Fireman's disc has disappeared, as the material surface of celluloid has disappeared from Lynch's work. But in this digital ether there lies a deeper, less visible materiality, the depth of the diegesis into which Laura Palmer's voice reaches, activating the space, and revealing its surfaces. The gramophone therefore functions as remediator: the void left by the apparently missing media is shown to have a material dimension of its own in the way that it opens up the alternate spaces for Laura's story to play out. Laura's re-emergence as Carrie Page is another articulation of remediation, her life becoming newly material again. At the same time, her voice carrying over into the darkness to close the series insists that this materiality need not be bound to a specific body in order to be recognized, that she can speak from the position of the *acousmêtre*, a body that is not containable in its multiplicity. In this sense, Laura, through Carrie, offers the possibility of female agency in the position of vocal disembodiment.

Laura's schizophonographic identity lies in the way that her voice exceeds the surface materiality that has governed Lynch's record players across *Twin Peaks* and his larger body of work. The absence of phonographic surface, here, is the marker of how Laura speaks across the boundaries of co-registrant times and spaces. Wrapped up in the idea of schizophonographics, then, is that the absence of explicit depiction of phonography can serve as the grounding that Laura's absent presence, her ghostly status, brings to the Twin Peaks universe. Laura has always articulated from this space, which depends upon one's position within it to interpret. This doesn't mean the space has no voice of its own, but that its voice cannot be pinned down and stabilized. This is agency, Laura as *acousmêtre*, revealed by the void at the heart of the gramophone. Laura is not the missing media in this equation; rather, the missing media reveals what Laura has always been, regardless of mediation or embodiment: present.

Coda: Immaterial Durability

An important and overlooked detail about the Palmer turntable in the original series is that it is both vintage and modern. While CDs had taken root in the late 1980s, LPs were still in mass production and many people did not make the switch right away, particularly the older generations. The clearest defining characteristic of the Palmer record player is its floor-standing and top-loading cabinet from the early twentieth century. The record player inside the cabinet, however, is a contemporary 80s deck. This modern gear housed in an older cabinet is similar to how today's digital audio devices, like Bluetooth streamers, are often wrapped in enclosures that recall older media like tabletop radios. The Fireman's gramophone could be seen the same way: an old gramophone container, complete with horn, housing a digital transmission device that we cannot see. This remediation is crucial to understanding the line that Season 3 draws back to the original series: old realities in new spaces.

It is also important that we no longer see any sign of phonography in the Palmer house in Season 3, the living room turntable replaced by a large flat screen TV that occupies much of Sarah Palmer's attention during the scenes set inside the house. The function of the Palmer TV, however, is similar to the record player that preceded it. It is a device prone to glitches that reveal its materiality, as when Sarah Palmer is shown watching a boxing match from the 1950s, a short segment of which is looping inexplicably and indefinitely. This is one articulation of the way that digital technologies are shown to be imperfect and unreliable in Season 3, instabilities that Jeffrey Fallis and T. Kyle King tie to the non-linearity of the digital realm that permeates the entire production from the hypertextual quality of the narrative itself to the non-linear editing process through which the show was constructed (new since the last time any new *Twin Peaks* material was edited in 1992) (2021, 53–55). But as we've seen, this kind of emphasis on technology's material imperfection, opening up spaces of spatio-temporal uncertainty, runs throughout the Twin Peaks saga and Lynch's work as a whole. It was to the sound of the Palmer turntable looping in the end groove that Leland, possessed by Bob, was revealed as Laura's killer as he murdered Maddy Ferguson in Episode 14. Further, it is perfectly logical that Lynch would continue his emphasis on such materiality in the digital age, for the immateriality of digital technology is a fiction perpetuated by metaphors like the "cloud" that mask the vastness of the material infrastructure that underlies our wireless connectivity in the twenty-first century. The images of Sarah Palmer engrossed in her endlessly repeating television screen in Season 3 speak to the continuum across the digital boundary line, which culminates in one final instance of looping in the Palmer living room in Part 17, perhaps the series' definitive articulation of Laura Palmer's own status as simultaneously amorphous and immutable.

Immediately following Laura's disappearance from the woods and the vanishing of her body from the shore, and before Cooper embarks on his final journey to find Carrie Page and return to the Palmer home, we see Sarah Palmer one last time. A wide shot of the living room rests for a long take as we hear Sarah moaning offscreen. The TV is off and the famous high school portrait of Laura is visible in the foreground, sitting next to a lamp on a circular end table, possibly the very same table from which Leland picked up the photo and danced with it in Episode 2 of the original series. After what feels like an eternity, the source of Sarah's distress unclear as her anguished vocalizations grow increasingly intense (and disarmingly similar to those emitted by Leland while he danced), she finally enters the frame, picks up the portrait, and walks toward the middle of the room. In a gesture that recalls her swiping the needle off the record to try and get Leland to stop his spinning all those years ago, she violently whacks some other photos off another side table before dropping to her knees and placing the portrait on the floor. Her swiping action cues an as yet unheard looping sound effect that stems from a source unknown but echoes the end-groove looping that scored Maddy's murder in this very spot. Here Sarah will attempt to annihilate the memory of her own daughter as she grabs a liquor bottle from the nearby coffee table and begins smashing the photo with all her might. In this moment, two prior instances of phonographic materiality merge, both resulting in the spilling of blood.

Laura may be gone from Twin Peaks, but Sarah can't make her picture disappear. No matter how hard she hits it, only the glass of the picture frame shatters while the print remains intact, another callback to Episode 2 when the frame's glass broke as Leland and Sarah fought over it. Sarah's agitated smashing is augmented with glitchy jump cuts and reverse photography that emphasize the looping of time itself, the glass continually reconstituting only to be smashed again while Laura's image remains stable underneath. The destruction of the frame that contains the image holds great symbolic power. Her high school portrait was always presented as framed in glass in the original series, but in the opening credits to Season 3 the image is already set free, floating in the mist hanging in the trees above Twin Peaks. When we see the portrait materialize within the diegesis, it is as an unframed print in a police evidence locker, taped to a cardboard backing. These gestures of unframing lead toward this final moment in which Sarah unbinds the image of her daughter, set to a sound effect that evokes the phonography at the heart of the tragedy in which the Palmer household is steeped. Phonographic materiality haunts the living room as Sarah attempts to banish the likeness of her daughter to the immaterial ether.

This scene marks the central tension of Season 3, its navigation of the beloved memory of the original show and the very different media world that we're living in today. It is essential that this scene falls directly between the end of Laura's story and the introduction of Carrie Page. Laura in that photo is both immutable and unknowable. That originary image can never be destroyed, even as the show destroyed it, freeing it from the container of the frame and setting Laura on new paths. But, for better or worse, nothing can destroy the memory of what she was before and this memory persists right through to the final frames of the series. The auditory callbacks of both the looping turntable and Sarah's blood curdling vocalizations suggest both the violence of Sarah's trauma over Laura's death and that, as the wife of her daughter's killer, she was perhaps complicit all along. Or that she is becoming complicit in the new reality shaped by Season 3, reshaping both her daughter's fate as well as her own. If we follow Mark Frost to his book *Twin Peaks: The Final Dossier* (2017), Sarah is, in fact, the girl from Part 8 who played host to the winged reptilian spawn as the Woodsman broadcast his hypnotic poem over the crackle of the KPJK turntable (136). As such, she is not only positioned as a victim herself, but also as another instance of Palmer possession by the forces responsible for unleashing Bob upon the world. When Carrie Page screams to close the Season 3 finale, it functions as a response to the sound of Sarah Palmer calling out the name "Laura" from somewhere deep in the diegesis. Does Page's scream express the horror of recognizing her true identity as Laura Palmer triggered by the sound of her mother's voice? Or perhaps a deeper recognition of Sarah Palmer's own shifting plight, never before considered? Or the reaffirmation of her own trauma as Carrie Page? All possibilities exist not only simultaneously as parallel tracks but are intricately connected through the narrative fabric woven by Season 3. As Page's final scream persists into the darkness, it loops back to the opening moments of the original series just as it points outward toward as-yet-uncharted territory. The darkness that closes the series is the darkness inside the cabinet of The Fireman's gramophone, a space no less material for being invisible, the space from which Laura's story has always been spoken, and from which it will continue to speak on its own terms.

References

Altman, Rick. 1992. "The Material Heterogeneity of Recorded Sound." In *Sound Theory, Sound Practice*, edited by Rick Altman, 15–31. New York: Routledge.

Anderson, Tim. 2008. "As if History was Merely a Record: The Pathology of Nostalgia and the Figure of the Recording in Contemporary Popular Cinema." *Music, Sound and the Moving Image* 2, no. 1: 51–76.

Batcho, James. 2018. *Malick's Unseeing Cinema: Memory, Time and Audibility*. New York: Palgrave Macmillan.

Bolter, Jay David, and Richard Grusin. 1999. *Remediation: Understanding New Media*. Cambridge: MIT Press.

Blake, Linnie. 2016. "Trapped in the Hysterical Sublime: *Twin Peaks*, Postmodernism, and the Neoliberal Now." In *Return to Twin Peaks: New Approaches to Materiality, Theory, and Genre on Television*, edited by Jeffrey Andrew Weinstock and Catherine Spooner, 229–245. New York: Palgrave Macmillan.

Chion, Michel. 1994. *AudioVision: Sound on Screen*. Translated by Claudia Gorbman. New York: Columbia University Press.

Chion, Michel. 1995. *David Lynch*. Translated by Robert Julian. London: British Film Institute.

Chion, Michel. 1999. *The Voice in Cinema*. Translated by Claudia Gorbman. New York: Columbia University Press.

Chion, Michel. 2003. *Un art sonore, le cinéma: histoire, esthétique, poétique*. Cahiers du cinéma.

Diduck, Ryan. 2017. "Get Coffee, Get Naked, & Die; or, Why I Prefer *Pawn Stars* to *Twin Peaks: The Return*." *Offscreen* 21, nos. 11–12 (December). https://offscreen.com/view/get-coffee-get-naked-and-die

Doane, Mary Anne. 1985. "The Voice in Cinema: The Articulation of Body and Space." In *Film Sound: Theory and Practice*, edited by Elisabeth Weis and John Belton, 162–176. New York: Columbia University Press.

Fallis, Jeffrey, and T. Kyle King. 2021. "Lucy Finally Understands How Cellphones Work: Ambiguous Digital Technologies in *Twin Peaks: The Return* and its Fan Communities." In *Critical Essays on Twin Peaks: The Return*, edited by Antonio Sanna, 53–68. New York: Palgrave Macmillan.

Frost, Mark. 2017. *Twin Peaks: The Final Dossier*. New York: Flatiron Books.

Garwood, Ian. 2016. "Vinyl Noise and Narrative in CD-Era Indiewood." In *The Palgrave Handbook to Music and Sound Design in Screen Media: Integrated Soundtracks*, edited by Liz Greene and Danijela Kulezic-Wilson, 245–260. New York: Palgrave Macmillan.

Getman, Jessica. 2021. "Playing with Sound: Fan Engagement with the Soundtrack of *Twin Peaks: The Return* (2017)." In *Music in Twin Peaks: Listen to the Sounds*, edited by Reba A. Wissner and Katherine M. Reed, 34–47. New York: Routledge.

Gitelman, Lisa. 1999. *Scripts, Grooves and Writing Machines: Representing Technology in the Edison Era*. Stanford: Stanford University Press.

Gorbman, Claudia. 1987. *Unheard Melodies: Narrative Film Music*. Bloomington: Indiana University Press.

Greene, Liz. 2012. "Bringing Vinyl into the Digital Domain: Aesthetics in David Lynch's *Inland Empire* (2006)." *The New Soundtrack* 2, no. 2: 97–111.

Greene, Liz, and Danijela Kulezic-Wilson, eds. 2016. *The Palgrave Handbook to Music and Sound Design in Screen Media: Integrated Soundtracks*. New York: Palgrave Macmillan.

Gunning, Tom. 2001. "Doing for the Eye What the Phonograph Does for the Ear." In *The Sounds of Early Cinema*, edited by Richard Abel and Rick Altman, 16–19. Bloomington: Indiana University Press.

Jameson, Fredric. 1991. *Postmodernism: Or, the Cultural Logic of Late Capitalism*. Indiana: Duke University Press.

Janisse, Kier-La. 2017. "In Heaven Everything is Fine: Murder and Martyrdom in the Lynchverse, from Peter Ivers to Laura Palmer." *Offscreen* 21, nos. 11–12 (December). https://offscreen.com/view/in-heaven-everything-is-fine

Jenkins, Henry F. 2006. *Convergence Culture: Where Old and New Media Collide*. New York: New York University Press.

Jordan, Randolph. 2007. "Case Study: Film Sound, Acoustic Ecology, and Performance in Electroacoustic Music." In *Music, Sound and Multimedia: From the Live to the Virtual*, edited by Jamie Sexton, 121–141. Edinburgh: University of Edinburgh Press.

Jordan, Randolph. 2009. "The Visible Acousmêtre: Voice, Body and Space Across the Two Versions of *Donnie Darko*." *Music, Sound and the Moving Image* 3, no. 1 (Spring): 47–70.

Jordan, Randolph. 2012. "Schizophonographics: First Cut." *Of Sound Mind* (October 26). http://www.randolphjordan.com/schizophone/schizophonographics-first-cut-2/

Kalinak, Kathryn. 1995. "'Disturbing the Guests with This Racket': Music and *Twin Peaks*." In *Full of Secrets: Critical Approaches to Twin Peaks*, edited by David Lavery, 82–92. Detroit: Wayne State University Press.

Kane, Dean. 2014. *Sound Unseen: Acousmatic Sound in Theory and Practice*. New York: Oxford University Press.

Kerins, Mark. 2011. *Beyond Dolby (Stereo): Cinema in the Digital Sound Age*. Bloomington: Indiana University Press.

Kittler, Friedrich A. 1999. *Gramophone, Film, Typewriter*. Translated by Geoffrey Winthrop-Young and Michael Wutz. Stanford: Stanford University Press.

Kulezic-Wilson, Danijela. 2015. *The Musicality of Narrative Film*. New York: Palgrave Macmillan.

Kulezic-Wilson, Danijela. 2021. "The Erotics of Cinematic Listening." In *The Oxford Handbook of Cinematic Listening*, edited by Carlo Cenciarelli, 368–384. New York: Oxford University Press.

Lastra, James. 2000. *Sound Technology and the American Cinema*. New York: Columbia University Press.

Leeder, Murray. 2017. *The Modern Supernatural and the Beginnings of Cinema*. New York: Palgrave Macmillan.

Mactaggart, Allister. 2010. *The Film Paintings of David Lynch: Challenging Film Theory*. Bristol: Intellect.

Nochimson, Martha. 1997. *The Passion of David Lynch: Wild at Heart in Hollywood*. Austin: University of Texas Press.

Peters, John Durham. 1999. *Speaking into the Air: A History of the Idea of Communication*. Chicago: Chicago University Press.

Reeves, Jimmie L., et al. 1995. "Postmodernism and Television: Speaking of *Twin Peaks*." In *Full of Secrets: Critical Approaches to Twin Peaks*, edited by David Lavery, 173–195. Detroit: Wayne State University Press.

Rennebohm, Kate. 2017. "You Can't Go Home Again: *Twin Peaks: The Return*." *Cinemascope* 71 (Summer): 62–64.

Richardson, John. 2004. "*Laura* and *Twin Peaks*: Postmodern Parody and the Musical Reconstruction of the Absent Femme Fatale." In *The Cinema of David Lynch: American Dreams, Nightmare Visions*, edited by Erica Sheen and Annette Davison, 77–92. London: Wallflower Press.

Rothenbuhler, Eric W., and John Durham Peters. 1997. "Defining Phonography: An Experiment in Theory." *Musical Quarterly* 81, no. 2 (Summer): 252.

Schafer, R. Murray. 1977. *The Tuning of the World*. Toronto: McClelland and Stewart.

Schwartz, Hillel. 2011. *Making Noise: From Babel to the Big Band and Beyond*. New York: Zone Books.

Sconce, Jeffrey. 2000. *Haunted Media: Electronic Presence from Telegraphy to Television*. Durham, NC: Duke University Press.

Silverman, Kaja. 1988. *The Acoustic Mirror: The Female Voice in Psychoanalysis and Cinema*. Bloomington: Indiana University Press.

Sjogren, Britta. 2006. *Into the Vortex: Female Voice and Paradox in Film*. Chicago: University of Illinois Press.

Stallings, Courtenay. 2020. *Laura's Ghost: Women Speak About* Twin Peaks. Columbus: Fayetteville Mafia Press.

Sterne, Jonathan. 2003. *The Audible Past: Cultural Origins of Sound Reproduction*. Durham, NC: Duke University Press.

Swain, Sara. 2017. "Circling the Void: *Twin Peaks* Returns." *Offscreen* 21, nos. 11–12 (December). https://offscreen.com/view/circling-the-void-twin-peaks-return

Van Elferen, Isabella. 2012. "Dream Timbre: Notes on Lynchian Sound Design." In *Music, Sound and Filmmakers: Sonic Style in Cinema*, edited by James Wierzbicki, 175–188. New York: Routledge.

Wilson, Steven. 2021. "David Lynch's Metaphysical Sound Design: The Acousmatic Personification of Judy." In *Music in Twin Peaks: Listen to the Sounds*, edited by Reba A. Wissner and Katherine M. Reed, 149–162. New York: Routledge.

Wissner, Reba A., and Katherine M. Reed, eds. 2021. *Music in Twin Peaks: Listen to the Sounds*. New York: Routledge.

5
Unsettled Listening
Tracking Vancouver's Contested Acoustic Profiles across Media

A mother and son of First Nations ancestry sit in the waiting area of a methadone clinic in the Downtown Eastside neighborhood of Vancouver, British Columbia, Canada. Their attention is directed toward an offscreen TV. A cartoon plays, featuring an instrumental version of "I've Been Working on the Railroad" that mingles with the operating sounds of the clinic and ambience from the street outside. The tune is punctuated by a metal clinking sound at the beginning of each bar, calling to mind the sound of driving railway spikes that once echoed just down the street, the City of Vancouver having been incorporated in 1886 as the western terminus of the Canadian Pacific Railway (CPR), accelerating the cycle of state-sanctioned erasure of Indigenous title to the land. The familiar voice of Bugs Bunny chimes in: "Uh, what's all the hubbub, bub?"[1]

As it happens, there is much hubbub indeed. The scene appears one third of the way through Antoine Bourges' film *East Hastings Pharmacy* (2012), a quasi-documentary set entirely within this clinic, staging interactions between methadone patients (played by locals and informed by their real-life experiences) and the resident pharmacist (played by actress Shauna Hansen). Vancouver's Downtown Eastside, notorious for its concentration of transients and public drug use, is also home to the largest community of Indigenous peoples within the city limits—a product of the long history of dispossession in the surrounding areas that forced people from many First Nations, with no place else to go, to concentrate in the heart of the inner city. The juxtaposition of the auditory railway construction motif and the image of the Native couple in the methadone clinic is profoundly unsettling. The fact that we are hearing a location recording of this couple listening to a Hollywood fabrication of the sounds that symbolize their loss of title to the Vancouver area is all too appropriate in a city that would come to be known as Hollywood North—more famous as a stand-in for myriad other parts of the world than for representing itself—its regional specificity endlessly overwritten with narratives that hide the city and its Indigenous presence from public awareness. The film's status as independent production amidst the environment of regular industrial shooting in the area is marked by the intersection of studio-fabricated sound effects and direct sound recording here, further complicated by the film's own hybrid of fiction and documentary modes. This hybridity speaks to the complexity of overlapping filmmaking practices in Vancouver today, a situation that mirrors the intersecting claims to land use and cultural propriety within the streets of Vancouver's Downtown Eastside. As such, this example stands as a rich indicator of the ways in which listening can attune us to the complex relationships between films and the places in which they are produced.

In this chapter I extend the premises of acoustic profiling, that have governed all my analyses in this book, to function as a mode of listening to soundtracks in an unsettling way so that we may better hear the integration of film and place. Vancouver makes a particularly fruitful case study to explore how this works. In her essay "Thoughts on Making Places: Hollywood North and the Indigenous City," filmmaker Kamala Todd stresses how media can assist the process of re-inscribing local stories into Vancouver's consciousness (2013). *East Hastings Pharmacy* is one such example, lending some screen time to urban Natives in the twenty-first century city. But Todd reminds us that audiences also have a responsibility "to learn the stories of the land" that have been actively erased in dominant media practices, and to bring this knowledge to our experience of the city in all its incarnations (9). Todd's call resonates with a process that critical geographer Nicholas Blomley calls "unsettling the city" in his book of the same name (2004). Blomley reveals Vancouver as a site of continual contestation and mobility across generations and cultural groups, and calls for an "unsettled" approach that can account for the multiple overlapping patterns of use that are concealed by "settled" concepts of bounded property. He advocates for ways of thinking about sites in the city through histories that have been obscured, a way to "re-place" them by revealing the places that they were and continue to be underneath the veneer of settlement (145). While Blomley doesn't address sound in his book, Dylan Robinson offers a corollary listening practice extending from Martin Daughtry's concept of "contrapuntal perception (hearing simultaneous contextual layers)," reoriented as a "practice of oscillation (moving between layers of positionality)" in order to "find greater levels of relationships between the strata of positionality" (2020, 60). In these spirits, I will use the term *unsettled listening* (Jordan 2014b) to describe a process of experiencing the city's contextual layers by way of the layers of positionality presented in media objects. An intermedial analysis of the city invites continual movement through a variety of listening positions framed by others so that we may not only learn to hear from the ears of others, but also to understand our own relationship to these alternate positions. Rick Altman taught us to hear any given sound event as a narrative by listening for the auditory markers of its propagation through physical space, and recording media, over time (1992). Unsettled listening invites us to hear through these physical properties of mediatic space to the resonating stories revealed by the overlapping and contradictory histories and patterns of use to which these spaces are put, all too often unacknowledged in the wake of settler colonialism.

The practice of acoustic profiling will now move into the domain of assessing community representation in films that engage, in one way or another, with real-world locations and the people that live there. Here I combine acoustic ecology's notion of the acoustic profile with a more general definition of profiling as a means of extrapolating information about something based on its known characteristics. As discussed in the introduction to this book, acoustic ecology has used the idea of acoustic profile to define the spatial boundaries of acoustic communities (Truax 2001, 66), bound together by common experience of the same sounds, as in the way parishes of old have been defined by the auditory limits of the church bell. Barry Truax extends this idea of acoustic community to examine not only listening but also communication by way of sound, offering a model for exploring the rich interplay of sounds within the limits of the profile that defines the area in which community exists. However, as I will discuss shortly, the geographical bias of this approach frequently excludes attention to the diversity that might exist within the community in question. When defining a community according to sonic geography it is thus essential to consider the constituents of that community and what it is that they are hearing when listening together to a given sound. Therefore, my aim here is to plug the static object of the acoustic profile into the active process of community profiling that attends to the intersectional diversity within a given geography.

In the pages that follow, I elaborate on how acoustic profiling works to unsettle listening through an intermedial analysis of Vancouver by way of its representation across a variety of media, particularly the sound documentation of the World Soundscape Project (WSP), the foundational project of the field of acoustic ecology that was born at Simon Fraser University (SFU) in the early 1970s under the direction of composer

R. Murray Schafer. As exemplified in *East Hastings Pharmacy*, the sound of trains is particularly loaded in Vancouver, and these sounds figured prominently in the WSP's construction of Vancouver's sonic identity. Their sound-based methodology yields valuable ways of thinking about urban issues and their manifestation in the media. Yet their mythology reveals a Eurocentric nostalgia for the days of settler colonialism, particularly when listening to the sound of industrial transportation. I demonstrate how listening to the sound of trains across the history of Vancouver's film production, informed by both the strengths and weaknesses of the WSP's methodology, yields an alternative history of the city's soundscape on film that reveals dimensions of local film practices and their intersection with the city's famous diversity unheard in the documentation of the WSP. By bringing issues of auditory representation from film and media studies to bear on the practices of the WSP, I unsettle their recordings to reveal the richness of the city's urban complexity and the ideologies governing their practices of documentation. This intermedial approach opens a new set of media documents to the WSP's ongoing research into the soundscape of Vancouver past and present, while offering film sound studies a new set of tools to listen to films across a variety of research areas.

I begin this chapter by detailing the process of acoustic profiling more specifically around issues of community representation, and then considering how one particularly loaded sound, that of the train, casts its profile across Vancouver—and British Columbia at large—through a variety of media representations. I start with an examination of how the WSP has staged the presence of train sounds in their archival recordings, literature, phonographic recordings, and radio broadcasts of the early 1970s to demonstrate their single-minded approach to defining one branch of Canadian culture around an imagined acoustic community defined by the shared experience of this sound. I will then move to an examination of three sets of films that make prominent use of trains to build an alternative history of their audibility in the Vancouver soundscape to inform my running critique of the WSP I'll start with representations of early twentieth century train life in and around Vancouver and the tendency toward whitewashing the relationship between this transportation technology and the Indigenous, Chinese, and Japanese laborers who laid the tracks and were then forgotten. Next I consider films that engage with this period through to the 1960s with an emphasis on the shifting status of labor around trains, from booming resource economy through Depression-era hardship and then the conflicting effects of urbanization in a city that increasingly rewarded white collar labor while pushing the resource industry well out of town, leaving a certain class of people stranded in the process. We'll then land back in the early 1970s to consider films by David Rimmer and Sylvia Spring that engage with the lived reality of downtown Vancouver in the same era that the WSP was making their first wave of recordings to reveal a dramatically more heterogeneous understanding of the city and its sociopolitical dynamics as they coalesced around the presence of trains. Finally I conclude by considering how the disappearance of train sounds from the Vancouver environment, lamented by the WSP as a precursor to the loss of the community they imagined, actually marks a return of Indigenous title to lands once taken away by the railway itself.

Acoustic Profiling

In the previous chapters I have worked through various angles on the concept of fidelity, shifting its hi-fi stereo culture emphasis on the notion of media transparency through to the authenticity opened up by performative documentary practices, the faithfulness of empathetic friendship articulated by sonic space, and the myth of vanishing mediation revealed by schizophonography in the cinema. In this final chapter I'd like to propose a new take, one that is tied specifically to a peculiar conflation of ideas in Schafer's evocation of the language of mid-century hi-fi stereo culture. Early acoustic ecology held the idea of schizophonia as a negative consequence of the electroacoustical transmission of sound, a position that has been roundly critiqued for its failure to account for the medial nature of human engagement with the world. Particularly interesting, however, is how schizophonia is bound up with Schafer's notion of the hi-fi soundscape, equating fidelity not only with a strong signal-to-noise ratio but also with the ability of sounds to travel a long way in an environment without being masked by density (1977, 43). The greater the distance from which we can hear any given sound, the greater the fidelity of the sound environment. This is an instructive conflation of fidelity and geographical range when considering the value of the acoustic profile concept: fidelity, in this construction, can map community. For my purposes here, this notion of fidelity can account for the way that sound within a given acoustic profile can articulate the communities that hear it.

Acoustic profiling formalizes the process of framing the issue of fidelity around the goal of unsettling a given geographical region to reveal continually shifting and multiple listener groups within. When applied to the analysis of sound media, the task is to hear how sound is used to establish a location, and then assess how faithful the staging of sound within this location might be to the communities that occupy the space. Tying the idea of the acoustic profile to the notion of faithful representation of a listening community offers a way of assessing fidelity on the basis of unsettling. As such, acoustic profiling as a mode of listening in film involves a cluster of activities. First, identify how a particular sound—or set of sounds—articulates the boundaries of a geographical region through its acoustic horizon, and what communities occupy this space. Second, in any given film or media produced in this region, listen for moments where auditory extension is used to define this acoustic profile. Third, identify how the spatial signature helps define the geographic particularity of these sounds and the point-of-audition from which these sounds are being presented. Fourth, identify possible ideological listening positions that the presentation of the sounds construct or refer to. Fifth, compare and contrast differing possible perspectives through the analysis of other media materials that engage the same profile region.

The result of the acoustic profiling exercise is to provide an alternative way of thinking about what constitutes fidelity in the representation of location in film when we have the goal of hearing the space with unsettled ears. In turn, unsettled listening provides a means of acknowledging the specifics of settler positionality through listening practice, an essential factor in resisting the idea of the "settler" as a fixed identity that "risks reifying a cohesive and essentialist form of subjectivity that does not take into account subtle gradations of relationship, history, and experience" (Robinson 2020, 39). For Dylan Robinson, the benefits of acknowledging the particularities of one's own settler positionality, and its differences from other settler positions, is in making the work of unsettling into "a process or state that fundamentally guides our actions and perception" (29). As we listen to the sounds of trains through a variety of settler positions in this chapter, we must also reflect on our own position within the deep layering of overlapping experiences that are revealed through this intermedial analysis, and understand that this layering is a living entity, ever changing and requiring sustained vigilance around our ongoing roles in the settling of the lands we occupy.

Acoustic profiling reveals an informative tension between what I have previously called "space replacement" in film sound design (2007, 132) and the notion of "re-placing" space as a mode of recovering lost histories of specific locations that have been overwritten by colonial processes of property inscription (Jordan 2018). Imported film treatments of a place like Vancouver follow the same principle, overwriting local specificity with its new script for space. *East Hastings Pharmacy* employs this strategy when filling the space of the Vancouver methadone clinic with sound produced in Hollywood decades prior. This replacement becomes literal when we learn that Bourges added the cartoon soundtrack in post-production, along with the ambient sound meant to reflect the street life outside.[2] Referring to this kind of overwriting as space replacement serves as both critique of, and engagement with, critical tensions in the World Soundscape Project's relationship to recording technology. In recognizing the artificial construction of auditory space in such an example, the opportunity to re-place this space opens up to the unsettled ear that listens for how the constructed soundscape engages with particularities of real-world place.

Space replacement in films shares an ideological goal of modernist architectural design sought to compartmentalize space discussed at length in Chapter 1 on Jacques Tati's film *Playtime*, to create quiet and neutral soundscapes that can be managed independently of the environment that surrounds them. In practice, perfect sonic isolation of a real-world space, and its infusion with a technologically imported soundscape, is possible under only the most ideal circumstances (such as an anechoic chamber at an institutional research facility). Schafer's notion of schizophonia imagines a kind of dystopia where such conditions prevail in daily life and end up disorienting people to the point of mental aberration. Space replacement describes the logical conclusion of schizophonia, much maligned for its anti-technological stance and proliferation of negative stereotypes of neurodivergence. Schafer's concept also points to a contradiction in his attitude toward technology, given that he championed the use of sound recording as a mode of documentation and analysis in the early days of the World Soundscape Project. He wanted to have his cake and eat it too, prescribing sound recording as a mode of objective documentation that functions unobtrusively in relation to the spaces it occupies, while decrying the use of sound technology to reconstruct these very same occupied spaces.

Of course neither extreme, of unmediated documentation or total replacement of a sonic environment, is truly possible. A sound recordist can only pretend to remain at a distance from their gear and the location they occupy together. Sound technology does not "reproduce" that which it records (Lastra 2000, 153), nor can media "vanish" from the process of representation (Sterne 2003, 218). Media, and its operators, always reveal their hand when engaging with place. At the same time, however, media engagement with place does not automatically constitute a distanciation from that place either. The distance between a location and the way it sounds in a piece of media is a function of the critical stance of the media-makers themselves; for Westerkamp, acknowledging the relationship between a sound recordist and their recording environment is the very basis of linking soundscape composition to acoustic ecology (2002). Importantly, the very idea of a particular location can be invented through the process of media engagement, as Michel De Certeau asserts when he argues that we write place by occupying space (1984, 93). To understand how media engages with place, we must not fall back on simple comparison between some imagined objective reality and the pieces of media that constitute an apparently impoverished reflection of this reality. Rather, we need an intermedial approach that recognizes that it is in the relationship between differing stories of place that we can critically assess what constitutes that place to begin with. To do this, we need to understand how all places are continually overwritten and replaced by competing practices, uses, and representations.

In films, space replacement is not only possible, but standard practice. The idea of space replacement is valuable as a way of describing an aesthetic strategy in film sound design, in which a given represented space can be supplanted by a shift on the soundtrack. Charting space replacements in work shot on location is one way to navigate how space is constructed in any given film, and to understand the filmmakers' approach to place when representing real-world locations. Space replacement as a sound design strategy becomes politicized in the case of cross-cultural treatments of a particular place, all the way from foreign productions to overlapping claims to space by local groups on the ground. To hear these overlapping treatments of place we need to rethink how the schizophonic replacement of a sound environment by way of film sound design offers a path to understanding how the distance between where one is and how it sounds can actually proffer a heightened critical engagement with these places. Space replacement as a sound design strategy can unsettle a place and open it up to multiple listening positions, re-placing them with the histories that form the basis of those positions in the first place.

Acoustic Profiling on Vancouver's Downtown Eastside

Let us consider *East Hastings Pharmacy* here in more detail. The cartoon that Bourges added to the sound environment of the methadone clinic is Robert Clampett's *Falling Hare* (1943), a good example of the noted history of cross-departmental production integration at the Warner Bros.' cartoon studios. The scene in question comes around two minutes into the film when a gremlin begins whacking the nose of a live bomb in time with the instrumental "I've Been Working on the Railroad" in an attempt to do away with enemy Bugs seated on top. With the image in play we understand from the beginning that the clinking sound is an allusion to railway construction from a different source depicted on screen, and in the production context this sound is just as likely to have been produced by one of music orchestrator Carl Stalling's percussionists as by sound effects editor Treg Brown. This integration can be heard in the way that the music's unspoken reference to railway construction charges each clink with the connotation of hammer on spike. James Lastra would say (by way of Christian Metz) that the clinking sound is "legible" as hammer on spike for the ease with which the sound can be recognized as emanating from this implied source (126). But this legibility is premised upon a lack of specificity that also allows the sound to become interchangeable with something else, as is the case in this cartoon. *East Hastings Pharmacy* capitalizes on this interchangeability by re-inscribing the clinking sound's railway connotations, first by stripping the original image and then by presenting this sound in the context of the dire social realities of Vancouver's Downtown Eastside as the city's sanctioned corral for the markers of urban poverty—and indigeneity—that officials don't want to spill out across the neighborhood's increasingly gentrified perimeter, which DTES residents have fought hard to keep at bay to preserve their long-standing community (Shier 2002, 11).

As one of a string of Warner Bros. cartoons placed in the service of WWII propaganda, the *Falling Hare* soundtrack also resonates with wartime xenophobia and imperialist expansion, branches of the same pathos that leads to the effacing of Indigenous culture from the consciousness of colonizing peoples. In Vancouver, this has taken the form of what Jean Barman (2007) calls "erasing Indigenous Indigeneity," the process of chasing the area's original peoples off the land while importing Aboriginal artifacts from elsewhere to maintain a Native chic deemed safe for immigrant consumption (as when the city paid "homage" to the vacated

Squamish residents of downtown Vancouver's Stanley Park by erecting Kwakiutl totem poles imported from 200km north on Vancouver Island) (26). This is an interchangeability of cultural heritage premised upon a lack of specificity, the same quality that allows "legible" sound effects to become synchretic with a variety of implied sources. This process is not unlike the interchangeability of urban spaces when shooting Vancouver for Seattle, New York, or Frankfurt, emphasizing generic qualities of globalized urbanization while suppressing recognizable soundmarks from the mix (such as the persistent sound of float plane propellers that populate Vancouver harbor, the grinding and screeching of trains in the downtown railyards, or the regular horn blasts from the local ferry runs just north of the city). As we'll hear, such interchangeability has also proven a viable strategy for local productions telling local stories, a tool for replacing space against the grain of bias toward location-derived recordings as marker of authenticity (Ruoff, 27–29).

The high-concept legibility of Warner Bros.' sound effects—used in *Falling Hare* to play on listener's expectations to comic effect—is further unsettled by its presentation within the context of documentary sound conventions in *East Hastings Pharmacy*. Bourges' film commits to regional specificity in part through the use of location sound recording. While Bourges stages the action inside the clinic, the film features location recordings of the rich street life audible and visible through the clinic's windows that proceeds unaffected by the cameras and microphones. This situation is all the more potent given that the location-recorded cartoon soundtrack and ambient sound effects were added in post-production, and so represent a highly conscious attempt to channel the acoustic environment according to the conventions of "authentic" sound in documentary film.

While the film uses location recording as a conscious stylistic choice to evoke documentary convention, it does so to engage meaningfully with the social situation in the Downtown Eastside, underlining Michel Chion's point that "rendered" film sound—fabricated in studio to evoke the qualities of a particular space—is just as capable of engaging the world authentically (or inauthentically) as "real" sound captured on location (95–98). By presenting this Hollywood cartoon as an embedded element within the soundscape of the clinic, using a provocative mix of location sound and studio fabrication, *East Hastings Pharmacy* unsettles Hollywood's usual practice of erasing local specificity, inviting us to think of runaway projects in the context of their foreign spaces of production and the local media practices that sit next to them.

Finally, this intersection of sonic styles points to the complex relationships that exist between the domains of independent and industrial production around Vancouver. In his book *Hollywood North* (2002), Mike Gasher argues for thinking about filmmaking in British Columbia as a resource industry, pointing to how the provincial government has offered business incentives for foreign film production similar to those in place for activities like logging and fishing. Here we can consider how the local film industry might follow the same unsustainable patterns of extraction as other resource industries, all premised upon wilful ignorance of Indigenous uses of the land. Yet, as David Spaner charts in *Dreaming in the Rain* (2003), the ability to make independent films in Vancouver has become largely intertwined with the availability of Hollywood-oriented industrial resources in town. Just as Hollywood didn't erase the independent film, colonization didn't erase Indigenous presence.

East Hastings Pharmacy offers a powerful example of how we can practice unsettled listening on the staged sound of *Falling Hare*, devoid of local context and connected to the railway only by inference, to reveal a rich integration with regional specificity as the cartoon's auditory resonances accumulate within its new spaces of propagation. In this way we can hear local media through its transnational network, including the First Nations, to understand the overlaps between seemingly contradictory modes of being within the city. In so doing, we can also hear through the misrepresentation of the Downtown Eastside as "Canada's worst neighborhood" (Sommers and Blomley 2002, 19) to the strength of the community that has long characterized the area for anyone who scratches the surface, an important first step along the path to unsettling the city as a whole.

Staging Trains in the World Soundscape Project

It is useful here to consider space replacement in films as a form of "staging," following the work of Karin Bijsterveld and her colleagues in their collaborative anthology *Soundscapes of the Urban Past* (2013). The authors argue that hearing history through the media offers tremendous and largely untapped potential to offer new depth to our understanding of specific places across time. They draw on some of the tools developed by the World Soundscape Project, such as their classification of sound into signals, keynotes, and soundmarks, to aid their analyses while also critiquing the WSP's pretensions toward objectivity in their documentation practices. The key challenge the authors pose is to understand that sound in radio, film, television, etc. is always staged for specific purposes, and that these purposes are often specific to the medium for which the sound is produced. The same holds true for the WSP's own documents, no less staged in their attempts at transparency. By bringing attention to the formal and aesthetic qualities of staging, and situating these within the cultural and historical contexts of production, rich comparisons can then be made across media to flesh out the roles that such media play in establishing the dynamics of particular places at any given historical moment. Thus re-placing a locale by way of overwriting its cinematic soundscape can be understood as a mode of staging, and in this way we can understand mediation as a form of unsettled engagement. I will demonstrate how this works through an assessment of the role of train sounds for the WSP and acoustic ecology more generally before moving onto a history of trains in the Vancouver soundscape on film.

Let's begin by traveling a bit south of Vancouver to Washington State, home of Gordon Hempton, one of the world's most active proponents of certain tenets of acoustic ecology. He makes his living recording the sounds of the world and advocating for the preservation of quiet in places like his designated "one square inch of silence," a spot in Washington's Olympic National Park that has the lowest ambient noise levels he has been able to find and document within the United States (2009). He laments the fact that there is scarcely a place on Earth where you can listen for longer than fifteen minutes without hearing a passing aircraft (13). As it happens, however, he's got a weak spot for the sound of trains.

The documentary film *Soundtracker* (dir. Nick Sherman, 2010) follows Hempton on a mission to record the singing of a meadowlark in conjunction with the rush of a passing train. He gushes over the value he ascribes to the train sound:

There's a certain feeling I get when I hear a train. They put out a lot of sound and then there's an echo that comes back and it helps define the space. You know, that's what a loud diesel truck does, that's what a jet does, but it doesn't really give you information about that space, it . . . almost violates the space. There's something about a train as it passes through and the way the horn goes off that it just reveals and then you know where you are.

Hempton has no official affiliation with acoustic ecology or the World Soundscape Project, but the notion of sound's capacity to reveal the places we occupy is crucial to the field whose main research goals have been to understand the auditory ecosystems of specific geographic locales. For Hempton and the WSP alike, practice is based on recording the sounds of the environment for the purposes of documentation and analysis. For Hempton, the use of recording as a tool to assist the revelation of place comes with a very strict ideology governing his practices in the field. In his own words:

> Some people might wonder, "Well if you want a bird and train in proper balance, why don't you get a train recording and a bird recording and mix it in the studio?" And I look at that person and I think to myself, "What a frickin' idiot." What would that person think if they were looking at a photograph that had the moon taken from one part of the world, and the forest from another part of the world, and a mountain from another part of the world, and made the perfect picture? Because it wouldn't be any kind of a perfect picture, it would be a stupid picture because it wouldn't be about where we are.

It's instructive to note the connection between the single-take approach to recording and making work that is "about where we are." He calls his pieces "sound portraits," and he goes to great length and expense to find just the right spots from which to create these portraits. Here he is very much in line with the early media practices of the WSP, whose recordings for the purposes of documentation and analysis became the first stages of the field's main artistic offshoot known as soundscape composition. As I charted in the introduction to this book, the WSP shifted from single-take recording practice with no overt acknowledgment of their staging practices to highly reflexive modes of sound composition using their single-take field recordings as the building blocks for highly composited works. Hempton occupies an intriguing middle ground here, open about his conscious shaping of the balance between elements he records as "portraits" while adamant that this balance be achieved *in situ*. We can find evidence of similar thinking in the WSP on some of their recordings, such as a recording made from the CN Pier on March 12, 1973, in which the catalog notes indicate an appreciation for how this particular recording allows for a rich interplay of elements in motion from the train yards, rain, the blast of Vancouver's nine o'clock gun, in which "signal patterns of whistles and bells appear in continually changing spatial perspective."[3] This is the kind of detail that film sound designers would build in the mix for the same aesthetic effect, here captured in a single-take location recording. It's instructive that the aesthetic results are appreciated in a compositional fashion while the production practices are rooted in the ideology of location.

The sounds of trains figured prominently in the WSP's *Soundscapes of Canada* series produced for CBC Radio in 1974, positioning them as a set of sounds that Canadians had in common, a traveling soundmark that extended an acoustic profile from coast to coast. In program three, "Signals, Keynotes, and Soundmarks," Schafer begins a discussion of the significance behind the sounds of these vehicles by playing us a typical whistle blast and asking how many Canadians would know exactly what this familiar sound means. In this example he is addressing the function of whistle blasts as signals that send messages to listeners—in this case, the announcement of a level crossing. Yet other levels of meaning are also important to the WSP team. In particular, they often emphasize sound's power to reveal the qualities of the natural and built environments of a place. In one example Bruce Davis calls our attention to how train whistles in Vancouver's rail yard activate the cityscape that surrounds it, asking listeners to "Notice the way the echoed sound answers back with a different version of the original chord as it bounces off the buildings around the yard." Here they get specific to the Vancouver context of the yard, which differs from other cities, and they frame the recording to emphasize the ways in which the spatial signature of the place is revealed by the sounds of the trains. This is very close to Gordon Hempton's sentiment concerning the power of the train's whistle to let us know where we are.

While the previous example addresses the physical properties of geographical space and the built environment, the WSP was also interested in a symbolic dimension to sound, tying the disappearance of certain sounds to the degradation of culture. Indeed, Schafer and the WSP have made a big deal out of changes to the design of signals like train whistles and foghorns over the decades, and what this means for the cultures that held them dear. In Schafer's concluding words to "Signals, Keynotes, and Soundmarks" he says,

> It takes time for a sound to take on rich, symbolic character—a lifetime perhaps, or even centuries. This is why soundmarks should not be tampered with carelessly. Change the soundmarks of a culture and you erase its history and mythology. Myths take many forms. Sounds have a mythology too. Without a mythology a culture dies.

Yet in defining a certain branch of Canadian culture around soundmarks like trains, the WSP necessarily exclude much else.

In fact, we could very easily flip the discussion to consider how the very presence of these sounds marks the degradation of so many other cultural streams present in Vancouver but unacknowledged by the WSP. As Mitchell Akiyama puts it, "created at a time when Canada's immigrant populations were exploding, when Indigenous activists were making important strides toward state recognition, *Soundscapes of Canada* was perhaps most notable for whom and what it left out" (2019, 115). Akiyama presents a thorough analysis of the *Soundscapes of Canada* radio program with an ear for its strategies of exclusion to create one version of Canadian national identity, which he ties to Benedict Anderson's term *unisonance* as a mode of rallying patriotism around common sounds (like national anthems) (119). Akiyama argues that there is an interesting tension at work between the WSP's commitment to regional specificity through attention to local soundmarks, supported by their emphasis on the content of recordings made on location, and their desire to turn these into symbols of national unity through tools of broadcasting. These tensions can be found operating in their regional work as well, such as their Vancouver case-study in which they attempt to extrapolate a city-wide community from locally sourced sounds. I will consider this Vancouver work more specifically now.

In the accompanying booklet to their LP release of *The Vancouver Soundscape* (1973), a few pages of "earwitness" accounts of the quietude of early settlement in the area are followed by E. Pauline Johnson recounting a Native legend about the inevitable conquest by the "white man" and then a dramatic announcement: "After the silence . . . the city was born," illustrated with a full-page picture of a logging train emerging from an old growth forest towing a full load of lumber (World Soundscape Project 1973, 8–10). This equation of the boundaries of the city being drawn through technologies of industrial transportation inflects the sonic narrative they put together on the record, and here we find a telling example of how the WSP have chosen to represent Indigenous voices. The first of the two LPs in the original release constructs an acoustic narrative of Vancouver's wilderness past and its transformation into major urban center. It begins with several tracks of ocean sounds, each fading in and out to suggest their status as fixed perspective single-take recordings rather than composition. This is the world as it was, they seem to be saying. Then they fade in on the sounds of birds and a trickling stream, and here the voice of Tsleil-Waututh elder Herbert George emerges, speaking in his native tongue about the process of building canoes, sprinkled with some English when referring to the "white man's tools" used in contemporary practice (1973). Midway through his monologue he is interrupted by the sound of a passing seaplane, which momentarily drowns out his voice, and those of the birds, after which the monologue continues in its untarnished Edenic idyll—until a foghorn blast indicates a shift to the fully built environment of the modern city. For the remainder of the side, the sounds focus on the harbor through bustling commuter voices on a local ferry that docks amidst crisscrossing sea planes and blasting boat horns. It is notable that here, on this first side of the LP, the sounds of trains are not included in their portraiture of the lo-fi density of an urban harbor. Instead, they open the second side of the LP with the sound of children playing down by the CN Railway yards, our entryway into the city proper, the train whistles granted special attention as musical sounds that carry deeper significance, a clear example of the WSP's selectivity in deciding which urban sounds should be admonished and which should be celebrated.

I believe that the WSP was well intentioned in attempting to give voice to the ancestors of the land while also railing against one of their least favorite modern-Vancouver sounds, the seaplane, a staple of the harbor town. Yet as I have pointed out elsewhere (Jordan 2015 and 2017), the choice to mix the disruptive sound of the seaplane into George's monologue contributes to the general trend of imagining the erasure of contemporary Indigenous presence in the face of urbanization. For Hildegard Westerkamp, this "deliberate sound design decision . . . highlighted the fragility of human language, of quiet and silence, and how easily these sounds and soundscapes can be masked or destroyed by such powerful sounds as aeroplane motors" (Westerkamp 2019, 55). But in making this choice, motivated by the WSP's particular ideas around good versus bad sound, they end up overwriting George's story of the land with their own. In this construction of the shift from primordial wilderness and Indigenous culture to the arrival of civilization and its noise pollution we lose the fact that George's very story, here, is a marker of contemporary Indigenous culture operating amidst the settlers: a continuing tradition of Indigenous canoe-building with non-Indigenous tools. Instead, George's story functions as a nod to past practice now rendered obsolete by the noisy modern modes of transportation that prevent him from being heard.

To the WSP's credit, they were very clear about their compositional strategies, with detailed liner notes about the separate recording elements used to make up specific sequences on the record. "I remember that we prided ourselves at the time of the transparency we offered to the listener," says Westerkamp, "wanting to demystify the editing or mixing process, in order to make a clear distinction between listening directly to the environment and listening to recordings of soundscapes" (2019, 55). This is an important early marker of the interest in a reflexive approach to soundscape composition that WSP members like Westerkamp and Barry Truax would go on to be known for. However, there is another layer of potential transparency that is clouded by the Herbert George segment, which has to do with the relationship between composition and the archive.

On *The Vancouver Soundscape* LP, George is only heard for a couple of minutes during the track entitled "Squamish Narrative." Yet the original interview in the WSP archive, conducted by Bruce Davis on June 5, 1973, is over forty-five minutes long.[4] The interview is structured around Davis asking George for place names in his native dialect with a push to record a longer story of some kind, which proves challenging as George has trouble recalling the language. Around all this, George speaks in English, offering rich details about the relationship between his people and the changing status of the land over the centuries. For one, George clarifies that he is of the Tsleil-Waututh tribe, not Squamish as indicated by the WSP in their liner notes. He also recounts a story about a warrior of legend who battled a double-headed snake at the northern end of Burrard Inlet, gateway to the area we now call Vancouver. Later he indicates that, during his mother's time, this story was co-opted by a local Catholic priest to explain how the railway passed through a difficult blockage in the mountains to facilitate the arrival of the missionaries in town, a telling admission about the intersection of local myth and its manipulation by Christian settlers as means to accessing the land. Davis eventually coaxes the canoe-building story out of George, and here we can see the single-mindedness of the WSP at work: their mission was to document an Indigenous language before it disappears, an example of the "salvage paradigm—a false ascription of the inevitable extinction of Indigenous cultural practices and the resultant desire to save them" (Robinson 2020, 153). And the compositional use of the canoe-building story on the record matches the salvage impulse behind the recording session. In so doing, the WSP omit a much richer account of the relationship between the railway and Indigenous entanglement with missionary settlers, a story that challenges the WSP's taste for train sounds at the expense of seaplanes and other forms of traffic.

So while the WSP might have been clear about how they deliberately mixed the George segment from separate recordings of birds and voice, this missed opportunity to engage more deeply with the realities of place speaks to a lack of transparency in their selection process when composing from their own archive of collected materials. In turn, this opens the question of what the best use of this interview would have been then, and what it should be now that it has been recently made available for public streaming through the SFU library. For Dylan Robinson, such use should proceed in the spirit of "ethnographic redress" and "compositional responsibility" (2020, 149–189), to free the Indigenous voice from its containment in the settler archive and make use of the recording in ways that would benefit George's community.

In their negative characterization of certain kinds of urban industrial sound while romanticizing others, the WSP staged their own communal sensibility around what sounds constituted the Vancouver acoustic community with which they identified, and what its threats were. What they miss, of course, is how their version of this acoustic community isn't shared within the profile charted by these sounds, particularly among those for whom relationships to early Vancouver soundmarks like trains and foghorns marked their own dispossession to the land. I will now investigate how other media representations, particularly film soundtracks, can reveal alternative relationships to the sound of trains that challenge the WSP's staging, revealing how even overtly fictionalized accounts of the city can provide access to truths obscured in the documentary practices of early acoustic ecology.

Tracking Terminal City

The sound of trains is particularly significant for downtown Vancouver, born as a railway town with the presence of trains defining the city in transformative ways over its subsequent first century. With this profile established we can then seek out films that use the sounds of trains within this region to ask: What signatures do these sounds reveal in these films? What perspectives do these signatures establish? What meanings are constructed through conscious or unconscious staging of sounds? And how can we listen for other perspectives across time and sources of media? In short, what do other people hear when they listen to the sound of trains in the Vancouver soundscape, and how do these perspectives enrich other media representations that emerge from the same acoustic profile? I will proceed in three sections, dealing first with Vancouver's early days as represented in documentary films that make use of archival footage of train travel and first-person testimonials. My focus will be on the relationship between the railroad and Vancouver's Chinese and Japanese communities, while questioning the role of sonifying images of trains from the silent era in these historical reconstructions. Secondly, I will examine a set of films dealing with the relationship between trains and British Columbia's resource industry, with particular attention to how these later films make use of location sound recordings in their examination of the shifting status of trains and labor in the province and its biggest city. Thirdly, I will consider a pair of films by David Rimmer and Sylvia Spring that bring us back to the Downtown Eastside in the early 1970s to reveal an unusually pithy examination of social realities on the ground around the same time that the WSP was making their first wave of recordings around the city, providing alternative perspectives on the use of media technology to document real-world space and the relationship between urban sound and the communities that live with it on a daily basis. I will then conclude with the question of how trains might articulate Indigenous presence in the city today.

Like the WSP, Vancouver filmmakers have also long been fascinated by trains. In my opening example from *East Hastings Pharmacy*, I made a point about the disappearance of the sound of railway construction coinciding with the onset of massive land appropriation by way of the government's dealings with companies like the Canadian Pacific Railway. Provocatively, these were also the days when filmmaking first came to the city. Lynn Kirby has provided beautiful examples of how the railway and the cinema proceeded on "parallel tracks" across the world in their early days (1997). There is no better example than British Columbia (BC) to illustrate such close connection between these technologies, the CPR itself being responsible for commissioning some of the first films ever to be shot in the province.

Film historian Colin Browne reminds us of the CPR's role in BC's film history in his documentary *The Image Before Us* (1986). It was made in the year of Expo '86, the World's Fair that many credit with putting Vancouver on the world stage, fast-tracking much of the gentrification that has been hotly contested over the decades, and providing an environment that would lead to Vancouver as permanent home for Hollywood North. The film highlights the function of filmmaking in these early days as closely tied to the tourism industry, constructing images of Vancouver and its surrounding areas designed specifically for this purpose (Browne 2000, 88–89). As Browne shows us a variety of excerpts from the earliest days of filmmaking in the region, all tied to trains in one way or another, the narrator explains, "Over the years, scenes like this helped define the familiar image of the Canadian West. If you saw enough movies, you'd begin to think you had a pretty good idea about what a place was like. With the help of the movies, Vancouver came to be seen less as a sort of genteel stopover and more as a destination in itself." In the absence of any major entertainment film industry in town until the 1970s, this meant that the images that the rest of Canada and the world saw of BC for most of the twentieth century were tourist propaganda pieces. This staging of the region's image for consumption abroad was inextricably linked to the dispossession of Indigenous peoples and non-European immigrants at the hands of the railway company that claimed much of the land and commissioned the films. So it is that Vancouver cinema was born to provide a particular image of the city designed to benefit the corporation that essentially owned the town and sought to profit from tourist dollars. This is an important beginning for a provincial cinema that has long been handled by the government as one of the region's resource industries along with logging, fishing, mining, and the like (Gasher 2002).

Browne's film depends upon the perceived authenticity of the archival images he presents, while making a point about how these images have been staged for a corporate vision of Vancouver. Significantly, the fidelity of the film's engagement with Vancouver is revealed by the soundtrack. The reflexive voiceover invites us to question the veracity of the images on the level of how they were staged. In this context, the addition of train sounds to sonorize the silent footage is loaded with questions that face all artists and researchers attempting to reconstruct the soundscapes of the past, also a favorite activity of the WSP. In *The Vancouver Soundscape* booklet, the WSP built a narrative around the role of the train in establishing the city, and setting the soundscape of its earliest days as the baseline against which encroaching modernity would instill an increasingly lo-fi environment, disrupting the soundmarks whose acoustic profiles helped establish Vancouver as a community (World Soundscape Project 1973). Without recordings of these early days, the WSP was left with the same options as any filmmaker working on a period piece to imagine what it sounded like. From the information they gleaned through their own research, the WSP might well have criticized Browne's choice of train sounds as inauthentic to details of period machinery and location-specific signatures. Yet like the cartoon sound in *East Hastings Pharmacy* with which I began this chapter, the rather generic quality of Browne's train sounds assists the process of unsettling the images under critique in the film to illustrate the reality that, from the very beginning, Vancouver has been staged in the media to enhance certain aspects of its social and geographical specificity while erasing others.

Browne's concern is general to Vancouver's position in the imagination of Canada and North America, replacing silent soundtracks in order to re-place the location about which the film is concerned. Filmmaker Karen Cho brings cultural specificity to questioning the fidelity of re-imagining the recorded past in her documentary *In the Shadow of Gold Mountain* (2004). Here she explores the neglected history of the thousands of Chinese workers who built the railroad (alongside Japanese and First Nations colleagues) imported as cheap labor and left too broke to return home upon completion, only to be ostracized by the Canadian government through state-sanctioned immigration and citizenship restrictions in an attempt to erase the history of their contribution to shaping the country until well after World War II. It seems appropriate that Vancouver's Chinatown was established nearby the downtown railyards, intersecting with the Downtown Eastside, parallel communities founded upon dispossession. As we watch archival images of Canadian train travel from the early twentieth century, we hear a recitation of F. R. Scott's 1966 poem *All Spikes but the Last*: "Where are the thousands from China who swung their picks with bare hands at forty below? Between the first and the million other spikes they drove and the dressed-up act of Donald Smith, who has sung their story?" Referring to the famous image of CPR co-founder Donald Smith posing with hammer over the final spike in the transcontinental railway (an image that persists to this day as background image to one page in the current Canadian passport, definitive arbiter of Canadian identity), the poet critiques the whitewashing of the history of railroad construction, the white male corporate class stepping in at the last minute for a photo-op to claim the glory of the railway's completion while erasing evidence of the diversity that went into it.

To assist in her excavation of the realities of the railroad's construction, Karen Cho draws on a rich array of found footage that calls attention to myriad different ways the Asian diaspora has been represented—or not— over the decades. As in Browne's film, her reconstruction of the soundscapes of this troubled past raises loaded questions about the relationship between memory and history, this time made specific to the Chinese community. The clinking sounds we hear in this clip likely stem no more from location recordings of railway construction than did the corollary sounds in the Bugs Bunny cartoon heard in *East Hastings Pharmacy*. Yet they are loaded here with an unsettling resonance up to the daunting task of Cho's film. If the sounds don't sit quite right in their generic legibility, they reveal cracks in the façade of these whitewashed images of the CPR at the turn of the century.

While Cho appeals to the gaps in the fidelity of collective memory within the Chinese community and its representation by white authority, Michael Fukushima takes a personal approach to memory in his animated short *Minoru: Memory of Exile* (1992). Here he recounts his own experiences as a child when his community of Japantown—once neighboring Chinatown and also filled with many descendants of the railway workers—was destroyed in 1942 after the BC government rounded up all people of Japanese descent and sent them, by train, to internment camps in the interior. The voiceover narration describes his vague recollection of boarding a train to New Denver as the hand-drawn images show us a young boy at a train station filled with bustle of rushing passengers, gushing steam, conductor whistles, and thundering engines. The immediacy of these station sounds quickly gives way to the distant sound of a train whistle echoing through the mountains upon his arrival in the camp. The image here shifts from the vibrant colors of the animated rendering of the train voyage to the appearance of an aged-looking archival photograph of New Denver, and here the lonesome train calls from afar simultaneously foreground the isolation of his new home at the time, and the temporal distance from this moment in his recollection many decades later. The trains that brought so many Chinese and Japanese to Vancouver now reenacted their role in the facilitation of exile, an association that any railway company would want us all to forget. This angle did not figure into the WSP's accounts of the cultural importance of train sounds in Vancouver either, one example of how their documentation of such sounds is not faithful to the cultural memory of the place. The geographical particularities of BC create a physically reverberant space, the kind of environment that yields the sense of where you are that Hempton and the WSP so often emphasized. In *Minoru*, this reverberant quality is staged to reflect physical and psychological distance from home. The acoustic profile of the train reaches as far as New Denver, but its function there insists upon the loss of a community once located in downtown Vancouver.

As an example of how the legacy of Vancouver's systemic anti-Asian bias persists, Mina Shum's *Double Happiness* (1994) explores the complexities of growing up Chinese Canadian in a Vancouver with a darkly racist past. Jade Li (Sandra Oh) is an aspiring actress who discovers she is most sought after as an ethnic stereotype when casting agents at an audition ask her to do an accent. After playfully asking what kind of accent they'd like while showcasing some of her range, the stern visages starting back at her make it clear that they're not amused. Begrudgingly, in broken Chinese-inflected English, she assures her potential employers: "Yes, a very good Chinese accent I can do for you." Just as the agents smile at each other in approval, the sound of a train whistle erupts on the soundtrack. The whistle bridges a cut to Jade on the street outside jumping for joy in her belief that she has landed the part, the train now seen rushing past her against the shipping docks in the background. The sound of a passing train here is both celebratory and an unsettling reminder of the price Jade pays for her success on the back of her community, echoing through the city as an indicator of the intersections between industry and dispossession that resonate throughout Vancouver's reverberant spaces, offering a rich meditation on how things have improved in the city while, in other ways, staying very much the same. The film is reflexive about the media's role in perpetuating sonic stereotypes while offering a nuanced corrective. Her casting agents attempt to replace regional specificity with generic racial branding, as per the norm in Hollywood, which Shum resists in her application of location-recorded train sound amidst this narrative moment illustrating the complexity of resistance in Vancouver's Chinese community.[5]

Resource/Replace

In all but the final example discussed so far, the sounds of trains have been sourced separately from the images provided, whether attached to the archival footage from silent films in *The Image Before Us* and *In the Shadow of Gold Mountain*, the mixture of hand-drawn animation and archival photographs in *Minoru: Memory of Exile*, or the location-shot live action in *East Hastings Pharmacy*. Each of these soundtracks can be thought of as re-sourcing its images, providing a new sound source independent of what was shot. In so doing, the locations for these films are re-placed: sound is deliberately staged to comment upon the images they present in order to expose nuances of place would be left obscured with only the images in play. Each of these films deals with sounds that are gone, many of them extinct before the possibility of location sound recording, and others lost to the vagaries of history. This is one pathway to acoustic profiling. In this section I will discuss a set of films that play with the boundaries between such re-sourcing of sound and location recorded material to yield a different relationship between film and place. And I will take this opportunity to play on the word *resource* to construct this cluster around the relationship between trains and the resource industry in the first half Vancouver's twentieth century.

Philip Borsos' film *The Grey Fox* (1982) offers a meticulous period reconstruction of the early days of British Columbia, dramatizing the story of "gentleman bandit" Bill Miner, Canada's first train robber active in the first few years of the twentieth century. In the film, Miner gets the idea to move his operations from stagecoaches to trains after a slightly anachronistic screening of *The Great Train Robbery* (1903) at a local tavern. The technologies of trains and the cinema were both new to Miner upon his release from a thirty-year jail term in 1902, and the film makes a point of locking the two together as symbols of the modernizing world that ends up doing Miner in as he retreats to the interior of BC when Vancouver was just a fledgling town to the south.

The period reconstruction for *The Grey Fox* was aided by the fact that BC maintains a heritage railway in Kamloops, site of Bill Miner's eventual capture after fleeing the United States. To this day they run regular tourist rides on restored turn-of-the-century steam trains, and they include a recreation of the famous robbery that led to Miner's arrest.[6] As in the earliest days of train travel in BC, here the mode of transport is tied to the tourism industry, offering visitors a taste of the past through the maintenance of vintage technology. This facilitates shoots like *The Grey Fox* which, in its own way, functions as a promotional film for the region with its spectacular footage of the BC interior and recreations of the exhilarating train-mounted film footage that formed the staple of the early twentieth century travelogues. The rich attention to train sound detail, thanks to new recordings of vintage trains, helps to sound out British Columbia's past that continues to resonate in the present.

The WSP was always interested in tracking down examples of old technologies at risk of obsolescence, including a 1993 recording of Vancouver's Royal Hudson steam train, serving at that time as a heritage excursion car much like the one further north in Kamloops. The interest in recording as preservation is, of course, ideologically loaded. But the continuing operation of technologies like steam trains allows for continuing investigation into the relationships between these sounds, the communities in which they arose, and their shifting status today. As described above, the train occupies a special place in the heart of the WSP, even as this technology might otherwise fit into the anti-modernization thrust of much of their discussion on the effects of transportation sound on urban living. *The Grey Fox* is heavily nostalgic in its romanticization of the train, but it is also consciously critical of the era it depicts and the relationship it develops between new technologies, the industries they make possible, and Bill Miner's desire to profit from both while remaining outside the system. The film itself also stands as a marker of the shifts in these relationships, part of an entertainment industry made possible by government subsidy and whose work of recreating the past depends upon the tourist industries in place on its shooting locations. As I will demonstrate, the relationships are bound together by the role of sound in the film's deployment of place.

A compelling moment early in the film draws parallels between three new technologies: the film projector, the automobile, and the train, each made the subject of Miner's startled wonder at the new world he faces. At the end of the screening of *The Great Train Robbery*, while the robbers on screen fire their pistols up in the air, Miner nearly jumps out of his seat when a member of the audience provides his own sound effect, firing a real pistol through the ceiling of the tavern. This is an intriguing parallel to the film's own approach to providing sound effects for the technologies we see depicted on screen, recorded as much as possible from vintage sources as we hear immediately thereafter. Cut to a direct frontal view of the projector resembling the front end of a train with headlight blazing into the night as the rhythmic sound of the film threading through the gate recalls the rolling of wheels over the tracks. Then another direct cut to an automobile passing Miner outside, creating a sound bridge into the early combustion engine whose chug-a-chugging is remarkably similar to the projector heard just prior, both of which call to mind the sound of the trains that open the film and which follow here directly as we cut again to Miner watching a train go by. It is the sound here more than anything else that threads these three technologies together, each framed as an element that catches Miner first off-guard and then in a state of marvel as he contemplates his career move.

The role of film technology and its relationship to sound within the diegesis is important here. Film is new to Miner. Falling short of the apocryphal story of audiences fleeing in terror upon their first sight of the Lumières' train in *Arrival of a Train at La Ciotat* (1896) a few years prior, Miner nevertheless puts faith in the real-world plausibility of what he sees on the screen and seeks to emulate it outside. At the same time, the tavern patron firing his gun into the air helps to solidify the connection between what Miner sees on screen and hears in the environment around him, a process of sonification that is similar to what Borsos does with the sound of the projector itself across the bridge through to the car and the train. These old technologies are supported by new real-world recordings, and the symbolic connection between film and new transportation technologies carries Miner with it. But he has trouble going with the flow. The film then leaves projectors and automobiles behind, but goes on to stage dramatic renderings of train travel through the mountainous region that intersects with Miner at key points in the story. Here the sound of the trains is made visceral, the impact of the footage brought to a level of intensity that would be unattainable through image alone, and key to the drama that unfolds around Miner's gradual undoing in this new technological environment.

Midway through the film, Miner is lying low in Kamloops as US detectives are on his trail. Against his better judgment, he accepts an offer to rustle horses for a colleague who threatens to blow his cover if he refuses. In an audiovisually spectacular sequence, he and two henchmen run the horses over the hills along a rail line. The sequence intercuts footage of Miner and the horses in golden hour sunlight with shots from the top of an approaching engine car presenting exhilarating views of high-speed travel along the tracks. The cutting on the soundtrack is especially dramatic, shifting back and forth between the galloping hooves and the all-encompassing steam blasts and heavy metal rolling of the train. When the two finally come together, the pairing provides a startling meditation on the shift from organic horses to iron horses. Miner attempts to outrun the train while remaining on the tracks, but ultimately it is futile and several of the horses grow scared enough to take off down a steep cliff, separating from Miner, one of them breaking a leg in the process. The sound of the train fades into the distance, and a gunshot provides final punctuation to the sequence as Miner puts the injured horse down. This sequence stands as a clear dramatization of our growing realization that Miner is unable to keep up with the times. He thought he had planned around the train schedule on this line, but this train turns out to have been a work train running logs, scheduled separately from the regular commuter trains.

The logging train also marks a shift in the relationship between this mode of transportation and the labor it enables. Later in the film, Miner accompanies the town photographer, Kate Flynn (Jackie Burroughs), on a call out to document the scene of a grisly crime: a man stabbed his wife and child to death in their tent before running off and turning the knife on himself a short distance away. The corporal turns to Miner and says, "Damn Chinamen. You can never understand what's going on in their heads." This is a revealing line, alluding to Chinese presence in British Columbia following the end of their work on the railroad, and the anti-Chinese sentiment that would steadily increase in the years to follow. But Miner is sympathetic: "Well I wouldn't be too harsh on them. You know they're a world away from home." As an outsider himself, Miner recognizes the problem of integration and assimilation, and here we are invited to imagine that this horrific scene arose from the duress under which they were living, with no place to go and no means of support. Miner's eventual downfall is thus positioned in relation to his status as a foreigner, unable to plug into the system that sustains those around him.

The difficulties faced by Indigenous peoples and the Asian community following their dispossession at the hands of the railway would become increasingly widespread across the general population as the Depression era set in. As labor became a buyer's market, exploitation ran rampant across industries, not the least of which being film. The 1930s were the era of the "quota quickie" films made in the provincial capital city of Victoria by American producers hiring British Nationals living in BC to sell to the British market. In an interesting symmetry of art and life, some of these films, like *Lucky Corrigan* (1936), tell decidedly local stories of Depression-era hardship. Here an undercover law enforcement agent investigates corruption in logging camps on Vancouver Island where workers are being dangerously exploited in the face of dismal prospects at earning a living anywhere else, much less the urban centers of Vancouver and Victoria. On his way north to the camps, the agent hears a train in the distance, which he hops to catch a ride up to the camp.

The sound of the train is tied to the promise of industry as source of sustenance as well as emphasizing the distance separating urban areas and sources of income. As one of the first synchronized sound pictures produced in Canada, the sound of the train also opens up questions about sound production practices on Hollywood films produced in foreign countries, an area for expanded investigation that could open such films up to serious consideration in soundscape research into British Columbia's past. The film is especially provocative because of how its own narrative, in reflecting real Depression-era issues, also foretells the effect its own producers would have on BC's overnight film industry that would vanish as fast as it came, leaving film production crews stranded without work and forced to find new means elsewhere (Morris 1978, 194–195). Indeed, the effect of departing industry is a common theme in urban studies literature on BC and, in particular, the Downtown Eastside neighborhood in Vancouver.

After the war, official accounts of Vancouver's economic boom as a modernizing city would be continually tempered by increasing awareness of the downside to urban prosperity. This tension can be found in comparing early postwar representations of Vancouver. Consider a city symphony–style film like Stan Fox's *In the Daytime* (1949), one of Canada's earliest experimental films featuring a sequence that casts the morning rush hour on commuter trains as a positive example of urban vitality, set to a rousing orchestral score meant to evoke the romantic drama of train travel rather than location recording of urban street sounds. While not long after, Allan King's documentary *Skidrow* [sic] (1956) emphasized proximity to stationary train cars down by the docks as a function of urban poverty as it followed the lives of a few aging denizens of downtown. The film features early use of location recording made possible by modifying a silent camera for sound (Browne 2000, 106), resulting in a grittier representation of the urban soundscape, and laced with mournful music cues and narration to poetically underscore the grim subject matter.

A few years later Larry Kent stepped into the relative void in narrative filmmaking that opened up after the 1930s and began producing independent works, beginning with a twenty-minute short called *Hastings Street* (1962/2007). Filmed on location in the Downtown Eastside it was left unfinished for forty-five years until a soundtrack was created by Marc Benoit and a group of his students training for industry post-production audio at the Art Institute of Vancouver in 2007. The soundtrack thus acts as a period piece, fabricating a soundscape to accompany the vintage images and, in so doing, raising questions about the authenticity of sounds like that of a passing train as character Charlie (Alan Scarfe) is released from prison and goes in search of legitimate employment in the resource industry.

As I have discussed at length elsewhere (Jordan 2014b), the film is especially interesting in how it pairs images from the early days of independent film in Vancouver with sound produced in the context of the city's twenty-first century status as Hollywood North, tracing the increasing overlap between industrial and independent filmmaking in Vancouver today, and providing an example of how filmmaking has marked a return of industry to the downtown core from which other industries fled, as Charlie discovers in the film and has to return to a life of crime in order to eat. The passing train thus acts as initial promise of a clean life for Charlie outside of town while also foreshadowing his inability to escape skid row.

Larry Kent would revisit the theme of urban poverty in his first feature, *The Bitter Ash* (1963), chronicling the financially precarious lives of Colin (Philip Brown), Laurie (Lynn Stewart) and their infant son as they live in a low-rent house down by the railyard, the kind that were once built to house railway workers. The location is introduced with lingering shots of trains in the yard, complete with location sound recording,[7] emphasizing the gritty reality of the young couple's plight while also symbolizing Colin's yearning to escape to a more vibrant metropolis to pursue his playwriting career. The film ends on the front porch of this house as a fight breaks out between Colin and Des (Alan Scarfe), a factory worker facing the obsolescence of his job in the face of incoming automation. Kent brings in the sound of the trains from the adjacent yard as punctuation for the violence spawned by these circumstances, at once a clever solution to the budgetary lack of Foley effects on the film as a whole, and a poignant symbol of the lot these characters are made to endure. Here Kent provides an example of how location-sourced sound can be inflected with dramatically different meaning from that given to such sounds by the WSP. Taken on their own, the train recordings could serve as valuable documentation of a moment in Vancouver's history rarely captured. All the more poignant, however, is the staging of the trains to articulate the violence of this situation, sounds that could just as easily have been described as nostalgic markers of a time now lost to changing technologies and neighborhood demographics.

The Bitter Ash provides a remarkable counterexample to *Hastings Street* on the point of urban sound. While most of the soundtrack in *The Bitter Ash* consists of dubbed dialogue and a musical score, the film's train sounds, used to bookend the film, are recorded on location and function similarly to the train sounds in *The Grey Fox* in that they are documentary recordings of real-world trains used for dramatic effect within the narrative. In the *Bitter Ash*, however, the setting is the present, holding the location recorded train sounds in a different status than in the period reconstruction of *The Grey Fox*. *Hastings Street* thus provides an interesting middle ground, with genuine 1962 imagery but a soundtrack that functions as a period piece, newly recorded material, calling into question the role of perceived authenticity in using vintage recordings rather than newly recorded material. *Hastings Street* looks old but sounds new, thanks to the production quality on the soundtrack regardless of the authenticity of the sounds employed. In *The Grey Fox*, on the other hand, the period detail is largely authentic, but both the sound and the image are marked by the time in which the film was produced. And so across these examples we run the gamut of possible spatial and temporal relationships between sound and image. These varying relationships yield different modes of understanding the status of the train in Vancouver, and British Columbia at large, in relation to the resource industry. Taken together, we find a history of the relationship between trains, the resource industry, sound, and image on film that is endlessly slippery and reconfigurable, resisting the stable narrative that the WSP imagined possible through the art of listening, unsettling the function of trains within this landscape along the way.

Vancouver Is...

We arrive now back in the early 1970s, when the WSP was formalized and began making their first wave of Vancouver recordings. I end this chapter by discussing a set of films by David Rimmer and Sylvia Spring, working both together and separately around this time, which pose a contemporaneous challenge to the staging of Vancouver by Schafer and his colleagues at this historical moment. Trains figure prominently in Rimmer's two *Canadian Pacific* experimental shorts (1974–75) and Spring's feature fiction film *Madeleine Is....* (1971). Before these, however, the two collaborated on a short documentary for the CBC entitled *Know Place* (1968) about an alternative education program for high-school-aged kids in Vancouver. Here they focused on the self-directed nature of the learning environments, highlighting the school's emphasis on place-based learning and, in particular, one student's work with experimental soundmaking techniques using amplified household objects and tape machines. Her sounds run throughout most of the film, using alternative listening practices to frame voiceover testimonials from students about the value of their experience at the school. At this same moment, R. Murray Schafer was designing pedagogical tools for bringing listening into his Simon Fraser University classrooms with an emphasis on environmental awareness. There was something in the air in Vancouver in the late 1960s, and *Know Place* serves as a telling precursor to Rimmer and Spring's interest in place-based filmmaking and their respective attention to sound, or lack thereof, in subsequent works about Vancouver.

David Rimmer's pair of *Canadian Pacific* films (1974–75) are silent experimental works that meditate on a classic Vancouver view over the downtown railyard, across the water, and up to the North Shore mountains. Rimmer filmed the view across the seasons and dissolves between different takes to create a continually shifting view of the landscape through sun, rain, fog, snow, and back again, all while maintaining awareness of the window through which we are looking. Both films are punctuated by a final dissolve to a night view in which the camera and the room's interior are reflected back from a window now darkened on its exterior side. Catherine Russell argues that this reflexivity presents an "inhabited view," an ecologically situated presence by emphasizing the view's construction by way of the mediating agents: both the window and the camera (2006, 149). "Nature is not 'out there,' existing independently of humans and technologies, but is intimately bound up with them at their mercy and as their support" (149). As such Russell argues that the film breaks free of the "garrison mentality" so often tracked in Canadian art. Instead of presenting the view of a hostile exterior world from the vantage point of a safe bunker, Russell suggests that Rimmer's studio acts as a space that is open onto the external world, not a protective shelter but instead a part of how we inhabit this landscape (155). Schafer wouldn't agree, this being a classic example of the glazed soundscape (as I discussed at length in Chapter 1). By now, it should be clear that I would land on the side of Russell in this case, as the running argument of this book has been about the role of mediatic reflexivity in fostering heightened engagement with place, which stands as a critique of early acoustic ecology's shyness from acknowledging the role of technological mediation in their staging of the Vancouver soundscape. However, Schafer's notion of the glazed soundscape resonates with critiques of what Lance Berelowitz calls "the view imperative" in Vancouver real estate, the condo market taking over the landscape in the 1980s through to the present day, providing views for those who can afford it while also affording them the option of silence in which to enjoy it, a privileged remove from the urban space of the city (2005, 25). In 1974–75, however, Rimmer's views were attached to low-rent artist lofts in the seedy part of town, and would not have afforded the sound insulation usually reserved for pricier real estate. He would have heard the trains through his window, and this has implications for the socioeconomic class from which Rimmer's film speaks. So what would Rimmer have heard, and why does it matter?

Interestingly, filmmaker Richard Martin added the sound of trains to images from *Canadian Pacific* in a segment from his documentary on Vancouver's experimental film scene entitled *Backbone* (2013), in which Rimmer is interviewed about the work. In Martin's quest to contextualize this film within a specific region at a specific time, he drew on the archive of the World Soundscape Project for the sound design, making use of the recordings of this very rail yard made in 1973 discussed earlier in this chapter. For those who value location shooting and recording as a marker of authenticity in engagement with place, it's a match made in heaven. Yet it prompts a couple of important points: Rimmer intentionally left his film silent as part of its effect, and the impulse to sonorize flies in the face of the ardency with which a few experimental filmmakers hold their ability to make silence a conscious choice for their films. But it also points to a question we might have asked of Gordon Hempton discussed above: just what, exactly, does the sound of a train reveal about space? Rimmer's images reveal by way of their mediality, which is clearly on display. The silence offers one way of replacing the soundscape, allowing the image to re-place the landscape through Rimmer's cinematic articulations. What about the World Soundscape Project's train recordings heard in Martin's re-presentation? The pairing strikes an unsettling balance, given what we now understand about the WSP's lack of reflexivity and Rimmer's own overtly self-conscious framing of the view here. To unpack the implications of this pairing, I conclude with a longer discussion of Sylvia Spring's use of footage from these same downtown Vancouver train yards in in her film *Vancouver Is. . . .*[8]

Best known as the first narrative feature to be directed by a woman in Canada, Sylvia Spring's *Madeleine Is . . .* finds the titular Madeleine (Nicola Lipman) recently transplanted from Quebec and eager to explore the social experiments for which the west coast metropolis had become famous. Early in the film, Madeleine and her self-styled radical boyfriend Toro (John Juliani) stand in her loft near the Downtown Eastside, looking out across the Canadian Pacific Rail yard set against the waters of Burrard Inlet and the North Shore mountains. The view is nearly identical to David Rimmer's in *Canadian Pacific*, and the couple is of the same marginal artist class that Rimmer was when he shot his film. Toro is fascinated by the trains coupling in the yard, watching them frequently, which later fuels his sexual desire for Madeleine as he calls her attention to their sound just outside their bedroom window. He mimics their sound as they lay in bed, prompting Madeleine to attempt empathy for her boyfriend's odd sexual interest in the trains. But she prefers the scenic backdrop that lay behind the trains, and the implied quietude therein. Here the sound of the trains marks a point of tension between the couple that will play out along the lines of their ideological differences around issues of social politics.

Toro is positioned in relation to heavy industry, and Madeleine with the wonders of nature: two gender-stereotyped poles that are intertwined in utopian accounts of Vancouver's harmony between civilization and the wilderness (Berelowitz 2005, 25). These positions are underscored by Madeleine's recurring dream in which she fantasizes about a young man who always appears by the water without a hint of civilization anywhere to be seen. When challenged by Toro on these escapist flights of fancy, she answers: "at least my fantasies are innocent," pointing to his sexual quirks as evidence of corruption by the very system he wants to challenge. Ultimately these gendered characterizations break down. Toro has been using Madeleine's loft as the base of operations for his plan to organize the transient members of Vancouver's young hippie community into a vehicle for systemic change, ultimately seeking to leave the city and start fresh on one of the islands off the coast.

Meanwhile Madeleine becomes increasingly entrenched in the street culture of an older generation who are homeless by dint of the city's changing relationship to industry rather than by privileged choice, the kind of people documented in Allan King's *Skidrow* and dramatized in Larry Kent's *Hastings Street*. Toro rejects these older social problems as unsalvageable. While he seeks to escape, Madeleine engages with her new urban home, reversing the relationship between their character psychologies and associated settings.

At the insistence of one of her homeless acquaintances, Madeleine begins to paint portraits of the elderly street people of the Downtown Eastside, an activity requiring active participation by her subjects and ultimately reflected back to the community through a showing at a local gallery. This reciprocal approach to documentation positions art as a mode of community activism, a facet of Hastings Street life that continues today. Although the gentrification of surrounding areas concentrated social problems in the Downtown Eastside, and some artist collectives have evacuated the area for safer and more profitable neighborhoods since *Madeleine Is . . .*, artistic and political activity remain (Shier 2002, 15). The recent redevelopment of the Woodward's block, once the thriving heart of the area's commercial district and then left abandoned upon the store's closure in 1992, now incorporates Simon Fraser University's School for Contemporary Art and is set to increase cultural activity: for some a remedy for the neighborhood's decline;

for others the feared herald of further gentrification. In the Woodward's atrium hangs Stan Douglas's large format photograph *Abbott & Cordova, 7 August 1971*, a critique of the violent police break-up of a hippie counterculture protest that occurred only months after *Madeleine Is...* was released. The film foreshadows the dispersal of the hippie life that once challenged city by-laws, to other neighborhoods and ultimately to the rural islands and interior—following Toro's proposed trajectory. In so doing, the film also comments upon the distinction drawn between different communities housed within this same space. As Jesse Proudfoot puts it, "The more iconic figures of the Downtown Eastside were the working-class men living in the neighbourhood's residential hotels—those men who look on like detached spectators from the peripheries of Douglas's mural" (2012, 90), the men that Madeleine was more interested in helping than the hippie newcomers that Toro would put to his own use.

The film charts Madeleine's shifting positions by way of strategic location shooting and creative employment of sound. There is a wealth of sequences shot downtown, treated with different stylistic approaches to capture a range of tonal qualities including: the calm of a morning yoga session across from the train yard; the bustle of a heavily trafficked commute to work; a free-jazz sprint through the neon night following a fight with Toro; a psychedelic meditation on the city's imposing architecture prior to a dream-therapy session; and a melancholy tour of the street life in sepia-toned stills as Madeleine begins her documentation project. As such the downtown core is presented as a heterogeneous space resisting easy categorization when set against the interstitial spaces of the beach or the remove of the Gulf Islands.

The sound of the railyards provides a particularly interesting case for the shifting status of Madeleine's physical and psychological geographies. We see these trains several times throughout the film, but each time they sound different. The first time the sound is presented naturalistically, most likely location recordings of the yard as Toro watches through the window and, shortly thereafter, listens from the bedroom. Following this scene, Madeleine wakes up the next morning and performs some yoga on the roof overlooking the yards. Here, however, there isn't a hint of realistic train sounds. Instead, we hear a mellow folk music track entitled "Morning Sunlight," written for the film by Ross Barrett and sung by Melinda Whitaker to suit Madeleine's meditative state. The sound environment bends to her psychology while the images remain grounded in location-based realism.

Later in the film, as Madeleine is on her way to a group dream therapy session to help her sort out her visions, the film presents a series of dramatic shots of the cityscape from oblique and imposing angles as a foray into experimental electronic sound effects by Don Young runs on the soundtrack. She peers over the railing of a plaza down on the train tracks and we get her point-of-view shot of the trains once again, but this time rendered as a strange and alienating part of the landscape into which she had earlier seemed to fit. Her interest in therapy is part of her final push to break free from Toro, and his association with the trains is now turning sour for her. Her own narrative arc is here tracked by a gradual shift away from a realistic presentation of the rail yards through to two very different musical treatments pushing toward the abstract. The views of the trains do not hold stable in this film, and as Madeleine becomes more plugged into her new city she also becomes increasingly distant from her romantic relationship down by the tracks.

Madeleine's personal unsettling comes to a peak with perhaps the most significant location of the film: the West End condo high-rise occupied by David (Wayne Specht), the corporate man that Madeleine befriends as a manifestation of the boy from her fantasies. David is emblematic of the rising professional class that would go on to claim the gentrified views of Vancouver's classic mountain backdrop in high-rises like these, increasingly encroaching upon the scenery for all those removed from the waterfront. Indeed, his building is filled with "moozak," the "schizophonic musical drool in public places" that so irritated the WSP (Truax 1978, 78). From inside David's apartment we hear nothing of the city outside. But the film refuses essentialism, and it is David, not Toro, who recognizes Madeleine's talent for capturing the essence of downtown street life in her painting. While Madeleine doesn't end up choosing either man as partner, the film is provocative in allowing for David to be a positive influence in Madeleine's life, keeping any strict lines from being drawn between the various conflicting worlds that intersect in the film. In the end it is the film's willingness to acknowledge overlapping claims to the city's spaces that speak most to Madeleine's character, its title leaving her self-definition open to situation-specific fluctuation that could just as easily be applied to the city itself. From David's glazed soundscape, with its privileged view, Madeleine discovers herself and her ability to engage ever more deeply with her own neighborhood and break free of Toro's toxic influence once and for all, lending support for the ecological reading of David Rimmer's sonically isolated view in the *Canadian Pacific* films.

Coda—Unmarking Sound

As sensitive as Sylvia Spring is to the nuances of the Downtown Eastside of the early 1970s, neither *Madeleine Is . . .*, nor any of the other films discussed in this chapter since *East Hastings Pharmacy*, represent Indigenous peoples even as they pass across a wide variety of social perspectives, styles, and historical periods. Madeleine's line in the sand between older working class and newer hippy arrivals in the area points to systemic neglect for another category, the *lumpenproletariat* class of "undeserving" poor that increased in numbers as the "deserving" class of retired resource workers diminished over the decades since *Madeleine Is . . .* was released (Proudfoot 2012, 92). Sadly, it is in this category that we find the majority of the neighborhood's Indigenous people, like the mother and son in the east Hastings methadone clinic that opened this chapter, overlooked by society to the point that dozens of women can disappear from the region without any serious police investigation until far too late, haunting the spaces of the Downtown Eastside with their invisibility (Oleksijczuk 2002, 98–99). This invisibility has been replicated by media representations of the area as well.

Let us end this chapter by rethinking the WSP's own narrative of Indigenous erasure at the hands of modern urban transportation. If, as Schafer suggests, the disappearance of soundmarks like train whistles can indicate the dying of a culture that held these soundmarks dear, what might that mean for communities that were less positively oriented around these same soundmarks? While the downtown railyards are still in operation, the network of rail lines that still crisscross the city have been decommissioned over the years, ensuring that the sound of trains is no longer the daily occurrence for most Vancouverites that it once was. In the WSP's quest to preserve endangered sounds for the posterity of culture, they captured once such train sound no longer heard in the city. On February 15, 1973, they recorded a passing train that ran along the shoreline of False Creek under Burrard Bridge, formerly on the land of Kitsilano Indian Reserve, established as Indian Reserve No. 6 in 1877. The first land to be appropriated from the reserve was for this rail line in 1899, running across the Kitsilano Trestle Bridge until it was torn down in 1982. The original agreements regarding appropriation of Native reserve lands for railway thoroughfares stipulated their return to reserve status should the railroads be put out of use. After twenty years in the courts, with competing claims by the Squamish, Tsleil-Waututh and Musqueam Nations, redress has actually come to pass for a small section of land surrounding the bridge corresponding to the original railway right of passage, awarded to the Squamish Nation in 2002 (Barman 2007, 29).

The WSP listened to trains through nostalgia for settler colonialism, and it is fitting that the disappearance of their soundmarks restored Indigenous title to the land on this spot in False Creek. This opens the possibility for a newly productive use of the WSP's archive, not as evidence of the sounds of culture now gone, but as pointers to how the disappearance of some of Vancouver's key settler sounds can map a revitalization of culture in the city. In her short film *Indigenous Plant Diva* (2008), Kamala Todd emphasizes how Indigenous culture can thrive in the modern city, tracking the herbal medicine practices of Cease Wyss of the Squamish Nation as she walks Vancouver with her daughter to pass on her knowledge of local plant life. For my purposes here, the most telling image comes near the end of the film as she poses for a still shot down on a decommissioned rail line now overgrown and ripe for harvest. This image also challenges the stereotype of urban Native culture as necessarily of the *lumpen* class so easily ignored on the Downtown Eastside. Sometimes it's what we don't hear that is most telling, and films can highlight this absence of sound through their strategies for re-placing location shot imagery on their soundtracks. Informed by alternative histories of the city's soundscape revealed through medial engagements with the acoustic profile mapped by the sound of trains, the unsettled ear can hear the disappearance of this sound as the return of culture to a space from which it had been erased, and perhaps even the end of the whitewashing that has characterized so much of twentieth century Vancouver. What the future holds in this regard remains unheard.

For the early WSP it would have been inconceivable to think that they could present their arguments about Vancouver's sonic environment without the aid of location recording as proof of engagement with place. This is why they privileged this brand of documentation in providing evidence for the elements of the environment that they found most worthy of discussion. Along with this privilege came a mode of presentation that, while acknowledging their mediatic interventions into their recorded documents, was largely un-reflexive about how their biases informed their construction of the Vancouver soundscape. The WSP's approach teaches us the importance of listening carefully to the ways in which sound interacts with geographical space to map the spaces in which acoustic communities emerge. At the same time, examining the limitations of their methodology opens questions about how best to modify their approach to pay greater attention to the multiple overlapping histories of place presented in the alternative listening positions available across a variety of cinematic representations. This is the job of acoustic profiling.

Treating film soundtracks as documents on par with the files of the WSP offers an alternative history of the Vancouver soundscape that unsettles the place to reveal rich and troubled histories that continually overlap. This is particularly evident in the sound of trains, a sound that signaled the birth of the city, carved out its paths of dispossession, and now marks new avenues to reconciliation. For founder R. Murray Schafer, trains signified a version of Canadian culture that ignored a great deal of Canadian experience. Using the tools of acoustic profiling to reveal alternative histories of the city's soundscape, and the varied settler positions that inform these histories, the unsettled listener can hear the overlaps between different filmmaking practices in the city, and between the city itself and the films produced there. Acoustic profiling allows us to listen beyond the physical attributes of geographical space to become immersed in the simultaneity of multiple histories that, even if they can't be picked up by a microphone on location, reverberate loudly through the city's environment at all times.

References

Akiyama, Mitchell. 2019. "Nothing Connects Us but Imagined Sound." In *Sound, Media, Ecology*, edited by Milena Droumeva and Randolph Jordan, 113–129. New York: Palgrave Macmillan.

Altman, Rick. 1992. "The Material Heterogeneity of Recorded Sound." In *Sound Theory, Sound Practice*, edited by Rick Altman, 15–31. New York: Routledge.

Barman, Jean. 2007. "Erasing Indigenous Indigeneity in Vancouver." *BC Studies* 155 (Autumn): 3–30.

Berelowitz, Lance. 2005. *Dream City: Vancouver and the Global Imagination*. Vancouver: Douglas and McIntyre.

Bijsterveld, Karin, et al. 2013. *Soundscapes of the Urban Past: Staged Sound as Mediated Cultural Heritage*. Bielefeld: Transcript Verlag.

Blomley, Nicholas. 2004. *Unsettling the City: Urban Land and the Politics of Property*. New York: Routledge.

Browne, Colin. 2000. "Afterword: Fugitive Events." In *Cineworks 2000: Twenty Years of Independent Filmmaking in British Columbia*, edited by Justin MacGregor, 85–120. Vancouver: Cineworks Independent Filmmakers Society.

Chion, Michel. 1994. *Audio-Vision: Sound on Screen*. Translated by Claudia Gorbman. New York: Columbia University Press.

De Certeau, Michel. 1984. *The Practice of Everyday Life*. Translated by Stephen Rendall. Berkeley: University of California Press.

Gasher, Mike. 2002. *Hollywood North: The Feature Film Industry in British Columbia*. Vancouver: University of British Columbia Press.

Hempton, Gordon, and John Grossman. 2009. *One Square Inch of Silence: One Man's Search for Natural Quiet in a Noisy World*. New York: Free Press.

Jordan, Randolph. 2007. "Film Sound, Acoustic Ecology, and Performance in Electroacoustic Music." In *Music, Sound and Multi-Media*, edited by Jamie Sexton, 121–141. Edinburgh: University of Edinburgh Press.

Jordan, Randolph. 2013. "Vancouver Is . . . " In *World Film Locations: Vancouver*, edited by Rachel Walls, 44–45. Bristol: Intellect Books.

Jordan, Randolph. 2014a. "Unsettled Listening: Integrating Film and Place." *Sounding Out! Blog*, August 14. Available from: http://soundstudiesblog.com/2014/08/14/unsettled-listening-integrating-film-and-place/]

Jordan, Randolph. 2014b. "Seeing Then, Hearing Now: Audiovisual Counterpoint at the Intersection of Dual Production Contexts in Larry Kent's *Hastings Street*." In *Cinephemera: Archives, Ephemeral Cinema, and New Screen Histories in Canada*, edited by Zoë Druick and Gerda Cammaer, 232–255. McGill-Queen's University Press.

Jordan, Randolph. 2015. "Unsettling the World Soundscape Project: Bell Tower of False Creek, Vancouver," *Sounding Out! Blog*, September 3. http://soundstudiesblog.com/2015/09/03/unsettling-the-world-soundscape-project-the-bell-tower-of-false-creek-vancouver/]

Jordan, Randolph. 2017. "Unsettling the Soundtrack: Acoustic Profiling and the Documentation of Community and Place." In *The Routledge Companion to Screen Music and Sound*, edited by Miguel Mera, Ron Sadoff, and Ben Winters, 590–602. New York: Routledge.

Jordan, Randolph. 2018. "Re-placing the Urban Soundscape: Performative Documentary Research in Vancouver's False Creek." In *Critical Distance in Documentary Media*, edited by Gerda Cammaer, Blake Fitzpatrick, and Bruno Lessard, 257–278. New York: Palgrave Macmillan.

Kirby, Lynne. 1997. *Parallel Tracks: The Railroad and Silent Cinema*. Durham, NC: Duke University Press.

Lastra, James. 2000. *Sound Technology and the American Cinema*. New York: Columbia University Press.

Morris, Peter. 1978. *Embattled Shadows: A History of Canadian Cinema 1895–1939*. Montreal: McGill-Queen's University Press.

Oleksijauk, Denise Blake. 2002. "Haunted Spaces." In *Stan Douglas: Every Building on 100 West Hastings*, edited by Reid Shier, 96–116. Vancouver: Arsenal Pulp Press/Contemporary Art Gallery.

Proudfoot, Jesse. 2012. "The Derelict, the Deserving Poor, and the *Lumpen*: A History of the Politics of Representation on the Downtown Eastside." In *Stan Douglas: Abbott and Cordova, 7 August 1971*, edited by Stan Douglas, 88–107. Vancouver: Arsenal Pulp Press.

Robinson, Dylan. 2020. *Hungry Listening: Resonant Theory for Indigenous Sound Studies*. Minneapolis: University of Minnesota Press.

Russell, Catherine. 2006. "The Inhabited View: Landscape in the Films of David Rimmer." In *Landscape and Film*, edited by Martin Lefebvre, 149–166. New York: Routledge.

Ruoff, Jeoffrey K. 1993. "Conventions of Sound in Documentary." *Cinema Journal* 32, no. 3: 24–40.

Schafer, R. Murray. 1977. *The Tuning of the World*. Toronto: McClelland and Stewart.

Shier, Reid. 2002. "Introduction." In *Stan Douglas: Every Building on 100 West Hastings*, edited by Reid Shier, 10–17. Vancouver: Arsenal Pulp Press/Contemporary Art Gallery.

Sommers, Jeff, and Nick Blomley. 2002. "The Worst Block in Vancouver." In *Stan Douglas: Every Building on 100 West Hastings*, edited by Reid Shier, 18–58. Vancouver: Arsenal Pulp Press/Contemporary Art Gallery.

Spaner, David. 2003. *Dreaming in the Rain: How Vancouver Became Hollywood North by Northwest*. Vancouver: Arsenal Pulp Press.

Sterne, Jonathan. 2003. *The Audible Past: Cultural Origins of Sound Reproduction*. Durham, NC: Duke University Press.

Todd, Kamala. 2013. "Thoughts on Making Places: Hollywood North and the Indigenous City." In *World Film Locations: Vancouver*, edited by Rachel Walls, 8–9. Bristol: Intellect.

Truax, Barry, ed. 1978. *Handbook for Acoustic Ecology*. Vancouver: ARC Publications.

Truax, Barry. 2001. *Acoustic Communication*. 2nd edition. Westport, CT: Alex Publishing.

Westerkamp, Hildegard. 2002. "Linking Soundscape Composition and Acoustic Ecology." *Organised Sound* 7, no. 1: 52–56.

Westerkamp, Hildegard. 2019. "The Disruptive Nature of Listening: Today, Yesterday, Tomorrow." In *Sound, Media, Ecology*, edited by Milena Droumeva and Randolph Jordan, 45–64. New York: Palgrave Macmillan.

World Soundscape Project. 1973. *The Vancouver Soundscape*. Sound recording and book. Burnaby: Sonic Research Studio, Dept. of Communications, Simon Fraser.

Conclusion

A Position Piece

I last saw my father, Robert Christopher Jordan, on December 14, 2019. He was eighty-six years old at the tail-end of a long and slow transition into dementia, living in a senior care facility on campus at the University of British Columbia, where he used to teach classical guitar in the music department and where I completed my undergraduate studies in film and philosophy. Having lived in Montreal for twenty years by that point, I was back in Vancouver to make location-specific field recordings as part of my work as sound designer on the *Impostor Cities* project, Canada's official entry to (what was supposed to be) the 2020 Venice Architecture Biennale.[1] I had spent the morning recording ocean and forest sounds on Tower Beach at the northern edge of campus, so named because of two concrete structures that once held powerful lights used to survey the harbor during WWII. I then popped in to see Pop before heading to the other side of the city to make recordings at Simon Fraser University, where he performed regularly in the 1960s and where I landed for my postdoc in 2012. He did not recognize me but was happy for the company. Then the world shut down, and a few months after that he died of pneumonia, unrelated to COVID-19.

A year later, R. Murray Schafer also died. I mention this here because there is overlap with my father's story. Schafer and my father differed in age by only four days, both born in late July of 1933. They were of the same era, and thus shared some common position in their ideologies. When Schafer was at Simon Fraser University (SFU) laying the groundwork for the World Soundscape Project (WSP) in the late 1960s, my dad performed on campus with soprano Phyllis Mailing, who was married to Schafer at the time, and with whom my dad also cut a record produced by the Canadian Broadcasting Corporation.[2] It was my dad who taught me how to listen from the position of a classical musician, with music lessons from a very early age and a home rife with the stickling tension that surrounds the model listener in the tradition of Western art music. Later I would also understand how this

Figure C.1   Robert Christopher Jordan.

listening position was very much connected to my dad's status as British expatriate who felt most at home in British Columbia amidst Canada's largest concentration of British nationals. He was a child in England during the war, and came over to Canada in the early 1950s, a commonwealth country with British royalty emblazoned on our currency. There was a sense that this land was waiting for my dad with built-in community, easing his transition between worlds and assisting in the position that he was able to achieve here over the years. And so I was born into a sense of entitlement over the land based on my colonial heritage, and understanding this has been crucial when coming to terms with Schafer's work.

When I first encountered Schafer's writing about environmental sound, after leaving Vancouver for Montreal (as described in the introduction to this book), my first impression was that this was a very different model for listening that offered freedom from the tyranny of the constraints I had associated with the demands of classical music. Later I would come to understand that Schafer's own methodology essentially imposed the Western art music model that I had grown up with onto everyday sounds, which perhaps explains why I was so comfortable in changing the objects of my attention while maintaining the same listener orientation. I would also come to understand how Schafer's own settler positionality informed this listening model, now the subject of many critiques of Schaferian acoustic ecology (some of which are detailed in this book). I don't presume to speak for Schafer in this regard, and certainly his status as Canadian born puts him in a different position than my father with respect to his own settler heritage. I don't know if Schafer and my father ever spoke, though I imagine they would have crossed paths on many occasions. I wonder where their ideologies would have overlapped around the relationship between music, sound, and culture, and where they would have diverged. They certainly would have shared a disdain for Muzak and traffic noise, the low hanging fruit of soundscape awareness. But my dad sure loved his hi-fi stereo rig, an impulse that I have inherited, and it is on my own rig that I now listen to *The Vancouver Soundscape* LP, released in the year of my birth.

Thinking about the role that positionality plays in Schafer's work has helped me understand my own position by way of my dad, and this path to self-reflection sits as a subtext to the progression of my analyses across this book. The trajectory begins in France with *Playtime*, moves to Canada's remote north in *Picture of Light*, and then lands in the Pacific Northwest for the last three chapters, starting in the US with *Last Days* and *Twin Peaks*, and finally arriving in Vancouver on the Canadian side. With this geographical journey from western Europe to North America's west coast, my critical attention has also moved from specific interest in the composition of films and sound works as recorded objects (the art model), to the way that these objects engage with the specificities of place (the documentary model), and finally to the role of listening practice in making sense of both (the activist model).

Across the book's trajectory of my own critical movement, one theme has stood out above all else: the tension between mediation and the myth of its potential to vanish. In all of my analyses, the goal has been to demonstrate a form of mediality that exposes the fabrications that limit our capacity to understand how positionality constructs both the objects we pay attention to and the way we pay attention to them. As a theoretical tool for recognizing this mediality in play, I have used the term *acoustic profiling* to reveal how filmmakers articulate the acoustic profiles of their narrative spaces and, by extension, position their audiences within these spaces. Acoustic profiling allows us to reframe the issue of fidelity, shifting away from its typical orientation around the relationship between a recorded object and that which it is said to record, and toward an immersive process that dissolves the boundary line between the two. In short, the goal of my analyses has been to make apparent the material conditions of spatial orientation that are often concealed by formal convention in films and media and their guiding ideologies; I want to reveal the mechanisms by which mediation is said to vanish in the myth of vanishing mediation.

Each chapter proposes a specific term designed at once to address the particularities of the film(s) in question within a specific chapter and the generalities of vanishing mediation that traverse the book as a whole. Since vanishing mediation is about drawing a line in the sand to demarcate distinct spaces that are then said to fold onto each other, my analyses pay critical attention to the way that films set up acoustic profiles across various thematic demarcations of boundary. The question for all films is this: to what extent do the spaces on either side of a given boundary line extend into each other, and how can this extension be tracked with attention to sound? In some examples, like *Playtime* and *Last Days*, these lines are diegetically physical. I use the term *audible transparency* in reference to the architectural quality of the simultaneously transparent and reflective windows of *Playtime* that demarcate the spaces of modernity and their hindrance to community engagement. Modernist glass walls are meant to be invisible, but Jacques Tati makes us hear them so that we can think critically about their role in shaping experience. The term *reflective empathy* suggests how the doorways of *Last Days* modulate empathy between friends gathered in a single house, echoed by the ways in which soundscape composition is integrated into the sound design, challenging established ideas about how compilation soundtracks function in film. *Playtime* and *Last Days* thus share an interest in putting the architectural design of cinematic space on display, reflecting upon the perceptual and emotional positions of the people that occupy them.

In other cases, as in *Picture of Light* and *Twin Peaks*, the boundary lines are tied to media technologies and their capacity to foster audience engagement with the worlds they represent. I use the term *immersive reflexivity* to explain Peter Mettler's explicit attention to the line between cinematic sound and image in *Picture of Light*, exploring asynchronicity in attempting to render audible the specifically visual phenomenon of the aurora borealis. Mettler puts the technology of filmmaking on display to challenge the idea of film as a window or doorway out onto the world before the cameras; instead, he demonstrates how the technology itself is what shapes the world and our experience of it. And the term *schizophonographics* illustrates how vanishing mediation itself can be visualized to reveal the fraught nature of the fidelity thesis, as when phonograph turntables in David Lynch's *Twin Peaks* dissolve spatiotemporal boundary lines to provide transparent access across times and places, as well as charting shifts in listener orientation across the dividing line between the pre-digital and digital eras. *Picture of Light* and *Twin Peaks* therefore share an interest in the visualization of recording technologies that are frequently meant to disappear when experiencing their records, suggesting that mediation itself is what allows for deep engagement rather than acting as distanciating barrier.

In the book's final chapter on the films and media of Vancouver, British Columbia, my attention is on the ways in which one listener position can overwrite the multiple positions active within a particular region, the way the biases of the WSP imagine the particularities of place in lieu of myriad other possibilities. Here, *unsettled listening* refers to the process by which we can employ attention to listener positionality across a range of films and media to better understand the complexities of overlapping experience within a specific place, offering the potential to rethink our own positionality in turn. All of the films discussed in this book make their medial moves by foregrounding the fabricated nature of vanishing mediation, putting on display the material qualities of the boundary lines we are otherwise supposed to ignore. It is the fiction of vanishing mediation that is the true boundary line under consideration here, which stays in place as long as it can remain invisible. Listening to the way that sound articulates space in these films makes this boundary line appear so that we may then acknowledge its limitations en route to dissolving its power.

My process of asking continual questions around the mechanisms by which boundary lines are meant to be rendered invisible has led to the conclusion that the myth of vanishing mediation itself is one expression of the settler impulse to claim space with one particular definition of place. In this respect, there is another possible line to draw through all of these films to delineate their particular approaches to the construction of geographic locales. The Paris of *Playtime* was constructed entirely on an elaborate set; the Pacific Northwest of *Last Days* was shot in upstate New York; *Twin Peaks* was shot (in part) on location in the Washington State setting of an otherwise fictional town; and not until we arrive in Vancouver do we find films that are dedicated to dealing with the true particularities of a real-world environment.

I am struck here by another line of intersection through the work of the WSP at the time of its formation: the arrival of Hollywood filmmakers in 1960s Vancouver, the start of an established presence that would eventually brand the city as "Hollywood North." Just as my dad was establishing his acoustic profile over the city, with the founding of the Guitar Centre, Vancouver's first space for the study of the classical guitar, and as Schafer was introducing environmental sound into university music curricula, Hollywood was introducing Canadian regional specificity to international audiences, while almost invariably presenting these spaces as other places. This is an extension of the settler mindset that I did not address in the final chapter on BC film, but it is a pertinent angle to frame my concluding thoughts on how acoustic profiling has informed my creative practice as well as my scholarship. Like my imagined conversations between Schafer and my dad, I wonder how the WSP members would have interacted with Hollywood filmmakers around town.

In August of 1971, a Universal Studios production team set up shop on campus at SFU for *Groundstar Conspiracy* (1972), a sci-fi thriller starring George Peppard. It's about a man named Welles, or perhaps Bellamy, who has had his memory wiped clean after being used as a mercenary by a covert government operation housed at a top-secret military establishment, played by the campus itself, designed by Arthur Erickson, with its distinctive elevated Academic Quadrangle resembling the Pentagon. This film set some important precedents as an early touchstone for Vancouver as Hollywood North and the inevitable overwriting of the city that came along with it. SFU never plays a university on film. A film like *Groundstar* offers ample points of identification for "insiders" who can see through the projected "placelessness" of the narrative (Matheson 2005, 133) and view the film as a goldmine of documentary footage of a city on the cusp of the major changes that the WSP would attempt to track. Yet this identification is challenged by the film's continual aims to erase that veracity in favor of narrative demands, not unlike the plight of the protagonist whose own memory has been wiped to service a political narrative. "I still don't know who I am," he laments at the end of the film surrounded by Erickson's modernist concrete angles, a question that could just as easily have been posed by the city itself as it set about defining its own path in the wake of modernity's onset in sister cities across the border.

What would WSP team members have said to the *Groundstar* production team that summer as they roamed campus, learning the ropes on their newly acquired sound recording equipment in preparation for the start of their official documentation process the following year? Perhaps the WSP would have been interested in the professionalism of the filmmakers' recording techniques, while disapproving of their continual attempts to reposition their shooting locations as other places. Hypotheticals aside, there is indeed a fascinating tension in play between the way the WSP went on to present their home city and the way this city is presented in films like *Groundstar*. The WSP was transparent in its distaste for the lo-fi masking sounds of the modern city, like the ventilation systems that muddied the soundscapes of Arthur Erickson's visually impressive design. Of course this aspect of the local soundscape is the first thing to get dumped by Hollywood filmmakers in search of hi-fi soundtracks that allow for maximum speech intelligibility. So when we listen to SFU campus in *Groundstar*, we hear no evidence of the qualities that the WSP would critique. While this marks a difference in staging across the WSP's documentation of these lo-fi sounds and the hi-fi fabrications in Hollywood films, there is an ideological commonality here: it's almost as if Schafer had modeled his notion of the hi-fi soundscape on the speech intelligibility model of film soundtracks. In this way, film conventions idealize these biases of the WSP.

Hollywood's erasure of lo-fi masking sounds works as part of a generic international convention that, in turn, services their genericization of local specificity. Yet the reality is that the ventilation at SFU is a location-specific sound. In *Groundstar*, this specificity is overwritten. For the WSP, that ventilation, along with corollary sounds like ubiquitous traffic noise, are markers of an increasingly generic global urban soundscape, with the rise of car culture and modern architecture emerging quickly in many parts of the world following WWII. The irony is that the WSP includes these sounds in their presentation of the city to demonstrate the loss of regional specificity, while Hollywood erases these sounds to capitalize on this very same loss. In both cases there is an impulse toward vanishing mediation. The WSP wants that layer of noise to vanish, leaving their ideal soundscape underneath. Hollywood makes those layers of noise vanish, leaving their own ideal soundscape underneath. In both scenarios, neither party invites critical thinking about the biases that inform these idealizations of what places should sound like.

The ideological commonalities and tensions between the WSP and mainstream film convention became the basis for my work on the *Impostor Cities* project. Helmed by David Theodore, Thomas Balaban, and Jennifer Thorogood, the project is premised on the reality that, in films, Canada is most often presented to the world in disguise. The multi-screen exhibition stages excerpts shots of well-known Canadian architectural sites (like Erickson's SFU campus) and strings them together across a variety of film appearances to highlight all the ways that these recognizable buildings are dressed up to look like they live somewhere else. My task in designing the soundtrack for the installation was to imagine how this "impostoring" process, as we call it, can be reflected acoustically. So I took the above-described overlap in the ideologies governing both acoustic ecology and Hollywood filmmaking as the basis for my aesthetic approach, which involved blending location recordings of these real-world sites with the soundscapes designed for them in the films in which they appear.

When I stood on SFU campus that day in December 2019, the place was barren and the ventilation shafts were blowing deep and loud. Yet in the middle of the Academic Quadrangle, there was a reflective quality to the sound that allowed it to blend with other environmental sounds, particularly the calls of crows flying from tree to tree within the boundaries of the structure, their voices echoing in their responses to each other as well as off

Figure C.2 Randolph Jordan with microphone on Simon Fraser University campus.

the reflective surfaces created by the unique four-sided structure. The quadrangle thus functioned like a multichannel mixing console, gathering all sounds in the environment, layering them over one another while assigning trajectories of reverberant movement through the space. The *Impostor Cities* installation begins with this recorded environment playing over images from *Groundstar Conspiracy*, *Battlestar Galactica* (2004–2009), and *Stargate SG-1* (1997–2007) all shot within the quadrangle, as I build in certain features of these impostorized soundscapes to offset the location-specific realism, including dialogue from *Groundstar* in which Bellamy speaks of his identity crisis.

My location recordings were made with an ambisonic microphone spreading nineteen recording capsules over a spherical surface to allow sound capture in 360 degrees, which would then be mixed into the fifteen-channel installation of the exhibition. In this way, something of the architectural specificity of Erickson's design would be made apparent to exhibition listeners, with the idea that listener positionality would be literalized as visitors to the Canadian pavilion move through the space and be continually

Figure C.3 Ambisonic microphone in the Academic Quadrangle on SFU campus.

reoriented with respect to the locations presented in image and sound, each screen and speaker reflecting and diverging from each other in an endless array of possible configurations. In building Hollywood constructions into the mix, my aim was to use the language of Hollywood's sonic fabrication to reveal the mediation in play in their spatial representations, exposing the tension between exploiting a particular location for its existing qualities while simultaneously advocating for their disappearance.

I attempted an even more direct address of the tensions found in the WSP's work in the film component of my *Bell Tower of False Creek* project (2017), about which I have written at length elsewhere (see Jordan 2014–2015, 2015, and 2022). This dates back to 2013 when, as part of my postdoctoral work at SFU, I was revisiting recording locations used on the *Vancouver Soundscape* LP on the fortieth anniversary of its original release. Under Vancouver's Burrard Bridge, spanning False Creek that separates the downtown core from the rest of the city to the south, I encountered a loud metallic clanging sound, which I traced to a pothole behind a metal divider on the bridge's surface that sounded every time a car passed across. I remembered a section from the *Vancouver Soundscape* release in which the sound recordists conversed with Schafer about their process, mentioning their frustration regarding bridge traffic noise obscuring their attempts at capturing the tinkling masts of boats in the marina. This is a perfect example of how two sounds representing modern realities of the city, a bridge for automobile traffic and a marina for pleasure craft, are given opposite value designations. Both, however, are markers of the settler colonialism that installed these facilities on unceded Indigenous lands, and this practice of preferential treatment became the locus of my own attempt to represent this space on film.

Burrard Bridge sits within a stone's throw of the Vancouver Academy of Music where I took music lessons from the age of three and where my dad was on faculty for many years. Vanier Park is the music school's front yard, and I have fond memories of playing out on the grass while my dad worked and my siblings finished their lessons. I knew nothing of Indigenous land claims as a child. But on one of my return visits to town after moving to Montreal, a newly erected Senákw welcome pole next to the bridge alerted me to Indigenous presence on the land. Later I learned about the original reserve status of the area, its piecemeal dissolution for projects like the railway and the bridge, and the return of a portion of the land to reserve status in 2002 (discussed in more detail at the end of Chapter 5). Walking the edges of Vanier Park, it struck me that the sound of the clanging bridge

Figure C.4 Seńákw Welcome Pole next to Burrard Bridge carved by Darren Yelton in 2006. Still from *Bell Tower of False Creek* by Randolph Jordan.

pothole was audible in a way that mapped out the general boundaries of the original reserve, an acoustic profile the WSP would dismiss as generic modern city noise erasing local specificity, but that here serves as an unsettling marker of the region's history around Indigenous dispossession. Further, I learned that the electronic billboard next to the bridge, erected shortly after the totem pole, also marked Indigenous presence as a revenue generating installation for the Squamish band made possible by the newly reinstated reserve status of the land. In this way, the traffic on the bridge, with all its noise pollution, was now servicing twenty-first century Indigenous needs.

Taking some inspiration from Hildegard Westerkamp's composition "Kits Beach Soundwalk" (1989), wherein she plays with shifting relationships between the foreground sounds of the ocean and the cityscape in the background, my film aims to reframe the classic WSP opposition to traffic noise around its positive connotations for reconciliation. To do this, I juxtaposed the voices of WSP members talking about the problems of Burrard Bridge traffic noise with my own recordings of the dramatic clanging sound from a variety of locations around the space now marked out as reserve. On the image track I presented the bridge from many different positions that also chart the limits of the reserve, with a centerpiece section that foregrounded the two poles that mark twenty-first century indigeneity on the land.

Figure C.5 Electronic billboard next to Burrard Bridge. Still from *Bell Tower of False Creek* by Randolph Jordan.

In the middle section I included a segment of the WSP's interview with Tsleil-Waututh elder Herbert George. My intention here was to offer a corrective to the usage of the interview in the "Squamish Narrative" track on the *Vancouver Soundscape* LP that I critiqued in Chapter 5, where they had presented George speaking in Squamish amidst the sounds of birds and water to narrativize the obfuscation of Indigenous presence by way of modern transportation noise, represented by a passing sea plane. In the excerpts I used in my film, George speaks in English to recount a complex story around the arrival of the railroad that illustrates the ways in which settler colonialism intertwined with local mythology as part of the story of modern transportation in the region. I included a bit where interviewer Bruce Davis asks George to repeat himself when a passing car interferes with the intelligibility of his speech, demonstrating the irony around aiming for hi-fi clarity in their recordings so that they would have the building blocks to dramatize lo-fi density in their presentation of the material. My aim in the film was to liberate George's voice from the constraints of the WSP's bias, to let him tell his story in the context of the film's exploration of the positive connotations of traffic noise for indigeneity in Vancouver. Yet in so doing I, too, am guilty of trapping George's voice within another media construct that, for all my good intentions, is no less inflected with my own settler positionality, the kind of typical settler encounter with Indigenous soundmaking that Dylan Robinson critiques in his book *Hungry Listening* (2020, chapter 4).

I had to make this work to understand my own settler hunger while listening on Indigenous land, revealing the legacy of my own colonial heritage that comes with a sense of entitlement over this space that I had visited since childhood but never really known. My process of self-reflection has been assisted by the model for acoustic profiling laid out in this book. In the end, my film aimed to chart the acoustic profile of the traffic noise in order to track the problems inherent in the WSP's presentation of Vancouver, and speak to their complicity in extending the settler narrative around Indigenous erasure. I learned how to build acoustic profiling into a filmic presentation of space from the films that I have analyzed through the framework of acoustic

Figure C.6 WWII ruins at Tower Beach on campus at University of British Columbia. Polaroid by Randolph Jordan, December 14, 2019.

ecology. Now it is time to move this knowledge to the field of action, to account for my own complicity in the problems of hiding the mediation that underwrites settler encounters with Indigenous space. That is to say, *all* space.

Back to UBC's Tower Beach on the day that I last saw my dad, where I listened to the harbor for sounds that would be useful to my work on *Impostor Cities*. It was in the era of cemented colonization and globalizing urbanity that my dad arrived on BC's west coast. In spite of the constrictions of the listening practices that I was taught at an early age, the lessons of my dad's positionality now resonate in unexpected ways. Here, in 2019, well after the completion of *Bell Tower* and much of the writing for this book, I heard more than just material for an artistic composition. The interplay of the waves on the shore with eagles flying overhead and the sound of the seaplanes in the distance was an eerie echo of the "Squamish Narrative" segment on the *Vancouver Soundscape* LP, the basis for suggesting the disappearance of Indigenous voices. Listening this morning, however, I was in a better position to hear the ways in which this land has been unsettled. The emptiness of the concrete ruins from WWII worked like shells on the seashore, their imposing monumental status that once announced the cementing of settler colonialism enabled by WWII was now belied by their hollowness, functioning in a similar way to the echoic properties of the SFU quadrangle, ready to take in whatever the land speaks and hold these layers of positionality in solution.

Directly above these towers, atop the cliffs that mark the edge of UBC campus, sits the Arthur Erickson designed Museum of Anthropology and its large collection of totem poles. In the short WWII propaganda film *Gateway to Asia* (1945) produced by the National Film Board of Canada, a totem pole appears on screen as the narrator expounds, "Mute witnesses of an earlier culture watch the beginnings of a new era bring down their world around them," referring to the resource extraction industries that brought settlers to the west coast, industries that would then be put in service of defense against the threat to these settled lands from new enemies in the Pacific Rim. Now, eighty years on, it is these concrete tower structures on the beach, built as part of that defense strategy, that look silently on as reconciliation begins to acknowledge the living indigeneity of this place. The Museum of Anthropology was built on the foundation of the bunker that housed the guns that would have used the light towers on the beach to set their sights. Looking out through the wall-size glass panels, much like those featured in the Paris of Jacques Tati's *Playtime*, the museum's totem poles are dramatically framed against the backdrop of the fabulous harbor view. The transparency of the glass provides the appearance of unbroken connection with the land; but like the modern architecture that Tati plays with in his film, the containment in the museum is painfully audible. Hildegard Westerkamp once critiqued this museum as an "acoustic dump" for its combination of ventilation noise trapped within its glazed interior, which contributes to silencing the voices of the many First Nations objects housed therein, stripped of their context and function within the communities from which they came (2019, 56–57). The 1976 article in which Westerkamp made these critiques went unpublished after a draft caught the attention of both the museum director and the architect himself. She recounts how her thinking was dismissed for its aura of "suppressed hysteria" (57), likely tied to her status as a woman, one of the many instances of sexism she experienced as the only female member of the WSP—and an important reminder of how, even within the WSP, positions were far from equal. But even if Erickson and the museum director had taken Westerkamp's critiques seriously, you can't fix the problem of the voiceless totem poles through changes to the acoustic design of their "graveyard," as Coast Salish artist Lawrence Paul Yuxweluptun once called the museum (CBC 2007).

Decades later, in the summer of 2019, not long before my last visit, a Haida mortuary pole held by the museum was returned to its people by request of the band's Repatriation Committee (Rowley 2020). This pole, at least, has had its voice reinstated, its acoustic profile no longer inhibited by the museum's settler ideologies given architectural shape through the building's modernist design. This repatriation was enabled by recommendations put forth in the 2015 report by Canada's Truth and Reconciliation Committee. To arrive at points of action like these, voices need to speak up to expose instances of harm, and people need to ready to listen. In Westerkamp's critique we find the potential for the kind of listening originally prescribed by the WSP to move into a more action-oriented mode for the present day. Attention to the acoustic profile of the museum reveals how the sonic by-products of a settler architectural imperative are connected to the process of disenfranchising Indigenous voices. The practice of acoustic profiling in this context could be repositioned away from opening dialogue around "fixing" the museum's aesthetics and toward productive action for redress to the communities harmed by the museum's foundational mandate. The museum itself might then one day sit empty, like the light towers on the beach below, a monument to a mode of settler positioning on the land that would now mark a distant past, the voices it once silenced able to speak again. In this spirit, it is my wish that the tools for acoustic profiling detailed in this book, premised on intersecting the strengths and weaknesses of acoustic ecology and film sound studies, can yield a mode of listening to film and media objects that reposition our thinking around the relationship between sound, space, and culture, and put us all in a better position for reconciliatory action.

References

Canadian Broadcasting Corporation (CBC). 2007. "The Ideas of Lawrence Paul Yuxweluptun." *CBC Ideas* (April 4).

Jordan, Randolph. 2014–15. "Bell Tower of False Creek." *Soundscape: The Journal of Acoustic Ecology* 14, no. 1 (Winter/Spring): 16–20.

Jordan, Randolph. 2015. "Unsettling the World Soundscape Project: Bell Tower of False Creek, Vancouver," *Sounding Out! Blog*, September 3. http://soundstudiesblog.com/2015/09/03/unsettling-the-world-soundscape-project-the-bell-tower-of-false-creek-vancouver/

Jordan, Randolph. 2022. "Pole Positions under Vancouver's Burrard Bridge: Exposure and Intersection on Indigenous Land in *Bell Tower of False Creek*." In *Place Matters: Critical Topographies in Word and Image*, edited by Jonathan Bordo and Blake Fitzpatrick, colour section 2. Montreal and Kingston: McGill-Queen's University Press.

Matheson, Sarah. 2005. "Projecting Placelessness: Industrial Television and the 'Authentic' Canadian City." In *Contracting Out Hollywood: Runaway Productions and Foreign Location Shooting*, edited by Greg Elmer and Mike Gasher, 117–39. Maryland: Rowman and Littlefield.

Robinson, Dylan. 2020. *Hungry Listening: Resonant Theory for Indigenous Sound Studies*. Minneapolis: University of Minnesota Press.

Rowley, Susan. 2020. "Yahguudangang: A Haida Pole Returns Home." *Museum of Anthropology* (May 26). University of British Columbia. https://moa.ubc.ca/2020/05/yahguudangang-a-haida-pole-returns-home/.

Westerkamp, Hildegard. 2019. "The Disruptive Nature of Listening: Today, Yesterday, Tomorrow." In *Sound, Media, Ecology*, edited by Milena Droumeva and Randolph Jordan, 45–64. New York: Palgrave Macmillan.

World Soundscape Project. 1973. *The Vancouver Soundscape*. Sound recording and book. Burnaby: Sonic Research Studio, Dept. of Communications, Simon Fraser.

Notes

Introduction

1. This shot runs from 24:25 to 25:14 on the Region 1 DVD (ISBN #0-7831-2791-X).
2. This shot begins with Nathan (Nathan Tyson) and Carrie (Carrie Finn) running to seek a hiding place at 1:14:31 and finishes with the beginning of the end credits at 1:17:46. The excerpt of Frances White's piece that runs for the duration of this shot begins at approximately 4:40 on the track as presented on her CD *Centre Bridge: Electroacoustic Works* (2007, Mode Records, mode184).
3. For excellent examples of medium-specific sound staging techniques in historical context, see Neil Verma's analysis of mid-twentieth century American radio drama style in *Theater of the Mind* (2012), and Eric Dienstfrey's reappraisal of the development of early multichannel sound for the cinema in *Making Stereo Fit* (2023).

Chapter 1

1. *The Tuning of the World* was reprinted in 1993 by Destiny Books under the title *The Soundscape: Our Sonic Environment and the Tuning of the World*. The text and pagination are identical across the two versions. Across this book I refer exclusively to the first version in order to maintain grounding in the 1970s context of its original publication.

Chapter 2

1. For a thorough examination of all the permutations of Eisenstein's interest in sound/image synchronization, see Robert Robertson's *Eisenstein on the Audiovisual* (2009).
2. Parts of this section have been adapted from my essay, "Brakhage's Silent Legacy for Sound Cinema" (2001) in which I conduct a longer discussion of Brakhage's interest in the "musical" quality of images alone.

Chapter 3

1. This excerpt from "Doors of Perception" begins at 9:06 in the release version that originally appeared on the compilation CD *Radius #4: Transmissions from Broadcast Artists*

(1995, What Next, WN0019), and re-released as part of the soundtrack album *Last Days: A Tribute to Mr. K.* (2006, Avex Records, AVCF-22746).
2. The trilogy refers to *Gerry*, *Elephant*, and *Last Days*. Chang was writing before the release of *Paranoid Park*, which some believe now constitutes the final entry in a quadrilogy. Yet I have also seen the word *trilogy* used to describe *Elephant*, *Last Days*, and *Paranoid Park*, leaving *Gerry* out of the equation. There are important relationships between all four of these films, but my discussion in this chapter focuses on *Last Days* because of its extensive use of the work of Hildegard Westerkamp.
3. This shot begins at 13:52 in the Region 1 DVD release of the film (2005, Alliance Atlantis, ASIN #B000AYEL10). The excerpt from "Doors of Perception" heard here starts at 5:50 in its CD release.
4. This sequence begins with Scott answering the door at 27:46 on the Region 1 DVD release. Blake turns on the TV at 29:31, followed by a cut to the Friberg twins, and then back to Blake at 30:30 at which point the sound of "Doors of Perception" cuts in with the location sound and the Boyz II Men track. The excerpt from "Doors of Perception" heard here begins at 14:10 in the CD release. As Blake begins his crawl toward the door at 31:25 in the film, a lengthy cross-fade to another section of "Doors of Perception" begins, bringing in an excerpt that begins at 19:00 in the CD release layered with the previous excerpt. As Asia opens the door at 32:16 in the film, the first segment of "Doors of Perception" ends and the second continues until Asia leaves the room and closes the door.
5. The concept of *dialogism* is developed extensively in the essays that comprise Bakthin's *The Dialogic Imagination* (1981) and *Problems of Dostoyesvky's Poetics* (1984).

Chapter 4

1. To identify specific episodes I will be following the generally accepted practice of referring to Seasons 1 and 2 (1990–91) as "the original series" with individual episodes numbered from 1 through 29. The pilot episode (1990) will be referred to simply as "the pilot," which precedes Episode 1. For the 2017 series, I will use the label "Season 3" as opposed to "The Return," the latter of which initially used by Showtime for promotional purposes but has not carried through to official releases of the program. I refer to each installment of Season 3 as "parts" numbered 1 through 18 rather than "episodes," following the filmmakers' wishes that the full season be considered a single film rather than an episodic series.
2. A case in point: *Listen to the Sounds* was adopted as the subtitle for *Music in Twin Peaks* (2021), a collection of essays edited by Reba A. Wissner and Katherine M. Reed.
3. This scene is included in *The Missing Pieces*, a collection of deleted scenes from *Fire Walk with Me* included in the *Twin Peaks: The Entire Mystery* Blu-ray box set released in 2016. You can view the YouTube video here: *Twin Peaks: The Gramophone Click Revealed*, https://www.youtube.com/watch?v=Wp205_aLym4

4. This fact is a reflection of the way in which Chion has adapted the more general term *acousmatic* from its earlier musical context developed by composer Pierre Schaeffer. Borrowed from ancient origins, Schaeffer used it to describe the presentation of sound abstracted from the idea of source, whether this source be visual or traceable within the sound itself. Chion's use of the term in the context of audiovisual media necessitates that it becomes defined by its relationship to the image track, a transformation that requires a measure of theoretical maneuvering. For a detailed discussion of Chion's adaptation of the term, see my essay: "Case Study: Film Sound, Acoustic Ecology, and Performance in Electroacoustic Music" (2007).
5. Passages in this section dealing with the theorization of the *acousmêtre* have been revised from my essay "The Visible Acousmêtre: Voice, Body and Space Across the Two Versions of *Donnie Darko*" (2009).
6. See this Subreddit thread for examples of fan critique of Rebekah Del Rio's performance of "No Stars": https://www.reddit.com/r/twinpeaks/comments/6o6kx6/s3e10_did_anyone_else_rewatch_the_rebekah_del_rio/

Chapter 5

1. This chapter is heavily revised and expanded from two prior publications: a post on the *Sounding Out!* blog entitled "Unsettled Listening: Integrating Film and Place" (2014a); and a chapter in *The Routledge Companion to Screen Music and Sound* entitled "Unsettling the Soundtrack: Acoustic Profiling and the Documentation of Community and Place" (2017).
2. Details about the sound production for *East Hastings Pharmacy* were discussed during a Q&A period and private conversation with Bourges after a screening of the film at Anthology Film Archives in New York City, October 2012.
3. https://digital.lib.sfu.ca/soundscapes-1837/soundscape-cn-pier-main-street-trains-900-van55a1
4. The Herbert George interview is accessible in three parts, labeled as reels Van113a1, Van113a2, and Van114a1, publicly accessible at the following links through the Simon Fraser University library: https://digital.lib.sfu.ca/soundscapes-1521/soundscape-herb-george-interview-interview-1500-van113a1, https://digital.lib.sfu.ca/soundscapes-1522/soundscape-herb-george-interview-interview-continued-1700-van113a2; https://digital.lib.sfu.ca/soundscapes-1515/soundscape-herb-george-interview-interview-continued-1510-van114a1
5. During a master class with Mina Shum at the 2015 Festival Nouveau Cinéma in Montreal, Quebec, Canada, I asked her about the potential symbolism of the passing train in this scene. She said that it was just a coincidence, but approved of my reading. This is a good example of how an unsettled approach to listening in film can reveal relationships across elements that speak to real-world truths even if not consciously designed by the filmmakers.
6. See this promotional video for an illustration of the Kamloops Heritage Railway in action: https://youtu.be/Ft9a75QMtnk

7. Details about the sound production in Larry Kent's films were discussed with me in private conversation with the filmmaker on various occasions.
8. This section expands on my short essay "Vancouver Is . . ." for the Vancouver volume of the *World Film Locations* book series (2013).

Conclusion

1. The exhibition opened in a condensed form for the rescheduled Bienale in 2021, and is opening in full at the Museum of Contemporary Art (MoCA) in Toronto in June of 2023. Full project details here: https://www.impostorcities.com/
2. https://www.discogs.com/release/9105235-Phyllis-Mailing-Christopher-Jordan-Derek-Bampton-Untitled

Index

For the benefit of digital users, indexed terms that span two pages (e.g., 52–53) may, on occasion, appear on only one of those pages.
Figures are indicated by *f* following the page number

Abbott & Cordova, 7 August 1971 (Stan Douglas, 2008), 203–4
ableism, 17–18, 42
acousmatic
  music, 80
  sound, 156–57, 229n.6
acousmêtre, 24–25, 131, 146–54, 155–56, 157–59, 161–64
acoustic community, 18, 173, 174–75, 188
acoustic design, 1–2, 6, 20–21, 29–30, 54–57, 224–25
acoustic horizon, 18, 176
acoustic profile, 61, 64–65, 93–94, 100–1, 107–8, 117–18, 131, 139, 184, 188–89, 190–91, 192, 220–21
acoustic profiling, 15–16, 18–27, 36, 172–77, 193–94, 207–8, 213–14, 216, 223–24, 225–26
Altman, Rick, 3–4, 16, 17–18, 40–41, 141–42, 145–46, 163, 172–73
Arrival of a Train at La Ciotat (Lumière Brothers, 1896), 76, 195–96
audible transparency. *See* transparency: audible
audile technique, 39–40, 141–42, 151–52
auditory extension, 17–22, 30–31, 107–8, 111, 113, 139, 149, 158–59, 176, 184, 214
aurora borealis, 21–22, 61, 214–15

Backbone (Richard Martin, 2013), 201–2
Badalamenti, Angelo, 151–52
Bakhtin, Mikhail, 117–18
Battlestar Galactica (various, 1997–2007), 218–19
Bell Tower of False Creek (Randolph Jordan, 2017), 220–25, 221*f*–22*f*

Bijsterveld, Karin, 10–11, 17–18, 181–82
The Bitter Ash (Larry Kent, 1963), 199–200
Black Ice (Stan Brakhage, 1993), 84
Blomley, Nicholas, 25–26, 172–73, 181
Blue Velvet (David Lynch, 1986), 160
Bourges, Antoine. 229n.4, See also *East Hastings Pharmacy*
Brakhage, Stan, 64–65, 69–70, 77, 83–88, 90
  See also *Black Ice; Stellar*
Browne, Colin, 189–92, 198
  See also *The Image Before Us*
Bruzzi, Stella, 21–22, 61–62, 67–68, 70, 72–73, 76–77
Bugs Bunny, 171, 191–92
  See also *Falling Hare*

Canadian Pacific (David Rimmer, 1974/75), 200–3, 205–6
Canadian Pacific Railway (CPR), 25–26, 171, 189, 202–3
Chion, Michel, 17–18, 24–25, 30–31, 63, 79–80, 81–82, 86–87, 102, 103, 115–16, 117–18, 128–29, 131, 146–54, 162–63, 180, 229n.4
Churchill, Manitoba, 21–22, 61, 75–76, 78, 86–87, 89, 91
Cobain, Kurt, 22–23, 97–98, 112–13, 120
Columbine High School, 1, 4, 109
compilation soundtrack, 22–23, 98–99, 100, 113–14, 117, 214
"Crying" (Roy Orbison, 1961), 150–51

Davis, Bruce, 184, 187, 222–23
"Death to Birth" (Michael Pitt, 2005), 103–4, 109, 118–19, 121–23, 125, 143

Debord, Guy, 29, 38–39, 52
Del Rio, Rebekah, 150–52, 229n.7,
dérive (drift), 52–54
détournement, 52–54
dialogism, 117–18, 228n.5
diegetic sound
    internal diegetic sound, 103–4
    metadiegetic sound, 115–16
    vs. non-diegetic sound, 17–18, 19–20, 50, 103–4, 115–18, 153
digital media, 41–42, 79, 128, 129, 131, 133–37, 160, 164–65
    digital humanities, 6
    surround sound, 149–50
    vs. non-digital media, 23–24, 141–46, 163, 214–15
    See also materiality: digital media
Disque 957 (Germaine Dulac, 1928), 134–35
documentary
    conventions, 8–9, 64–70, 89, 108, 180–81
    films, 10, 13, 14–15, 16, 171–72, 182, 188–90, 191, 196–97, 198, 199–200, 201–2, 208, 216–17
    media practice, 6, 21–23, 117, 125, 171–72, 173, 177–78, 181–82, 183–84, 188, 203–4, 207–8, 213
    performative, 21–22, 43–44, 61–62, 66–68, 70, 73, 76–77, 91, 93–94, 175
    skepticism, 3–4, 61–63, 78–79, 93–94
    voiceover, 65–66, 69–74, 76–77, 190–91, 192
"Doors of Perception" (Hildegard Westerkamp, 1989). See "Türen der Wahrnehmung"
Double Happiness (Mina Shum, 1994), 192–93
Dune (David Lynch, 1984), 141

Ear Cleaning (R. Murray Schafer, 1967), 29, 54–55
East Hastings Pharmacy (Antoine Bourges, 2011), 171–74, 177, 179–81, 189–90, 191–92, 193–94, 206
ecomimesis, 12–13
Edison, Thomas, 144–45, 146–48
Eisenstein, Sergei, 81–83, 84–85, 87–88, 90, 227n.1

electroacoustic
    ecology, 41–42
    music, 1–2, 5, 21–22, 65–66
    sound transmission, 10, 14, 17–18, 20–21, 31–32, 37, 39–40, 41–42
Elephant (Gus Van Sant, 2003)
    comparison to *Last Days*, 22–23, 100, 108, 109, 111–12, 228n.2
    use of sound, 1, 2–3, 4, 5, 18–19, 105
Elephant Man, The (David Lynch, 1980), 134–35
empathy
    anempathetic sound, 115–16
    between audience and film, 22–24, 117–19
    between characters, 19–20, 99–100, 107–8, 109, 112, 120, 202–3
    empathetic sound, 115–16
    as formal strategy, 117–19, 124–25, 175, 214
    reflective empathy, 22–24, 99–100, 118, 124–25, 214
    sensory empathy, 115–16
Eraserhead (David Lynch, 1977), 23–24, 133–34, 135–36
Erikson, Arthur, 216–18, 224–25
    See also Vancouver, British Columbia: Museum of Anthropology; Vancouver, British Columbia: Simon Fraser University

Falling Hare (Robert Clampett, 1943), 179–80, 181
fidelity, 65, 99–100, 128–29, 175–76, 190–92, 213–14
    discourse, 8–9, 10–12, 15–19, 21–26, 31–32, 39–41, 129–30, 131, 214–15
    faithful representation, 8–9, 15–16, 17, 31–32, 173, 176, 192
    hi-fi stereo culture, 9, 10–11, 20–21, 23–24, 31–32, 39, 41, 56, 141–42, 175, 212–13
    hi-fi vs. lo-fi soundscape, 9, 16–19, 31–32, 41, 42–43, 45–46, 175, 185–86, 190–91, 216–17, 222–23
    original vs. copy, 8–9, 15–16, 40–41, 141–42, 145–46, 160–61, 163
    perceptual fidelity, 15–17, 147–48

reproduction vs. representation, 3–4, 15–16, 40–41, 145–46
signal-to-noise ratio, 18, 175
vanishing mediation, 9, 20–21, 22–25, 26–27, 39–42, 92–93, 99–100, 131, 136–37, 141–42, 143–44, 146, 148–49, 154, 175, 177–78, 213–15, 217
Foley effects, 199
Friedberg, Ann, 37–38, 47

Gambling, Gods and LSD (Peter Mettler, 2002), 68–69
Gateway to Asia (Tom Daly, 1945), 224–25
George, Herbert, 185–88, 222–23, 229n.1
Gerry (Gus Van Sant, 2003), 228n.2
gesture
  metaphorical, 49–50, 57, 58, 130
  musical, 80, 89, 90–91
  physical, 33–34, 45–46, 49–50, 63, 140–41, 165–66
glazed soundscape. *See* soundscape: glazed
The Great Train Robbery (Edwin S. Porter, 1902), 194, 195
The Grey Fox (Philip Borsos, 1982), 194–95, 199–200
Groundstar Conspiracy (Lamont Johnson, 1972), 216–17, 218–19

Hastings Street (Larry Kent, 1962/2007), 198–200, 203
Hempton, Gordon, 182–84, 192, 201–2
hi-fi stereo culture. *See* fidelity: hi-fi stereo culture
hi-fi soundscape. *See* fidelity: hi-fi vs. lo-fi soundscape
Hollywood, 134–35, 177, 180, 192–93, 197, 217–18, 219–20
  classical, 73, 152
  Hollywood North, 171–73, 181, 189–90, 198, 216–17
human scale, 10–11, 16, 106–7, 109, 121–22, 125
hypermediacy, 142–43

identification (audience), 22–23, 67, 112–13, 114–15, 117, 118, 144–45, 161–62
  affiliating vs. assimilating, 114–19, 120
  extratextual, 117

The Image Before Us (Colin Browne, 1986), 189–90, 193–94
immersive reflexivity. *See* reflexivity: immersive
Impostor Cities (2021), 211, 217–19, 224, 230n.1
indexicality, 69–70, 92, 143–46, 160, 163
In the Daytime (Stan Fox, 1949), 198
In the Shadow of Gold Mountain (Karen Cho, 2004), 191, 193–94
Indigenous peoples
  activism, 185
  dispossession, 171–72, 174–75, 181, 188–90, 197, 206–7, 220–26
  Indigeneity, 179, 224–25
  labour, 174–75
  reconciliation, 225–26
  representation in media, 10–11, 88–89, 172–73, 179–80, 185–88, 206, 207, 222–24
  See also voice: Indigenous
Indigenous Plant Diva (Kamala Todd, 2008), 207
Inland Empire (David Lynch, 2006), 133–35
International Style (architecture), 20–21, 29–31, 32–33, 38–39
"Into the Night" (Julee Cruise, 1989), 135–36
Ivan the Terrible (Sergei Eisenstein, 1944), 82–83
"I've Been Working on the Railroad" (trad.), 171, 179

Jameson, Fredric, 39–40, 133–34, 159, 160
Jordan, Robert Christopher, 212*f*
  as "Dad," 211–13, 216, 220–21, 224, 230n.2

Kassabian, Anahid, 22–23, 114–17
Kent, Larry. 194–95, 230n.7, See also *The Bitter Ash*; *Hastings Street*
"Kits Beach Soundwalk" (Hildegard Westerkamp, 1989), 221
Know Place (David Rimmer and Sylvia Spring, 1968), 200
Kulezic-Wilson, Danijela, 105, 133, 142–43

234   INDEX

Lady Blue Shanghai (David Lynch, 2010), 133–34
Last Days (Gus Van Sant, 2005), 19–20, 22–24, 97–125, 143, 213, 214, 215, 228n.2
Lastra, James, 3–4, 15–17, 40–41, 145–46, 147–48, 163, 177–78, 179
listening
   hungry Listening, 10–11, 222–24
   practices, 3–6, 8, 10–11, 14, 16–17, 29–30, 31–32, 33, 54, 172–73, 176, 200, 213, 224
   reflective listening, 14, 99–100, 114–15, 117, 124–25
   unsettled listening, 25–26, 43–44, 172–73, 176–77, 180, 181, 207, 208, 215
   See also positionality: listener; soundwalking
location
   recording, 1–2, 13, 21–22, 78, 101, 102–4, 105–6, 108, 109–11, 113, 115, 171–72, 177–81, 183–84, 185, 188–89, 190–92, 198–200, 201–2, 204–6, 207–8, 211, 216–21, 228n.4
   setting, 7, 13–14, 18–20, 173, 176–77, 191, 193–94, 205–6, 217–18
   shooting, 65, 87–88, 178, 193–95, 201–2, 204, 207, 215
lo-fi soundscape. *See* fidelity: hi-fi vs. lo-fi soundscape
Lucky Corrigan (Lewis D. Collins, 1936), 197
Lynch, David. *See Blue Velvet*; *Dune*; *The Elephant Man*; *Eraserhead*; *Inland Empire*; *Lady Blue Shanghai*; "No Stars"; "Slow 30s Room"; *Twin Peaks*

M (Fritz Lang, 1931), 98–99
Madeleine Is... (Sylvia Spring, 1971), 200, 202–6
materiality
   the body, 163
   dematerialization, 37–38
   digital media, 129, 131, 145–46, 154, 164–65
   film, 84, 163–64
   glass, 36–37, 43–44, 48–49, 55–56, 57
   medium-specific, 23–25, 129, 158–59
   phonography, 128–29, 130, 133–34, 135–44, 148–49, 154, 164–66
   See also materializing sound indices
materializing sound indices, 102, 111–12, 120–21, 128–29
McCartney, Andra, 10–11, 41–42
media convergence, 129
mediality
   in *Canadian Pacific*, 201–2
   definitions, 12–16, 17, 18–19, 20–22
   in *Last Days*, 99–101, 106–7, 118, 124
   medial move, 12, 18–20, 30–32, 64–65, 130, 207, 213–14, 215
   medial writing, 12–13
   in *Picture of Light*, 21–22, 62–63, 68–70, 76–77, 83–84, 91, 93–94
   in *Playtime*, 20–21, 31–33, 36, 39, 42–44, 47, 56, 58
   in *Twin Peaks*, 129, 135–37, 139, 146, 155–56
medium specificity, 17, 23–24, 129, 133–34
   See also materiality: medium-specific
metadiegetic sound. *See* diegetic sound: metadiegetic sound
Mettler, Peter, 86
   See also Gambling, Gods and LSD; *Petropolis*; *Picture of Light*
Minoru: Memory of Exile (Michael Fukushima, 1992), 192, 193–94
modernism, 20–21, 29–30, 31, 32–33, 36–39, 43–46, 47–48, 50–51, 54–55, 56, 57–58, 177, 214, 216, 225–26
   See also Erickson, Arthur
Mon Oncle (Jacques Tati, 1958), 47, 51, 56–57
"Morning Sunlight" (Ross Barrett, 1971), 204–5
Mountain, Rosemary, 80
moving visual thinking, 64–65, 77, 85–87, 90–91
   See also Brakhage, Stan
Mulholland Drive (David Lynch, 2001), 150–52
Museum of Anthropology. *See* Vancouver, British Columbia: Museum of Anthropology
musical performance, 22–23, 49–50, 100, 101, 103–4, 109, 115–16, 118–19, 120–23, 125, 143–44, 151–52, 211–12

Musqueam Nation, 206–7

neurodivergence, 23–24, 42, 160
New Denver, British Columbia, 192
Nichols, Bill, 21–22, 61–62, 67
noise abatement, 1–2
Norman, Katharine, 14–15, 99–100, 114–15, 117
"No Stars" (Rebekah Del Rio, David Lynch, Angelo Badalamenti, 2011), 151–52

on-the-air sound, 17–19, 135–36
offscreen sound, 87–88, 103, 105–6, 119–20, 121, 149, 153, 165–66, 171. *See also* acousmêtre
"On Bended Knee" (Boyz II Men, 1994), 103–4, 109–13, 119, 120–21
O'Rourke, Jim, 65–66, 71–72, 74, 78, 80, 87–88

Paranoid Park (Gus Van Sant, 2007), 105, 228n.2
"Pennsylvania 6-5000" (Glenn Miller Orchestra, 1944), 136
perceptual fidelity. *See* fidelity: perceptual
performativity. *See* documentary: performative
personal noise, 104, 106–7
Peters, John Durham, 134–35, 143–45, 160
Petropolis (Peter Mettler, 2009), 73
phatic writing, 12–13
phonography
 in David Lynch films, 19–20, 23–25, 132–35
 as representational style, 13, 15–16
 theories of, 141–48, 160
 in *Twin Peaks*, 128–31, 135–41, 164–66, 214–15
 See also schizophonographics
Picture of Light (Peter Mettler, 1994), 19–20, 21–22, 23–24, 61–94, 213, 214–15
Playtime (Jacques Tati, 1967), 19–21, 23–24, 29–58, 177, 213, 214, 215, 224–25
positionality
 Indigenous, 26–27
 listener, 10–11, 16, 17–18, 25–27, 40–41, 43–44, 141–42, 163, 215, 219–20

settler, 3–4, 11, 26–27, 29–30, 43–44, 172–74, 176, 185–86, 187–88, 207, 212–13, 215–16, 220, 222–26
unsettled, 178, 180, 181–82, 207, 208, 224
See also unsettled listening
postmodernism, 39–40, 133–34, 146, 159–62, 163
psychogeography, 20–21, 52, 53, 54–57

Rashomon (Akira Kurosawa, 1950), 16
realism, 8–9, 15–16, 65–66, 68–69, 73, 81–82, 122–23, 130, 149, 204–5, 211
reflective empathy. *See* empathy: reflective
reflective listening. *See* listening: reflective
reflexivity, 12–13, 31–32, 83–84, 89
 in documentary, 19–20, 21–23, 61–62, 65–66, 67–68, 69–70, 71–72, 73–74, 76–77, 86–89, 190–91, 192–93, 200–2
 in fiction film, 2, 5, 29–30, 53–54, 55–56
 immersive reflexivity, 21–22, 23–24, 61–65, 66, 70, 71–72, 78–79, 84, 91, 92–94, 214–15
 in soundscape composition, 106–8, 183–84, 186–87, 207–8
 See also mediality
Rimmer, David, 174–75, 188–89, 200–3, 205–6
 See also *Canadian Pacific*; *Know Place*
Robinson, Dylan, 10–11, 222–23
Rothenbuhler, Eric, 143–45, 160
Russell, Catherine, 68–70, 200–1

Schaeffer, Pierre, 80, 229n.6
Schafer, R. Murray
 applications of, 20–21, 24–25, 29–30, 36–39, 42–44, 45–46, 56–57, 93–94, 113, 121–22, 125, 131, 150–51, 200–1, 206–7, 216–17
 critiques of, 2–3, 10–11, 16–18, 43–44, 106–7, 177, 185, 208, 212–13
 history of, 13, 29, 173–74, 200, 211–13, 216
 methodology of, 1–3, 9, 11, 13, 18, 175, 184, 220
 theoretical intersections with, 16–17, 39–42, 54–55, 141–42, 146–47, 160

schizophonia, 10, 16–18, 20–21, 39–42, 56–57, 64–65, 93–94, 113, 131, 154, 160, 163, 175, 177

schizophonographics, 23–25, 131, 136–37, 155–64

Seńákw totem pole, 220–21

settler colonialism. *See* positionality: settler

Shatz, Leslie, 4, 5, 105, 107–8, 111, 124–25

Shum, Mina, 229n.2, See also *Double Happiness*

signal-to-noise ratio. *See* fidelity: signal-to-noise ratio

Silverman, Kaja, 73, 152

Simon Fraser University (SFU). *See* Vancouver, British Columbia: Simon Fraser University

Situationists, 20–21, 29–30, 31, 38–39, 43–44, 51–56, 58

See also *dérive; détournement;* psychogeography; Unitary Urbanism

Sjogren, Britta, 73, 152–54, 156–57

Skidrow (Allan King, 1956), 198, 203

"Slow 30s Room" (Dean Hurley and David Lynch, 2017), 140–41

soundmark, 17, 179–80, 181–82, 184–85, 188, 190–91, 206–7

sound recording. *See* location: recording; World Soundscape Project: ideology and methods

soundscape
  composition, 1–3, 5, 7, 13–15, 22–24, 54, 62–63, 94, 97–104, 105, 106–8, 111, 113–15, 117, 122–23, 124–25, 183–84, 186–87, 214
  glazed, 20–21, 36–37, 42–44, 45, 200–1, 205–6, 224–25
  research, 3, 6, 8–9, 10–11, 21–22, 25
  terminology, 9, 16
  See also hi-fi soundscape; lo-fi soundscape; *Soundscapes of Canada; The Vancouver Soundscape*

Soundscape Vancouver 1996 (World Soundscape Project). See *The Vancouver Soundscape*

Soundscapes of Canada (CBC Radio, 1974), 184, 185

Soundtracker (Nick Sherman, 2010), 182–84

soundwalking, 4–5, 54–55, 104, 106–7, 124–25

Soviet Montage, 64–65, 73, 77, 78–79, 81–82, 84–85, 86–87, 227n.1

space replacement, 39–40, 41, 177, 178, 181–82

spatialization
  of music, 97–98, 100–1, 113–14
  of voice (*see* acousmêtre)

spatial signature, 17–18, 105–6, 110, 111–13, 119–20, 121–23, 176, 184

Spring, Sylvia, 174–75, 188–89, 200–3, 206 See also *Know Place; Madeleine Is...*

"Squamish Narrative" (World Soundscape Project, 1973), 187, 222–23, 224

Squamish Nation, 179–80, 187, 206–7, 220–21, 222–23, 224

staging, 17, 21–22, 25, 174–75, 176, 181–82, 183–84, 188–91, 192, 193–94, 195–96, 199, 200–1

Stargate SG-1 (various, 1997–2007), 218–19

Stellar (Stan Brakhage, 1993), 84

Sterne, Jonathan, 4, 6, 9–10, 12, 39–40, 41–42, 69–70, 106–7, 141–42, 177–78

Synchromy (Norman McLaren, 1971), 79

synchronization
  asynchronous sound, 19–20, 65, 66–67, 73, 78–79, 81–83, 86–87, 93, 214–15
  counterpoint, 64–65, 81–84, 89
  creative examples of, 34–35, 65–66, 86–87, 88, 98–99, 102–3, 111, 123, 125, 179–80, 197
  free counterpoint, 81–82, 86–87, 88–89
  harmonic counterpoint, 90–91
  lip-sync, 89, 90–91, 146–47, 150–51, 152
  non-synchronous sound, 64–65
  occult nature of, 93–94
  orchestral counterpoint, 81
  spatial synchronization, 149
  theories of, 64–65, 72–73, 78–80, 81–85, 146–47, 153–54

Tati, Jacques. See *Mon Oncle; Playtime*
Thompson, Emily, 20–21, 37, 39, 56–57

Todd, Kamala, 172–73, 207
trains, 25–26, 74, 76, 102–3, 173–75, 176, 179–80, 181–86, 187–208
transparency
  as accountability, 181–82, 186–87, 188, 216–17
  audible transparency, 20–21, 23–24, 56, 58, 214
  of glass, 19–21, 30–33, 36–39, 42, 43–44, 45, 46, 47, 48–49, 53–54, 99–100, 123–24
  of media, 11, 30–33, 36, 76, 141–43, 145, 175, 224–25
  sonic, 3–4, 20–21, 31–32, 36–37, 39–41, 43–44, 53–54, 142–43
  spatiotemporal, 57–58, 214–15
  transparent immediacy, 142–43
transsensoriality, 63–65, 77–78, 79–80, 82–83, 84, 85–87, 90–91, 93–94
Truax, Barry, 10–11, 13, 14, 16, 18, 39–40, 41–42, 114–15, 173, 186–87, 205–6
Tsleil-Waututh Nation, 185–86, 187, 206–7, 222–23
Tuning of the World (R. Murray Schafer, 1977), 29, 39, 227n.1
"Türen der Wahrnehmung" ("Doors of Perception") (Hildegard Westerkamp, 1989), 22–23, 97–99, 102–4, 105–8, 109, 110–12, 114–17, 227–28n.1, 228n.3, 228n.4
Twin Peaks (David Lynch et. al., 1990–2017), 19–20, 23–25, 42, 128–29, 141, 154, 155–56, 228n.1
  critiques of, 159–63
  The Final Dossier, 166–67
  Fire Walk with Me, 128, 130, 147–49, 155, 156, 158–59, 161–62
  Laura Palmer, 23–25, 42, 127–33, 135–40, 146, 147–48, 154, 155–67
  The Missing Pieces, 128, 228n.3
  original series, 130, 132–56, 158–59, 160–61, 162–63, 228n.1
  pilot, 127–28, 130, 132–33, 156–58, 228n.1
  Season 3, 127, 129–30, 132–33, 134–36, 139–41, 146, 156–58, 159–61, 162–67, 228n.1
  Sheryl Lee, 161–62
  See also phonography: in *Twin Peaks*

unisonance, 185
Unitary Urbanism, 51–52, 54–55, 57–58
unsettled listening. *See* listening: unsettled

Vancouver, British Columbia
  Burrard Bridge, 206–7, 220–21, 221*f*–22*f*
  Chinatown, 191, 192
  Chinese Diaspora, 174–75, 188–89, 191–93, 196–97
  Downtown Eastside, 171–72, 179–81, 188–89, 191, 197, 198, 202–4, 206, 207
  False Creek, 206–7, 220, 221*f*–22*f*
  The Guitar Centre, 216
  Indigeneity in, 171–73, 174–75, 179–80, 185–90, 197, 206–8, 220–26
  Kitsilano Indian Reserve, 206–7, 220–21
  Museum of Anthropology, 224–25
  rail yards, 184, 201–3, 204–5
  Simon Fraser University (SFU), 6, 29, 173–74, 188, 200, 203–4, 211–12, 216–19, 218*f*, 220, 224–25
  University of British Columbia (UBC), 211, 223*f*, 224–25
  Vancouver Academy of Music, 220–21
  Vanier Park, 220–21
  See also Hollywood: Hollywood North; *The Vancouver Soundscape*
The Vancouver Soundscape (World Soundscape Project)
  1973 release, 7, 13, 25, 62–63, 185–86, 187, 190–91, 212–13, 220
  Soundscape Vancouver 1996, 7, 13, 62–63
vanishing mediation. *See* fidelity: vanishing mediation
Van Sant, Gus. *See Elephant*; *Gerry*; *Last Days*; *Paranoid Park*
The Velvet Underground. *See* "Venus in Furs"
"Venus in Furs" (Velvet Underground, 1967), 103–4, 109, 118–22

visual music, 64–65, 77, 78–80, 82–84, 86, 89, 93
musical imagery, 80
voice
  disembodied (*see* acousmêtre)
  Indigenous, 188, 224–26 (*see also* George, Herbert)
  mediated, 17–18, 119, 134–35, 140–41, 144–45, 147–48, 151–52, 157–58, 221
  singing, 102–3, 109, 119, 122–23, 124, 150–52
  speech intelligibility, 71, 147–48, 216–17
  unamplified (*see* human scale)
  voice-off, 152–54
  voiceover narration (*see* documentary: voiceover)
  See also synchronization: lip-sync

"Walk Through Resonant Landscape #2" (Frances White, 1992), 1–2, 4–5, 18–19
Westerkamp, Hildegard, 2, 4–5, 10–11, 13, 14, 22–23, 54, 97–98, 104–8, 186–87, 224–26

See also "Türen der Wahrnehmung" ("Doors of Perception"); "Kits Beach Soundwalk"
"What a Wonderful World" (Louis Armstrong, 1967), 137–38
White, Frances. *See* "Walk Through Resonant Landscape #2"
World Forum for Acoustic Ecology, 3, 62–63
World Soundscape Project (WSP)
  ideology and methods, 6–8, 10–11, 13–14, 26–27, 62–63, 93–94, 173–75, 177, 181–82, 183–84, 188–89, 194–95, 199–200, 205–8, 211–12, 215, 216–17
  use of WSP materials, 17, 25, 201–2, 220–24
  See also *Davis, Bruce; Schafer, R. Murray; Soundscapes of Canada; Truax, Barry; The Vancouver Soundscape;* Westerkamp, Hildegard
World War II (WWII), 179–80, 211, 217, 224–25

Yelton, Darren. 221*f*